ISABEL B. BURGER is Administrative Coordinator of the Children's Theatre Association, Inc., Baltimore, which she founded in 1943. Recognized as a leading authority on creative dramatics and children's theatre, she has lectured and conducted workshops throughout the United States, as well as in Germany, The Netherlands, Scandinavia, and England. She has twice represented the United States at World Congresses of the International Theatre Institute (The Hague, 1953, and Dubrovnik, 1955). Mrs. Burger is a Life Fellow of the International Institute of Arts and Letters. Her articles have appeared in such journals as *Players Magazine, World Theatre, Instructor,* and *The Maryland Teacher.*

CREATIVE PLAY ACTING

Learning Through Drama

ISABEL B. BURGER
Administrative Coordinator
Children's Theatre Association, Inc., Baltimore

SECOND EDITION

THE RONALD PRESS COMPANY • NEW YORK

Copyright © 1966 by
THE RONALD PRESS COMPANY

Copyright © 1950 by
THE RONALD PRESS COMPANY

All Rights Reserved

No part of this book may be reproduced in any form without permission in writing from the publisher.

3c

Library of Congress Catalog Card Number: 66-21852
PRINTED IN THE UNITED STATES OF AMERICA

To My Mother

whose selfless love, gallant courage, and gentle understanding have filled me with a desire to bring to many children a small measure of the joy that she has brought to me

FOREWORD

History has proved that the drama, when it is an intrinsic and vital part of the lives of the people, is one of the most universal and effective instruments with which to build human understanding and interaction. That it is not more widely used today as an important element in the education of youth may be due to a lack of people able to see its full creative potential and to apply it successfully in meeting contemporary individual and social needs.

We discovered one of these people years ago in Baltimore, Maryland, where Isabel Burger and a committee possessed of courage and social foresight were exploring the territory of the mind and heart, providing dramatic media for creative expression, and developing educational techniques in the workshop of the then Children's Experimental Theatre.

This organization, now the Children's Theatre Association, Inc., affords an inspiring example of what can be done through drama in every community to spur progress in the art of democratic practice. The participating young people, while functioning in small units divided according to age levels, are all linked together by their methods of work and their common desire to increase their capacities for self-expression. They share work, rotate duties, and accept responsibility for both failures and achievements. The attitudes and atmosphere in this unique project facilitate the growth and development of the individual, the realization of latent skills, and the unfolding of the entire personality.

We have watched with satisfaction the expansion of the work of the Children's Theatre Association, and we have seen Mrs. Burger's methods and philosophy, as set forth in CREATIVE PLAY ACTING, bring well-deserved international recognition. This Second Edition is even richer in materials and suggestions for practical use than its predecessor. Every worker with youth will greet it as a vital and timely help in his efforts.

TAM and IVAH DEERING

Wildflower Acres
    Marysville, Washington

June, 1966

PREFACE

Every conscientious individual whose vocation or avocation is working with children has the same objective at heart—to further the development of the whole child, mentally, physically, and emotionally, in order that he may be more adequately prepared to take his place as a mature, contributing member of the social group. Carleton Washburne states this goal in these words: ". . . to open wide the minds of children and bring each child to the threshold of his own unique capacities." To the teacher of day or church school, the recreation worker, the playground or camp director, and the agency social group worker the following chapters are dedicated in the hope that they may offer new and practical ideas for programming through the medium of creative dramatics.

The author lays no claim to rank among the pioneers in the field of creative dramatics. As early as 1911 Alice Minnie Herts published a graphic story of experiments conducted in New York that proved the significant values of free dramatic expression. During the first two decades of this century a strong interest was evidenced in the educational philosophies of Pestalozzi, who had led an educational revolt in Europe in the late eighteenth century. The educational experiments of Edward Sheldon, Francis W. Parker, William Wirt, and John Dewey successfully testified to Dewey's theory that ". . . the primary root of all educative activity is in the instinctive, impulsive attitudes of the child, and not in the presentation and application of external material . . . spontaneous activities of children, plays, games, mimic efforts . . . are capable of educational use, nay, are the foundation-stones of educative method." These experiments paved the way for the general acceptance of creative dramatics as an educational tool. The influence of Winifred Ward's experiments at Northwestern University and in the Evanston schools from 1925 to 1950 cannot be overestimated. In more recent years substantial contributions to the cause of creative dramatics have been made by Hazel Robertson, Agnes Haaga, Geraldine Siks, Margaret Woods, Rita Criste, Barbara McIntyre, Emily Gillies, Eleanor York, and many others.

The purpose of this volume is to set forth practical procedures for organizing the creative dramatics project. These procedures are based on successful experiences in directing the Children's Theatre Association in Baltimore during the past twenty-three years and similar experiments with leaders, teachers, and young people in Germany, England, Holland, and Sweden conducted, for the most part, under the sponsorship of the United States Department of State since 1954.

The Children's Theatre Association, Inc., holds the unique position of being a member agency of the Health and Welfare Council of Metropolitan Baltimore. It acquired the status of a community service agency in 1943. During the two and a half years prior to that date, it had operated under the author's direction on the campus of The Johns Hopkins University as an educational experiment sponsored by the then College for Teachers.

The Current CTA[1] program includes eight weekly classes in creative dramatics in which approximately one hundred fifty boys and girls participate. The age groups range from third grade to college level. Although one of the functions of the agency is to produce each year, according to the highest professional standards, three plays for young people, the major objective is to further the mental, physical, spiritual, and emotional growth of the individual child through the group experience in creative drama. This aim is expressed in the agency's credo, "Playacting is the child's rehearsal for his role as a grown-up."

A further facet of the program involves adult leadership training. Since 1944 the Education Extension Service of CTA has sponsored two courses for teachers, youth workers, and recreation leaders. One, a thirty-three hour lecture-laboratory course in creative dramatics techniques, is offered during the winter semester. The other course, in the early spring, is a fifteen-hour stagecraft workshop led by the consulting designer for CTA. Both courses have been recognized by the City and State Boards of Education. The summer months have recently been dedicated to a statewide theatre program for children provided by the Showmobile. This is a completely self-contained theatre in a thirty-two foot trailer. It takes two plays on the road in Maryland and neighboring states, and in seven weeks plays to audiences totaling about 50,000. Mrs. H. Guy Campbell,

[1] Here and elsewhere the initials CTA will be used to refer to the Children's Theatre Association, Inc.

PREFACE

long dedicated to the cause of cultural enrichment in Baltimore, organized local business and industry interests and helped initiate this unique program in the summer of 1963.

It would be unfair to launch forth upon this Second Edition without expressing my indebtedness to some of those whose interest and help made it possible. I am grateful indeed to Miss Mary Elcock, formerly Director of the Greenwood School in Maryland and Camp Asquam in New Hampshire, for providing an opportunity for early experimentation and to The Johns Hopkins University for its sponsorship of the project during the first two years. Most hearty thanks are due to the late Mrs. Nicholas Penniman and the Vagabond Players of Baltimore, whose Green Room provided a workshop from 1943 to 1949. The Baltimore Bureau of Recreation and the Boards of Education of city and state deserve a word of praise for their many invitations to work with teachers and leaders; valuable data resulted from these experiments. I am deeply appreciative of the confidence that inspired administrators of fifteen colleges, universities, and community organizations, both at home and abroad, to invite me to conduct workshops and lecture-demonstrations. These experiences were of incalculable worth in reevaluating creative dramatics techniques and discovering new approaches. To children everywhere, but especially to those who have participated in CTA, I owe the greatest debt; their warm responsiveness, live imaginations, creative and spontaneous ideas have in truth written this text. An expression of sincere thanks goes to my friend and colleague, Celeste Bobbett, for her enthusiastic support and patience in editing the First Edition of CREATIVE PLAY ACTING and her valuable advice in preparing this revision.

If the methods employed successfully in the CTA project can provide guidance and inspiration to leaders and teachers elsewhere, and give further impetus to the use of this technique in promoting the development of the whole child, the efforts of many years will have been justified.

ISABEL B. BURGER

Baltimore, Maryland
June, 1966

CONTENTS

1	Creative Dramatics	3
2	The Project	12
3	Activity Pantomime	25
4	Mood Pantomime	33
5	Change-of-Mood Pantomime	43
6	Dialogue	55
7	The Short Play	70
8	The Long Play	80
9	Episodic Play and Pageant	95
10	Techniques for the Director	103
11	Staging the Play	114
12	Play Acting and Living	144
	Appendix A: Supplementary Exercises	150
	Appendix B: Stories for Dramatization	172
	Appendix C: Short Plays—*The Queen of Hearts; The King's Birthday*	177
	Appendix D: The Long Play—*Child of the Sky*	191
	Appendix E: Youth Speaks for Itself	216
	Bibliography	227
	Index	229

CREATIVE
PLAY ACTING

CREATIVE DRAMATICS

1

Educational principles and philosophies have shown startling changes and advances since the turn of the century. Special concern over objectives, and the methods by which they may be achieved, has developed in recent years. Young people must be helped to solve not only the problems developed by closer relationships of widely differing national groups, but also those resulting from the overt expression of sharply conflicting ideas on social order, world government, and standards of human behavior.

TOTAL GROWTH

Those who educate children to be worthy members of a society today assume a serious responsibility. They hold a golden opportunity in their hands—an opportunity to prepare young people to shape a brave new world. At the same time they face a rather awesome reality: It is they who must partially bear the burden if they fail to meet this challenge—if they fail to do their share in this gigantic undertaking.

The conscientious youth leader who recognizes the serious nature of his task makes a thoughtful beginning; he considers first his fundamental objectives. He will concur with the modern educational theories that emphasize total growth, rather than intellectual learning alone. What is this total growth? What are the basic attributes of a contributive citizen in today's democratic society? Besides a good foundation of factual knowledge, it is physical, emotional, and spiritual health that constitutes the goal. The well-rounded boy and girl should possess: (1) a healthy and well-coordinated body; (2) flexibility and fluency in oral communication of ideas; (3) a deep and sympathetic understanding of his fellow man; (4) an active creative imagination; (5) resourcefulness and independence; (6) initiative; (7) controlled and balanced emotions; (8) ability to cooperate with the group; (9) sound attitudes of behavior toward home, church, school, and community; (10) aesthetic sensitivity—a real appreciation for beauty of form, color, sound, line.

HUMAN DEVELOPMENT PRINCIPLES

How is all this to be realized? Not even the most skilled technological genius in today's push-button society has invented the button that, when properly used, will provide the precise amount of the ten characteristics listed above, arranged in exact proportions to guarantee perfection of human development. Like education, growth is an on-going process; it can be said to begin at birth or before and to end at the grave. Someone has described the living system as "open," for it is always in the process of becoming and is never completely at rest. Both heredity and environment contribute to a child's development; more specifically, it results from interaction of the two factors. Many difficulties arise during this developmental experience; the "growing pains" can be attributed to the conflicting demands made by the two aspects of the child's person—the individual and the social forces. From the very beginning, each child possesses a streak of individuality of his very own—certain inner potentials, dormant, eagerly awaiting fulfillment. As he progresses and attempts to establish relationships with others, he must often face a struggle. This is the sign of the growth of the "social" side of his person. He may have to subdue some of the spontaneous desires of the inner "self" in order to experience the satisfaction of acceptance by his peers, a need which must be fulfilled. According to Jersild[1]:

. . . it is necessary for a child to conform to the ways of his fellows, but it is also essential for him to preserve his individuality. . . . a growing person cannot reach his full development without encountering difficulties and somewhere along the road to maturity he is bound to be hurt . . . [he] finds himself through his relation with his fellows, but he loses himself and his dignity as a human being, if, in the name of social adjustment, he simply becomes a conformer, an "organization man."

Creative Dramatics and Human Development

As we re-evaluate goals, with the principles of human development in mind, the task takes on new complexity as well as greater challenge. It is important to provide experiences that will help children develop individually and socially, understand and accept themselves and their fellow creatures. Whatever the practice, it must

[1] See Bibliography, pp. 227–28, for sources not otherwise identified in the text.

offer opportunities for mental, physical, spiritual, and emotional growth, thus contributing to the development of the ten attributes listed in the discussion of total growth. All honest professional workers must adopt any medium that can be proved effective in accomplishing these purposes. Only the perverse and stupid fisherman persists in using the earthworm for bait, instead of trying the successful lure with which his comrades are catching the largest fish in the lake.

Specialists in schools and community centers all over the country have found, in the practice of creative dramatics, a significant means to broaden the scope of education, in the largest sense. Geraldine Siks writes: "Creative dramatics stimulates a child's awareness. It causes him to learn to look and listen, and from this to see, hear, and feel. It strengthens his sensibilities and builds a receptiveness to the world that surrounds him—to the world of people, nature, things—to moods, beauties, wonderings." She also discusses the power of the rich creative drama experience in building a sound philosophy of living: "He cogitates and thinks upon things far greater and more glorious than his immediate sphere of living. He strengthens his social and aesthetic attitudes and appreciations. In indirect but vivid ways, creative dramatics introduces children to a philosophy by which to live." Hughes Mearns also mentions the possibilities of creative dramatics in establishing high standards and behavior patterns. He says: "The fine playing of an evil role can be done only by those who are at the same time inwardly repudiating evil. We know, if others do not, that the play, better than the precept, establishes permanently an allegiance to the moral life." Besides the personal values so often noted, Eleanor Chase York (in Siks and Dunnington: *Children's Theatre and Creative Dramatics*) points to creative dramatics as a way of introducing children to the art of the theatre, and preparing them to become members of a discriminating audience of the future. In her words, ". . . an appreciation of children's literature and, ultimately, of dramatic literature is built. In fact, since drama is the meeting place of all of the arts, finer appreciations for the visual arts, music, and dance may also grow from experience in creative dramatics."

A clear understanding of the term *creative dramatics* is important, even essential, and yet somewhat difficult to come by. The author served on a Committee on Basic Concepts of the Children's Theatre Conference in 1955. From its study of definitions, as reported in the *Educational Theatre Journal* in May, 1956, comes this statement: "Creative dramatics, in which children with the guidance of an imaginative teacher or leader create scenes or plays and perform them with improvised dialogue and action. Personal development of the players is the goal, rather than the satisfaction of a child audience. . . ." The report goes on to subdivide creative dramatics into four categories: the dramatic play of little children; creative dramatization of a story told by a leader who also assists in developing the spontaneous dramatization; creative plays developed to a point where they approach formal plays; and creative dramatics as it is used for tryouts or group scenes in a formal play. Creative dramatics is certainly the counterpart of formal dramatics, as the term is generally understood. The creative scene, based on a familiar story, a life situation, or a plot developed by the children themselves, inspired by a poem, a piece of music, or a personal experience, is of the young actors' making and voiced in their own vocabulary. To summarize: It is the expression of thought and feeling in the child's own terms, through action, the spoken word, or both. Formal drama, on the contrary, is the expression of thought and feeling in the words of the playwright, presented according to his, or the director's suggestions for movement and interpretation. Although there is a place for formal theatre in the lives and experiences of young people, especially those who have been previously involved in creative dramatics, the latter provides obvious advantages in terms of child growth and development that are not implicit in practice of the more conventional forms of drama.

Glance for a moment at the goals mentioned earlier, the ten attributes, essential to the contributive member of society. Then imagine a group of twelve-year-olds freely playing the following scene, and judge whether the experience provides opportunity for growth in any or all of these directions. The story opens on the Oregon Trail, about 1844. John Sager, a boy scarcely in his teens, is sitting alone by the makeshift fire near the rude shelter he has constructed to protect his four younger sisters, including the four-months-old Henrietta, from inclement weather. He knows there is still a good distance to go, and many dangers to face, before they can reach the Willamette Valley, the destination John's father had dreamed of for so many years. The boy, head of the family now since mother and father both died during the long trek from Missouri, must make the decisions. There is no one to whom he may turn for help. The Sager cart, which had fallen behind the wagon train, somehow took the wrong trail. The youngsters are completely alone now—children in the wilderness. John, realizing that help would come from the Whitman Mission, if only the good Doctor knew the Sager children were in danger, has scrawled a message on birch bark, and sent it ahead some days before by a friendly Indian. Not until tonight, as he sits before the fire while the girls try to rest, does he feel lost, afraid, and hopelessly discouraged. In his hand he holds the birch bark, addressed to Dr. Marcus Whitman, which he had hoped would bring them aid. This very afternoon, during a reconnoitering trip, he found the lifeless body of his Indian friend lying only a few hundred yards east of the camp. John's message was clutched in the courier's hand. It seems to the small boy as though the end of the world has come. How can he tell his sisters?

Cathy, who was just a year younger, stirred in the tent. As she peeped out, she saw John's pathetic figure silhouetted against the fire. Something was wrong! Creeping silently over to him, with the baby held close in her arms, she whispered, "What is it, John? What's happened? We promised not to have any secrets, you know." Slowly the boy turned, opened his hand, and disclosed the bit of bloodstained birch bark. He watched her face grow pale with fear, her eyes widen in terror. Then—at that moment—he knew! He knew that he must be wrong! He knew that he must do as his father would have done, had he been here. He set his jaw determinedly and, with a quiet courage, he put his arm about his sister. Without the slightest tremor in his voice, he said, "It's going to be all right, Cathy. We'll make it. I know we will, if we stick together. It was Father's dream to stake his claim on the Willamette, and we're going to make that dream come true."

Here is a simple story about children, their courage, loyalty, and perseverance. As the boys and girls discuss it, making mind-pictures of the life and character of those stalwart pioneers—their great sacrifices, strong family ties—the children themselves are caught by the same spirit. As they play it, two at a time, the understanding of the relationship between John and his sisters deepens; a genuine emotion fills their hearts. They have unconsciously grown considerably in points 3 and 7 on the original list. They have also called into active service the creative imagination (point 4), in order to make the pathetic camp site of the lost children seem a reality. As each pair plays out the scene in its own way, new thoughts are expressed differently. Every child is thinking independently, in character, unhindered by lines that must be memorized, expressing his thoughts freely in his own words. (Impetus is thus being given to points 2, 5, and 6.) Young bodies are, in turn, tense with fear, drooping in despair, uplifted with determination; muscles, mind, and heart are working in unison, resulting in perfect coordination (point 1). The precursory discussion and the playing of the scene has been a real group process. The aggressor has learned to subordinate some of his ideas to those of the rest of the group. The reticent child has grown in stature as one of his suggestions is accepted by his colleagues. It is a real lesson in happy cooperation, a learning how to get along with people in the best possible manner (point 8). Implicit in the story itself are fine evaluations of loyalty, courage, perseverance, assuming responsibility, and service to others, all sound behavior patterns (point 9).

These attitudes, so important to the future happiness of young people, cannot be taught by lectures, reading, or memorized formulae. For too long a time a belief has prevailed in the fallacious pedagogy of the Herbartian psychology which teaches that a mind filled with ideas about truth will therefore be truthful. There is, however, increasing awareness of the fact that conditioning, not intellectual learning, cultivates social attitudes. As Tuttle points out:

> Next to actual conditioning of democratic conduct itself is vicarious experience approximating real life situations. . . . Because emotions are given overt expression in drama, approved principles of conduct are strongly conditioned. . . . This type of art, which has been so generally treated merely as a form of entertainment, has educational possibilities superior to any traditional teaching device of the schools.

In taking stock of the educational opportunities provided by the playing of this one short episode, it is evident that development has been stimulated along nine of the ten goals suggested. If material for the creative drama class is selected wisely, presented and handled by an intelligent, trained, and sensitive leader, there will always be such opportunities for the growth of the children participating.

Leaders working with children between the ages of twelve and sixteen should recognize the urgent need for a specific medium to develop controlled and balanced emotions (point 7). A child, during this period, is struggling to become an individual, to detach himself from the family group and find his place in the social group. To complicate further his task of readjustment, he is beset with a rising tide of emotional energy that is forever seeking some channel of liberation. The small child relieves himself in occasional temper tantrums or joyful physical outbursts. The teenager, on the contrary, seeking to surround his approach to the threshold of maturity with an aura of adult dignity, endeavors to repress his feelings. This constant suppression of strong emotional urges is contradictory to nature. Some young people find an occasional outlet through athletic participation. If legitimate outlets are not provided, illegitimate avenues may be the choice. The turbulent feelings of the adolescent rebel against being bottled up over too long a period. If the supply is not tapped now and then, through some healthy release, undue pressure will pop the cork and the heedless spill in every direction will appear in terms of actions labeled as delinquent behavior. Are not such manifestations as seeking the adventurous thrill concomitant with indulging in intoxicating beverages, clandestine meetings, experiments in sex, absorbing censored literary or theatrical fare, speeding in a borrowed automobile, sometimes even gambling and stealing, often the expression of rebellion of unduly restrained emotions?

Becoming another character in a dramatic situation involves feeling deeply the emotions of someone else. Through this very use of the complex emotional mechanism, a boy or girl may get a healthy release from his tensions. He will have "played them out" through the emotional pattern of another individual. No psychologist advocates the free unleashing of emotions, nor does he advise suppression. There must be both release and control. This directed outlet, provided through experiencing the emotions of another character, implies control. Perhaps Bill Smith, the boy who was playing John Sager in the pioneer scene just described, has been filled with tensions caused by an unhappy home situation. In the playing out of the despair and hopelessness, he will find release, but he cannot give way completely to his feelings. They are controlled because a new and more admirable emotion—that of courage and perseverance—takes possession of John and coincidentally of Bill. The whole experience has therefore been one of release and control set in fine balance.

One of the strongest points in favor of adopting the creative drama project in all group work with children is the warm reception accorded it by the young people themselves. All children love play acting. The play instinct is a part of every child's equipment in his early years. Through make-believe the child is striving to get the feel of the new world unfolding about him, and a better grasp of the complex situations that he is beginning to observe and is eager to understand. It is with real fervor and seriousness of purpose that he plays out the doctor's visit, the trip to the market, the fire engine that he saw across the street, and later the cowboys and Indians from his storybook. Any observer will note that, during this period of spontaneous dramatic play, the child is actively participating, every sense awake, every impulse alive. When creative play acting is included in an activity program, the natural play instinct with which every child is already endowed is made to serve educational purposes. The student's genuine enthusiasm over the very first project in creative playmaking will convince the most sceptical leader that he has made a happy choice of techniques.

EXPERIENCING TOTAL GROWTH

At the twelfth session of a creative drama class for eight-to-ten-year-olds, a conversation took place that will offer first-hand evidence of the free and eager participation of the whole group. These boys and girls had previously enjoyed dramatizing short scenes concerning the nursery rhyme characters; they had come to look upon them as old friends. Suddenly a loquacious brown-eyed child spoke:

"Let's put them all into a big play, shall we?"

"Sure," said her mischievous seat mate, "if you'll make it about the knave stealing the Queen's tarts." (He had been playing that villainous character, so there was an ulterior motive in his suggestion.)

"But we have to have a King for the Queen," said another.

"That's easy! We'll let King Cole be the Queen of Hearts' King."

"Yeah! And let's make him have a birthday!"

"And I know what! That's why the Queen was making the tarts . . . for his birthday."

"Well, what about Little Miss Muffet?" queried a starry-eyed little girl, seriously disturbed. She was championing her favorite role, which seemed in grave danger of being omitted from the story. It was obviously time for the teacher-director to step in. Little Miss Muffet must not be forgotten.

"Don't you think the King and Queen might have some little princesses?" the director said.

"Yes, of course," came the affirmative reply. "The Princesses Muffet!"

"Let's have four of them, and they can always have curds and whey on the King's birthday."

"Sure, 'cause they'd be too little to eat tarts anyway."

"But we have to have the spider . . . they're half the fun . . . spiders to scare us," said the same Little Miss Muffet, still worried.

"That's all right. We can have the spiders." The boy who spoke hoped to be the King. "They'll be the villains. They can spin their webs in the throne room and scare the Princesses, and the King'll send 'em to the dungeon."

Here indeed creative imagination was at work; independent thinking, resourcefulness, and initiative were developing by leaps and bounds. As the project continued to its culmination, timid, young voices became stronger; inhibited and awkward bodies relaxed, moving with marked improvement in coordination. There was a healthful give-and-take in planning the sequences. The result was the genuine happiness that comes from sharing successfully in carrying out a common project. The time would have been well spent even if this deeper understanding of real cooperation had been the only obvious benefit. But an individual sense of security, relaxation, and well-being was everywhere in evidence. Each inner self grew a little; individuals, on wings that had gained confidence, soared to new heights of originality. As Jersild notes: "The personal satisfaction that a child derives from being able to do something well is an important factor in his growing conception of himself."

SUMMARY

Dynamic changes in the world today present new problems as well as new opportunities for teachers and youth leaders. The education of the whole child must be the aim, rather than intellectual learning alone. Educational techniques should be sought that will be effective in developing the major attributes of the well-balanced, happy, contributive personality. Creative dramatics is a successful means to that end, because it is democratic in method, teaches through conditioning, sharpens imagination and sensitivity, deepens human understanding, adjusts emotional tensions, develops resourcefulness and initiative, helps to build sound patterns of behavior, and stimulates body flexibility and ease in oral communication. Its special value to the adolescent group in providing a healthy emotional outlet should be recognized. Such a program will be received enthusiastically by any group of boys and girls because it is based on the natural play instinct with which all children are richly endowed.

2

THE PROJECT

The opportunities for growth through the creative experience discussed in the previous chapter will not present themselves in the course of a dozen or more meetings devoted merely to rehearsing a play. A group of the same age level should meet with the leader at least once a week during the whole season. Freeing emotional tensions, relaxing tight muscles, stirring the creative imagination into activity and heightening sensibilities require time, patience, and a carefully planned program. The slim green shoot that appears in early spring requires days of sunlight, soft rain, fertilization, and loving care if it is to reach out and up to become the fully formed fragrant flower. The child, likewise, needs time, warmth, sympathy, inspiration, and guidance before he can unfold, stretch out, and increase his stature through creative thought and expression. His growth may be almost imperceptible in the beginning, but given proper time and problems that are not too difficult to solve at first, he will soon show evidences of well-rounded development.

PLANNING

Each of the next four chapters, therefore, is devoted to achieving a single step in this gradual process. The pantomiming of simple activities is followed by mood pantomime and exercises involving the expression of a change of mood. This practice lays a firm foundation for work with dialogue. Each of these steps makes progressively greater demands upon the creative instinct. The total plan is based on actual experiences recorded during class work with large groups of children of all ages. The method has been tried and tested. Whether boys and girls are eight or eighteen, it is advisable to utilize the same general procedures; only the subject matter of the exercises, or the manner of presentation, need be adjusted to suit the age level. Emphasis is always placed on the development of the whole child; the goal is the same regardless of age, size, physical maturity, or social background. Whether the project be initiated in a school, scout troop, Y-Teen club, summer camp, settlement house, or recreation center is of little consequence. All participants are children; all have generally the same basic needs, inhibitions, potentialities for growth. Every group requires, therefore, the services of a skilled leader who plans wisely and sets for himself the highest educational aims.

A few basic instructions for working out the exercises in the following chapters apply to all leaders. Because they are generally useful, they are mentioned here. Not until sufficient time has been spent on the first four steps (Chapter 3 through Chapter 6) are children ready to present a short creative drama, even informally for their own colleagues. It is impossible to set arbitrarily a definite time to be spent on each of the four procedures; readiness to advance is determined by the growth of the individual members within the group. Far less is any unit capable of presenting a more formal full-length play until the preparatory exercises have been dealt with adequately. Only after there is freedom of body and voice, and imagination creating actively, can children sincerely and joyously reproduce a story on the stage with worthwhile results, from the point of view of their own development or audience satisfaction. How many times have parents, aunts, and uncles, endured in agony the church or school play in which Mary or Johnny has a part! Stiff, frightened bodies, carefully memorized lines that stutter haltingly from dry throats as meaningless words strung together like beads—every one alike—the harrowing, silent moment when young eyes are turned beseechingly to the prompter's corner: These are the unpleasant memories connected with many children's productions. There is no entertainment, no joy, no growth, no benefit to anyone concerned —least of all to the young actors themselves. It is far better to eliminate drama from the program altogether, if it cannot serve some educational or recreational purpose.

THE PROJECT IN VARIED SETTINGS

Although the theory, philosophy, and order of procedure are the same for the practice of creative dramatics anywhere, the sensitive leader will be flexible, conscious of the emphasis in his particular group, and will adjust appropriately to the limits imposed by time, space, and agency policies. Suggestions follow for adapting creative dramatics technique to (1) the classroom, (2) the church school, (3) the summer camp, and (4) the recreation center.

The classroom teacher in the average elementary school has a rigid and demanding schedule to meet. Taken at face value, such a time sheet would not seem to allow a single moment for extracurricular activity such as creative dramatics. Only if the technique is utilized as an effective educational tool to assist the teacher in achieving his aims is its inclusion valid. If, however, the dramatization of certain short stories, old English or Scottish ballads, or tales from classic mythology will help vitalize the teaching of these subjects, surely a half-hour three times a week could justifiably be devoted to this approach. When the wise teacher analyzes the benefits derived from this experience, he will note that much more has been gained than a clearer understanding of the course content. The personal development of each individual student is patent; growths in fluency of language, body coordination, imagination, resourcefulness, and human understanding are some of the many gratifying results of the regular practice of creative dramatics. The time that can be devoted, in several classes a week, may be short, and must dictate the length of each creative drama lesson plan. The course content will also guide the selection of material for the dramatizations. Although the growth may be slower in this special adaptation of the project, the benefits are the same if the same procedures are followed; rewards to both students and teacher are great!

The church school teacher faces still another situation that calls for different adjustments. His basic purpose is to find the most successful means of helping young people to discover the redeeming power of God's love and to witness it in action in their lives. Drama has often proved a most effective tool in achieving these aims. If one would help children to become emotionally mature, contributive, secure adults, one must help them to live "religious" lives—lives free from the inhibiting chains of self-pity, self-pride, and self-hate. In order to find their real selves—accept themselves as they are, and therefore accept their fellow creatures—they must turn their center of interest from self to others about them. The ancient directive that one learns in the greatest of all *books*, to "love your neighbor as yourself", is implicit in the modern psychologists' recipe for developing the mentally healthy human being. For the word "love," they use "accept"; on close scrutiny the two seem almost synonymous. One must accept (love) one's self first, before he can ever accept (love) his neighbor.

In any skillfully planned creative drama project, the emphasis is on these objectives, for only when the child has accepted himself and his neighbor is he comfortable enough to create freely. It can be assumed, then, that such an approach tends to encourage "religious" living. It also follows that some minutes or hours of the church school or vacation day-school class that are devoted to creative dramatics experiences can be richly rewarding. Again the material may be appropriately selected from the general content of the course being taught. The same step-by-step procedure should be followed, if significant progress in human growth and development is to be achieved. The need for specific training in creative dramatics for church school teachers is, unfortunately, not often recognized by religious education directors, many of whom do not themselves clearly understand the values of this discipline. Much careful research is still needed in so complex a field, if the greatest benefits are to accrue from the hours devoted to this activity.

Creative dramatics is especially successful in the summer camp where the informality creates an appropriate climate. Children who are already living and working together daily have established a friendly rapport and group interaction. Out-of-door life, nature study, mountain climbing, swimming, and boating offer endless subjects around which to build interesting projects. A group can continue to work daily on a theme that has inspired a creative play; this continuity of effort is a distinct advantage. The results are often more spontaneous, better organized, and far more effective than those dramatizations created in the class that devotes a short time to creative drama once or twice a week. Camp dramatics is also likely to fail if it falls into the hands of well-meaning but unskilled counselors because the administrators are unaware of the special attributes and training that the good creative drama leader must possess.

Still other problems vex the average leader in a large recreation center where creative dramatics is listed on the schedule as a special "interest group." This kind of neighborhood center is generally financed by the city or state government on a limited budget. Two or three leaders are supposed to supervise the entire program, which may include children, young people, and adults involved in sports, crafts, music, dramatics, and other activities, carried on simultaneously in rather cramped facilities. Often the creative dramatics leader will find his group changing in number from week to week and including age ranges so great that it is impossible to find a common interest level. On certain occasions he must work in small quarters to make room for dance groups or the basketball team; almost always he competes with noise and distractions caused by telephone calls or office duties. No creative drama group can succeed under such conditions. The first requisite is space; the next is quiet, which is conducive to the development of concentration and imagination. Lastly, the group must be small enough to handle (maximum of twenty), all of whose ages are within two years (i.e., ages 8 to 10, 11 to 13, etc.). Only if the administration insists upon regular attendance for the creative drama group members will any real progress be possible. If these arrangements can be made and if the leader who has had proper training can be freed to concentrate his attention on the class, creative dramatics can make a significant contribution to the recreation center's program.

Whether a teacher is contemplating a creative dramatics project in a school, camp, or recreation center, an overall plan, made in advance, is essential. He will consider his final goal, the students participating and their socioeconomic background, the facilities in which he will work, and the total span of time to be devoted to the project, as well as the hours allotted to each session. After a careful study of these facts, he will outline lesson plans, again noting purpose and general content of each meeting. Like a good navigator, he will plot the safest and most direct course to his destination. Unexpected winds in the form of a spontaneous onslaught of creative ideas may, and should, cause him to shift direction now and then, but the overall plan, with compass set, will assure him of final arrival at his port-of-call!

USE OF MUSIC AND RHYTHM

To keep interest high and imaginations active, one may vary the lesson plan from time to time with music and rhythm exercises. Music's appeal to the emotions, its power to relax tense muscles, to develop mood and stimulate body reactions, admits no argument. Rhythm has always been an ultimate in one's total makeup. The ancient Greeks felt it so important that they founded their whole educational system on various forms of rhythm or "mousike," as they termed it. Besides its general endowments, music is a strong factor in the development of original thinking. Geraldine Siks writes: "Music has power. It arouses feelings that surge through old and young alike. Marching music always quickens the blood. . . . lullabies are soothing in their gentle rhythm . . . music stirs many different feelings." And of rhythm she says: "Rhythm is the basis for expression in all arts. It starts with the individual. Each artist expresses through a medium unique to his art. A painter expresses rhythmically in space with line and color. A musician expresses rhythmically in space with sound. . . . A child expresses rhythmically in space with movement."

Fortunate is the leader who can secure the services of a skilled, creative musician from time to time. (For general purposes a pianist is most practical.) This artist should share the leader's love for and understanding of children; their needs, actions, and reactions should guide his work. He must be prepared to improvise, inspired by the leader's story or the spontaneous mood created by the children. There is seldom an occasion when a set lesson plan in which every exercise is mapped out in advance can be followed. It is rarely possible, therefore, to prepare beforehand definite mood music patterns of a certain length and style. If the project is truly creative, an idea suggested must be permitted to grow into a dramatic situation as the children feel it (see Figs. 2–1 and 2–2). As their ideas are trans-

Fig. 2–1. The reaction of several characters to the same piece of news. (Credit: Edward J. Peterson.)

lated into active expression, a creative pianist's thoughts will also fall into a musical pattern; one stimulates the other. To insist that children create their story to fit a set musical composition is to hinder their freedom of expression.

Few leaders will be able to find, readily, a music director who is a skillful improvisator, and has a deep and sympathetic understanding of children. To recognize these qualities as needs, however, will help him in his quest for the ideal musician.

An incident that occurred during a class where music was used with eleven- and twelve-year-olds may point up the significance of the musician's ability to improvise. Responding to quick changes of mood was the study. This had been the only information given to the pianist before the start of the period. Twenty boys and girls listened attentively as the leader spoke.

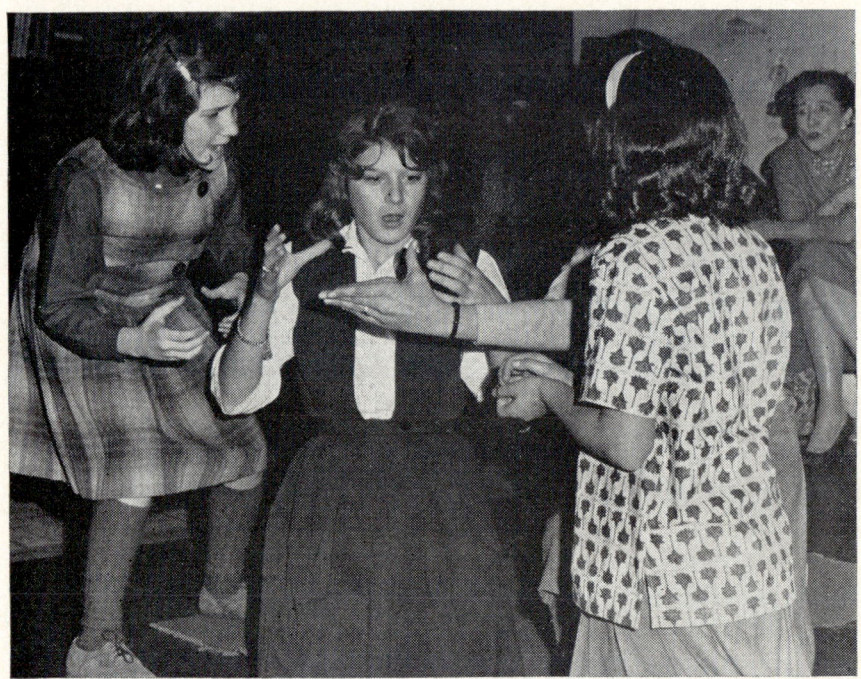

Fig. 2–2. The poor children receive a surprise gift. (Credit: Edward J. Peterson.)

"Let's pretend we're walking in the woods on a beautiful day in summer, or playing on the beach, or having a picnic at Grandmother's farm. How do we feel in summer?"

"Happy!" "Light as a balloon!" "Like you have wings." These were some of the replies offered spontaneously. The leader continued:

"That's right. And then what could happen that would make you feel just the opposite?"

"Oh, that's easy! A storm could come up and spoil everything."

"If you were playing on the beach, you could lose your best ring in the sand."

"Maybe while you were walking in the woods you'd hear the hiss of a rattlesnake on the path."

"Yes," said the leader, "any of these things might happen . . . something that would make us angry, or sad, or afraid. Which one shall we play first?"

One of the more intense youngsters suggested that they be walking in the woods when something happened to make them afraid. There was a general murmur of agreement. The signal was given to the musician, and immediately a group of volunteers was on the floor ready to play the situation. Had the director completely planned the episode, and the pianist composed his score in advance, all opportunities for creative development would have been lost. The music would have inhibited, rather than freed, the power of expression. Rhythm exercises may be used at any time, without the aid of a musician. The leader who has a natural feeling for rhythm can inspire interesting movement patterns with a tom-tom or other percussion instruments. The starting point for any work of this kind is practice in the natural rhythmic movements of walking, running, and skipping. Games that call for quick response to these three patterns, used interchangeably, are popular and challenging. They sharpen concentration powers and promote body coordination. During these early drills the observant leader can usually discover the child who has difficulty coordinating mind with muscular response; he will be able to offer special help where it is needed in future rhythm work. Use of simple patterns, 3-4, 2-4, or 4-4 times, are advisable. Nearly all children have a natural feeling for rhythmic expression, and most of them have had group singing or music lessons in school. To begin a day when 4-4 time will be the basic pattern used, one may start by having the whole group clap the rhythm, emphasizing the first beat. Then, in a large circle, they may walk and clap, or walk every beat and clap only on the first beat. In a short time, most children will recognize these steps as quarter notes because it takes four of them to complete a measure. To relate this ordinary walking rhythm to a life situation is the next task.

"Where am I walking when I walk in this kind of rhythm?" says the leader as he walks the room in 4-4 time.

"Oh, just anywhere . . . like downtown, or to school; no place special," says Billy nonchalantly.

"Do I feel any special way when I'm walking like this?" asks the leader. "Can you tell?" He continues to walk in exactly the same rhythm.

"Nope! Just sort of regular!" says Sally, starting to clap in time to the leader's movement. Suddenly the steps change, the leader begins to walk in half notes—on the first and third count of each measure.

He asks: "Now . . . now where might I be going? You're still feeling four beats but I'm only walking on every other beat. Do I feel different now? Who can tell me?" He is still walking half notes.

Finally Georgia speaks: "I know, I know! You're lost, that's what! You're lost and you're looking around to find the right number on the house. That's why you're going so slowly."

"No! That's not it! I think you just got a scolding and your mother sent you to your room and you're sad." Tim's conviction, as he speaks, gives evidence of his having recently experienced a similar sensation.

Before long a stimulating discussion arises about the different kinds of feelings expressed in walks to half notes, whole notes, and quarter notes. Soon various dramatic situations are suggested and rhythm patterns (always based on 4-4 time) are created to express them. Georgia, for example, continues to enlarge on her story of the little girl who was lost in a strange town.

> Well, first she's walking down the street slowly, looking for the number she has on her sheet of paper. That's the half notes. Then she stops and looks closely at the number on one house, 'cause she thinks it's the right one. That's a whole note. Then she realizes that the one she's looking for must be next door, so she hurries to that one. That's the quarter notes. Then she knocks on the door four times and that's more quarter notes.

The leader, recognizing Georgia's story as an accurate description of a situation demonstrating the reasons behind changing rhythm in movement, writes the four measures on the blackboard, using a simple code which the children can understand.

1st measure—walks down the street slowly	1-1-
2nd measure—stops to examine number	1---
3rd measure—walks quickly to next house	1111
4th measure—knocks on door	1111

When this is completed, an explanation is given concerning the need to use four measures to tell the story. If more are necessary, then other sets of four measures each must be added.

Soon a group or an individual will offer to play out the story rhythmically, while the rest clap or beat the rhythm. As children become more adept at this kind of rhythmic work, complex scenes may be developed. Many variations and approaches are possible. The leader can beat out a rhythmic pattern (4 measures) and ask for different story situations that it might suggest. Or one group may present a dramatic situation and another group try to develop the rhythm pattern that expresses it.

Transition is easy to a discussion of the relationship between the rhythm of one's movement and the feelings or circumstances that motivate it. (This advanced rhythm work should logically be introduced during the classes when mood and change-of-mood exercises are in progress. See Chapters 4 and 5.)

Music or rhythm may enrich the creative dramatics project in several ways:

1. To vary the program
2. To create or heighten the mood, or indicate change of mood in pantomime or dialogue improvisations

3. To suggest a story theme
4. To relax tense muscles and help to develop body coordination
5. To stimulate imaginative thinking and feeling

Used as background for the creative play, it may not only deepen the meaning but also serve to heighten climactic moments, anticipate dramatic incidents, and cover long pantomime scenes.[1] Although creative music can be a great asset to the program, the lack of music does not necessarily doom the whole effort to failure. A tireless search for the right creative musician is suggested, but the leader should not abandon all ideas of using music or rhythm because his quest is not successful. Tapes of certain mood music, carefully selected and timed, can often provide suitable background music for the created play.

A revealing episode that occurred during a rehearsal for a short play created on the ballad "King John and the Abbot of Canterbury," may substantiate the theory that background music is important to the children themselves. At this particular rehearsal the music director was not present. King John, played by Jimmy, age twelve, had great difficulty entering his court, greeting his ladies, and crossing to seat himself on the improvised throne. It had seemed a natural and simple matter before, but on this occasion he felt uncomfortable, and asked for permission to try it again and again. Finally in desperation, he cried: "No wonder I can't feel like the King of England, or walk like him either. There's no king music to get into your bones!" He had expressed it perfectly. Good background music should do just that—it should "get into your bones."

ATMOSPHERE

To enjoy a meal to the fullest extent, one must have spotless linen, good food, and pleasant surroundings; to get the most out of a trip, one must have the proper equipment, interesting company, good weather. The success of the creative drama class also depends upon the attendant cirumstances. The meetings must be conducted in an atmosphere of pleasant informality that breaks down fear tensions and at the same time stimulates eagerness, ambition, and respect for the job at hand.

The responsibility for creating this climate within the group rests almost entirely with the leader. A serious responsibility this,

---

[1] See Chapter 9 for detailed explanation. The same principles apply to other dramatizations.

and a privilege! The leaders of children can make any experience a powerful force for good or a hollow, empty time-filler. Much depends upon the attitude one has toward young people. As Socrates knew long ago, "One can only teach whom one loves." And perhaps the reverse is true, that one can only learn from one whom one loves. At any rate love, understanding, patience, enthusiasm, awareness, an ability to laugh, and a sense of magic and spontaneity are all attributes of the creative leader. Other qualities always found in a *great* individual, no matter what his occupation, are concern, a caring for humanity, a deep desire to grow along the lines where he himself is lacking, and an eagerness to help others achieve their full stature. Someone has said that the great leader is one "who can lead a line of boys along a stream of living water and cause them to want to drink." In the field of creative dramatics, the successful leader must have some basic knowledge and experience in drama, and some fundamental training. Although dramatic ability is a distinct advantage, it is not by any means a necessity. Geraldine Siks believes:

> A good leader knows and enjoys drama . . . she seeks new and continuous experiences in this art. . . . Until she experiences the beauty . . . and power of drama she cannot hope to have an attitude that motivates her into finding ways to share it . . . she searches until she finds an imaginative way to reach children . . . she cultivates a genuine play spirit.

Mrs. Siks is especially emphatic on the subject of spirit and enthusiasm:

> A leader's spirit may be characterized by physical vitality, but even more by emotional vitality, radiance, aliveness, intensity, and faith. . . . a leader cannot expect the magic of creativity and group dynamics to happen if she holds back because she is emotionally insecure, lacks confidence or energy, or is unprepared . . . a leader with spirit arouses, energizes, and incites children into creative expression . . . [and] realizes with Ralph Waldo Emerson that "Nothing great was ever achieved without enthusiasm."

It is the enthusiastic coworker, not the cold disciplinarian—the patient cheerful companion, not the impatient bored teacher—who will inspire the confidence and freedom on which the successful creative dramatics project thrives. In this kind of climate there will be no discipline problem.

Although there are as many ways of creating appropriate climate for creative dramatics as there are leaders, an explanation of an approach used successfully for many years in the Children's Theatre Association in Baltimore may prove helpful. Let us imagine a group of eight- to ten-year-olds gathered on a Saturday morning for a first creative dramatics session. Many of them have never seen one another before; they may come from sharply contrasting socioeconomic backgrounds. The leader begins. "How nice that we've all finally found our way to The Carriage House; and what a great morning it is!" A few general comments follow about where we come from, how far we had to go, whether The Carriage House was hard to find and the like. As soon as the majority of the group seems to have entered into the general conversation, and is comfortably settled on the rugs, couches, and chairs that have been previously set up in an informal style, the leader starts the conversation along a different line.

"My, it's fine to have such a big children's theatre family this year. Do you know how many we are?" They look about the room and mentally try to count. The leader continues: "We're all not here, you know. There are seven other groups like you and altogether we are about a hundred and fifty! Think of that! Some big, some little, and some middle-sized!" There are "ohs" and "ahs!" "Yes, indeed, I have so many children I feel like the old woman who lived in the shoe; but there's one difference, I *do* know what to do with all my children and she didn't. And I am glad for every single one of you!"

Then the talk of "family" begins, with such questions as: What makes a good member of a family? What is a good member of your scout group like? Why do you like certain people who are members of your class so much? Through guided discussion come spontaneous responses like these: "I like the people who aren't always interested in themselves." "The people that share their toys are fun." "The best friends I have in school are those who care about me and what I'm interested in." "In our family the ones that are best liked are the ones that help, and not the ones that always make excuses for not doing any work."

Before long certain basic principles and conclusions are agreed upon:

1. To be a good member of a family—our CTA family especially—I must forget "self" and try to think of others in the group.
2. I will try to be aware of ways in which I can help others to be happy, and so will be happier myself.
3. Since this is our "home" I will try to think of ways to take care of it because then I will enjoy it more.

A very short step takes the discussion to the next significant point. "What has forgetting one's self got to do with play-acting or pretending?" Frequently some will respond, "Well, if you pretend to be somebody else, you have to forget yourself . . . and really BE somebody else for a while." If this answer is not forthcoming, several other carefully worded questions will probably bring it forth. Thus, in a short time the friendly, family atmosphere is established. Everyone feels that he belongs; even if, in his inmost thoughts, he doesn't quite fit into the pattern of a "good" family member, he at least has the recipe for becoming one, and is ready to set out upon the endeavor in good spirit. Now, at long last, the group is ready to begin work on the first step, the pantomiming of simple activities.

SUMMARY

That growth through the creative drama process is gradual must always be kept in mind. Until the four preparatory steps have been taken, no group is ready to present even an informal play. Creative dramatics can be successfully practiced in many settings, including the classroom, the church school, the summer camp, and the recreation center. Music and rhythmic exercises can add immeasurably to the creative drama program. A large part of the success of any group depends upon the warm, friendly atmosphere created by the skillfull, trained, understanding leader, whose enthusiasm must generate eagerness and interest.

3

ACTIVITY PANTOMIME

At first glance, the title of this chapter may seem ambiguous, for the word "pantomime" means the expression or communication of an idea through action alone, without the assistance of the spoken word. This kind of play acting, however, may be performed on many levels, from a simple action like bouncing a ball or placing a flower in a vase, to a complicated scene, involving several incidents, which tells a complete story. It is to the first, or simplest form, that the term "activity pantomime" refers.

DEFINITION AND OBJECTIVES

Pantomime performed on this level may be termed dramatic play rather than drama. It has none of the limitations of form that one associates with drama; there is no conflict, no beginning, climax, or denouement. It is simply a kind of "make-believe," an outgrowth of the play instinct with which every child is richly endowed.

The emphasis throughout the periods devoted to this study is threefold: (1) activating the imagination, or learning to use the first of the two "keys" to the magic door of make-believe, *making a picture in the mind;* (2) developing concentration; and (3) freeing the body by encouraging natural response to an imaginary stimulus. It is the easiest way to make a beginning for, at the outset, the child is only recreating a familiar activity; he is not called upon to imagine any particular mood or emotional state. Whether he is pretending to skip rope, draw a picture, read a newspaper, or shovel snow, he need visualize only the objects that he is handling and the place where this action occurs. This kind of exercise may seem too simple to the initiate leader, but he will soon discover that it is a sufficiently difficult and challenging procedure to warrant the expenditure of considerable time.

THE START

In presenting the following suggested plan for the first pantomime class, one assumes that the group has already met long enough for members to have established a comfortable rapport with the leader and with one another (see "Creating the Climate," in Chapter 2). One general recommendation deserves attention; it should guide the tenor of every early session; dispense with unnecessary, routine formalities and attack the subject matter at once with a vigor that will stimulate enthusiastic interest.

A leader might say to a group of ten-year-olds, meeting the first period of a snowy school day in February, "What a cold trip we all had this morning, didn't we? My teeth are still chattering, aren't yours?" (This informal greeting will at once break down restricting barriers and create an atmosphere of friendly relaxation.) Several youngsters will forthwith volunteer remarks about the cars being stuck in the snow, or breakfasting before the open fire or finding ice on the milk bottles. The leader may continue, "That's the fun of starting off the day with creative dramatics. We can pretend all we want to and just forget about the cold. We can go to a sandy beach or a sunny garden, or feed the fish in the park. Which shall we do first?" Spontaneous suggestions will come pouring forth. It is finally decided, perhaps, to collect shells at the seashore, and the leader proposes that it be tried in groups of six. Two facts control his decision; first, eighteen children compose the group, and although the space is too small for all to work together, ample room exists for six to move about freely; second, he realizes the advisability of starting a new class with group work rather than individual exercises, thus encouraging the timid child to participate.

An open discussion follows, key questions being posed by the leader in quick succession. These questions help the children to recall specific details related to summers spent by the sea—the color of the water, the varying shape and size of shells, the delicious feel of burrowing in the sand with bare toes, the thrill of being showered with spray from an unexpected wave. In other words, before the children begin to play, the creative imagination will have started to work. The part of the room to be transformed into the beach and the ocean is now agreed upon, as are areas for the boardwalk and the cottage where the children are staying.

With the physical aspects of the scene in mind, the first group begins. No special time limit is set; the leader's judgment must guide him in terminating the action. When the appropriate time

ACTIVITY PANTOMIME 27

comes he may say, "Ah! That's fine! I'm sure we all have fine shell collections now, haven't we? Let's see yours, Mary." Mary, one of the timid ones, still encouraged to imagine by the question put to her, holds out her make-believe bucket and with great glee shows off its also make-believe contents. A short period follows, devoted to evaluating the work of the first group, in which all participate, including the young actors themselves.

Questions like this are likely to be forthcoming:

"Do we have to put our shells into a bucket? And how big is the bucket?"
"Can't we put the shells in our pockets?"
"Some people found so many shells! Can't we look for just two or three good ones?"
"I saw somebody go too close to the water. I hope he had his shoes and stockings off!"

Each of the questions is answered thoughtfully by the leader. He learns from these responses how specific he must be in explaining an exercise. Most of the participants can only feel secure if they completely understand what is expected of them. The ability to "make a picture in the mind" is dependent upon the exact knowledge of what one is to see.

The second group of six then try the same pantomime, and another critique follows. So it goes until each child has had his turn. This procedure can be mutually beneficial to players and observers alike, if it is intelligently guided. The audience members of the class learn to give concentrated attention to the work of their colleagues, as it becomes evident that their comments and constructive criticisms are welcomed and respected. The young actors, on the other hand, gain in stature through the valuable experience of learning to take these suggestions in good spirit. A friendly give-and-take between members of the class is established early and without too much effort. One gentle reminder may be in order. In any group, one or two children may tend to enjoy negative or cruel criticism of their neighbors. This must never be tolerated. The sensitive leader will handle this delicate situation wisely. He must say: "Perhaps you didn't watch carefully enough, Jane! I think I saw the shells Bobby put into his bucket quite clearly. We must remember, we are not being very good members of our children's theatre family if we make unkind remarks unnecessarily." He will refer casually but perhaps at some length, to the attitudes agreed upon at the first meeting of the group; he knows that Jane, like the others, wants very much to live up to them.

The period has started at a fast pace; there is alertness, excitement, and enthusiasm, because an immediate attack has been made on the heart of enthralling subject matter—the game of "let's pretend!" The same high level of interest can be maintained throughout the whole period, if the leader is well prepared in advance and has many ideas for activity pantomime at his fingertips. If this first meeting lasts for forty-five minutes, there may be time to try only two or three group situations. If the musician is present, however, at least ten minutes should be allowed for simple rhythmic exercises, including running, skipping, walking, or the clapping of various rhythms.[1]

THE FOLLOW-UP

The next few classes will proceed in somewhat the same manner. Although the leader is still devoting the sessions to the pantomiming of simple activities, he will endeavor to vary his approaches. His presentation must never seem dull or repetitious. Some of the techniques that have proved successful follow:

1. He may divide his class of eighteen into two groups of nine, by counting off by nines. The number ones in each group will raise their hands and take a good look at each other so that they will remember that they will be partners; the number twos, and number threes, etc., will do the same. The first group of nine will go to an imaginary store counter, which has been carefully indicated by the leader. This, he explains, is a most delightful unusual shop where toys and things to wear are sold, but without cost to the customer. He need only select what he wants and then take it along. As he turns from the counter he will handle his purchase, so that as he approaches his partner, the latter can see quite clearly. Then his partner will take the object, and will indicate by his handling of it whether he has discovered what it is. This exercise takes on the nature of a guessing game, but demands clear picturization and observation. When the first group has finished with its trip to the store, the second group of nine repeats the experience.

2. The leader may, after seating everyone in a big circle, join the group and say: "Now this is the most exciting day! It's a joint birthday! Imagine, everyone of us has a birthday today! Isn't that lovely?" There are some squeals of delight at the very incongruity of this statement. "And guess what?" She continues, "I have made you each a lovely box of fudge candy and have put it behind you. Whoops! Don't look . . . not till I describe the box to you. It's square, like this [he pantomimes], and has no wrapping. When I say 'Ready,' you reach behind you, get the box,

[1] See discussion of value of music, Chapter 2, pages 20–21.

ACTIVITY PANTOMIME

put it on the floor in front of you, lift the top off, fold back the two sheets of wax paper that cover the candy and then take a piece . . . and eat it . . ." He pauses for a moment—suggests that they close their eyes and make a clear picture in their minds of the box, its size and shape. "Now . . . all ready? Look!" And the pantomime begins.

3. This time the leader may walk around the circle (the children are still seated) carrying to each one an imaginary big tray laden with good things to eat and to drink. When he passes, each child will select something from the tray. He will not begin to eat or drink until all have been served. The thoughtful leader will remind his group that each must decide what he will select before the tray comes, so his mind picture will be clear. When all are served, the leader will stand off and watch the children enjoying their treats; he will try to guess what each one has chosen.

4. "Today," says the leader, "we will all imagine ourselves walking through a beautiful woods in the fall. The leaves are turning bright colors, and some are fluttering to the ground. What else might we see in such a forest?" Answers include squirrels, birds, flowers, interesting rocks, other animals, and perhaps even other people. When enough ideas have been presented, the whole group will rise . . . and close eyes for a moment, as they try to see the forest. At a signal such as, "All ready now? . . . let's walk in this beautiful forest . . . ," they will start to move. In such an exercise it will be necessary for the leader to indicate some sort of ending . . . since none is implied. After two or three minutes he might say, "Fine . . . shall we go home now?"

In most beginning pantomime groups certain difficulties will always present themselves. The wise adult will expect these things to occur and will be prepared to deal with them. Some of the less secure children, who are conditioned to behave according to a strict set of rules, will be afraid to work individually. They will constantly look at a neighbor to find out how he is doing an exercise, rather than run the risk of being criticized for not doing it correctly. They must be helped, gradually, to overcome this tendency by being assured that the leader is only interested in seeing the shape of Billy's shells, or the kind of leaves that Molly caught before they fell to the ground. They will be comforted to learn that there is no right way, for everyone sees different leaves, different shells, and handles them differently. Everybody's way is right as long as he really makes a picture in his own mind and sees his own objects. Another problem that one must anticipate is that of the unexpected giggle or exclamation, from those who observe. As soon as *this* occurs, the leader should stop the exercise and explain that since the noise made all the "pictures" disappear, we must start over again. This is a fine opportunity to go into the point in greater detail; all will agree that since the observers must soon be the performers, they will be as quiet as mice hoping that their colleagues will extend the same courtesy to them. It should be noted, however, that no concentrated observation can be expected unless appropriate material, guaranteed to interest the age group, is selected.

It is impossible to state arbitrarily the number of sessions that should be devoted to this simple pantomime. The experience of many groups indicates that there should be a minimum of three periods and a maximum of six. The frequency of the meetings, the alertness of the children, the number of inhibited or tense youngsters participating, and the creativity of the leader are all controlling factors. The appropriate time to progress to more difficult work must be determined by the growth and readiness of the members of the group. When most of them are moving with free coordination and are showing ability to "make a picture in the mind" with ease, then the time has come to go forward.

SUMMARY

Recreating, in pantomime, simple activities with which children are familiar, is recommended as the best method of beginning the drama project. The paramount objectives of this part of the program are: (1) activating the imagination by practicing the first "key" to play acting, "making a mind picture"; (2) developing the powers of concentration; (3) relaxing the body by encouraging natural response to an imaginary stimulus. It is most important for the leader to get into the heart of the subject at once, selecting an approach that will generate enthusiasm and friendly cooperation. The first exercises should be assigned to groups rather than to individuals, because it is easier to forget self when not working alone. Each attempt should be followed by a critique period, during which the young actors, as well as their colleagues and the leader, are free to discuss and evaluate the work. This practice offers an excellent opportunity to teach young people the importance of learning how to give and take kind, constructive criticism, rather than indulge in the cruel, destructive comments so often exchanged among children. The number of periods to be devoted to activity pantomimes may vary from three to six. The leader must try for variety in presenting program content during this time, so that the sessions will never seem dull or repetitious. Many factors control the decision to progress to more difficult work.

EXERCISES

The following suggestions, and those included at the end of the succeeding chapters, are intended merely to serve as models for the creative drama leader. No list is adequate for use during the three to six periods that will be devoted to this particular procedure, nor will any one of the lists indicated here be appropriate in its entirety to a special group of children. Before selecting suitable material for any program, the leader must consider the age level, general intelligence, experience range, social and economic status, and the primary interests of the young people participating. For example, children who have known only the activities related to life in a crowded urban area, whose only playground has been the concrete sidewalk, cannot be expected to imagine such experiences as planting seeds in a garden or raking leaves on the lawn. It is hoped that the examples listed below will suggest, rather than provide, fitting lesson content for the imaginative director. To save space, suggestions are given in the abbreviated form, merely listing the activity itself. This does not mean that the assignment would be introduced to the children in this manner. For example: One would not say in using Exercise 1 for the nine- to ten-year-old group, "Now pick violets in the woods." Here is a more interesting and exciting approach: "Let's imagine it's early spring. Have any of you taken walks in the woods in May or June, to look for wild flowers? Have you ever found little violets peeking out from under some dry leaves that are still lying on the ground? They have such dear little pansy faces; they almost look as though they're asking to be picked and taken home for your tiny little vase! Let's look about this forest (indicating a part of the room) and see if we can find some violets. Remember they have tiny short stems, and sometimes they're not easy to find. . . . Ready?" It is very important to help create this "mind picture" and also to interest them in a total situation or story, not merely the activity.

Eight- to Ten-Year-Old Group

1. Picking violets in the woods
2. Collecting shells on the shore
3. Gathering twigs for a fire
4. Feeding fish in the pond
5. Bouncing a new ball
6. Skipping rope
7. Dusting the table, floor, books in the bookcase
8. Building a house with blocks
9. Brushing the teeth, washing hands, combing hair
10. Putting dolly to bed
11. Making a sandwich for lunch
12. Eating an ice cream cone, lollypop, banana

Eleven- to Thirteen-Year-Old Group

1. Threading a needle
2. Writing a letter, sealing, stamping, and addressing it
3. Arranging flowers in a vase
4. Raking leaves on the lawn
5. Shoveling snow
6. Playing with a yo-yo
7. Practicing swinging a baseball bat or serving with a tennis racquet
8. Wrapping a gift for mother
9. Peeling potatoes, apples, onions
10. Crossing a stream on stepping stones
11. Hanging out two towels to dry
12. Cooking hot cakes

Fourteen-Year-Olds and Over

1. Trying on hats in a hat shop
2. Playing solitaire
3. Decorating for a party
4. Packing a suitcase for a trip
5. Fishing (baiting hook, casting)
6. Typing a letter
7. Making a phone call in a telephone booth
8. Painting a landscape in oil or water color
9. Purchasing a tennis racquet or baseball bat
10. Mixing ingredients for a cake, pie, or biscuits
11. Modeling in clay
12. Loading a wheelbarrow with soil for the garden

4

MOOD PANTOMIME

During the early classes no mention has been made of the expression of feeling through body action. Facility in "making a picture in the mind" of other places—the orchard, the beach, the dark forest, to which one can, in the wink of an eye, transport one's self—must come first. An easy transition can be made then to questioning the *feelings* of the city child when she is in the orchard or on the beach, or the lost boy scout's sensation when he is in the dark forest. How do their feelings affect their walk, their posture, their faces? Children are quick to note how the body droops from disappointment, swells in anger, shrinks with fear, lifts with joy. They will be unanimous in their answers to the difference in the walks of the sad boy and the happy boy. Interesting responses also come to questions concerning the color, line, and weight of positive and negative feelings, as well as the tempo.

"Jimmy's feeling, as he walked away from the railroad station where he said goodbye to his father, was blue, or maybe a blackish feeling. It was down instead of up and he felt terribly heavy! That's why he walked so slow!" This child has analyzed and expressed a human being's mood in terms of all the related art forms. In rhythm, he was slow, not fast; in color, he was blackish or blue; in line he was down (horizontal, not vertical); in form he was heavy, not light. Had the leader asked a question involving music or harmonies he would undoubtedly have heard that Jimmy was in a minor, not a major, key. This is a perfect example of the way in which a simple, creative drama exercise can become, under the guidance of a perceptive leader, an experience that relates all the arts and furthers aesthetic sensitivity.

Virginia, in describing Bobby's journey home from school with an "A" report card in his pocket says: "Bobby's feeling was bright yellow and orange! It was an *up* feeling and as light as a feather! If he'd had wings, he'd have flown. He was like a happy song!"

The next step is the discovery, together, that these feelings are accompanied by certain thought patterns. It is these thoughts that seem to send their messages straight to the heart; from there they are telephoned over hundreds of little wires (the nerves) to every part of the body, directing its moves. When Jimmy walks away from the station he thinks: "Gosh! Three whole months he'll be gone . . . my best pal! Nobody to play 'catch' with. Gee! I'm sure goin' to miss him!" These thoughts actually weigh him down, slow his steps, and turn his face into a thunder cloud. From this kind of explanation and many attempts at playing Jimmy or Bobby, one arrives naturally at the second "key" to the magic door of make-believe: "Think the thoughts of the character you're playing." It is obviously necessary to "think the thoughts" if the play-acting is to be real and believable.

SENSITIVITY

Every thought and feeling that gives color and meaning to life is absorbed through the senses. A sensitive individual is aware, concerned, and responsive; his senses reach out and absorb impressions, and he responds to these impressions. The technological, push-button efficiency of modern life tends to dull the senses; many people seem spiritually deaf and blind, and for some even the sense of taste and smell has become less acute. Dora Chaplin fears for children living under these influences. She says: "We are being doped into a cow-like immobility."

Modern living patterns *do* imply dangers; the senses seem either to be overstimulated to the point of neurosis, or so dulled by regular repetitive, conforming behavior that the human being takes on the appearance of a robot that has eyes that see not and ears that hear not. If children are to retain their natural sensitivity, they must be provided with experiences that keep the five senses alive and active. Since it has been agreed that all feelings come in through the senses, and this is the stage in the creative drama project when the expression of feeling is being studied, it seems an appropriate time to emphasize sense exercises. Furthering aesthetic sensitivity and an appreciation of beauty will also sharpen concern for human beings and deepen the meaning of personal relationships within the class.

One of the best ways to approach the subject of sensitivity with children is to encourage careful observation of sights, sounds, smells, tastes, and the feel of things. Questions such as these can be used as a starting point for sense exercises:

"What did you see today on your way to school?" "What colors did you notice most?" "What were the sounds and smells you liked most in the mountains?" "How were they different after the rain?" "What food do you think of first when I say: 'It's bitter . . . sour . . . sweet'?" "Shall we touch something with our hands that feels soft? What is it?" "What can our feet touch that feels soft . . . warm . . . cold . . . rough?"

Often one idea seems to crystallize in the minds of the children and they all start to create. The following "sense" question given to a class in late September once inspired a complete lesson. "Let's close our eyes and smell smoke! Can you tell me what you see, now? Take your time!" There was a pause; one could almost hear the thoughts whirring past.

"There's a big pile of leaves burning in our back field. Daddy and I have been cleaning up the lawn."

Then a little girl spoke. "The smoke's coming out of the oven! Mother's on the phone and she forgot she left the cookies in there."

A boy smiled as he said: "It's the smoke from grandfather's cigar. It's nice. I'm glad he came to see us!"[1]

The relationship of the smell of smoke to the vision of the imagined source of smoke provided three fine ideas that were later developed into interesting pantomimes.

Throughout the sessions devoted to these sense and mood exercises, the leader must constantly reemphasize the importance of the second key—think the thoughts; the right questions will help to drive the point home. For example: "There comes Janice, my little two-year-old sister limping up the path and sobbing. She has fallen and scratched her knee, poor thing. Let's each imagine she sees a little sister coming toward her." Several of the children fail to reach out sympathetic arms, fail to move toward the imaginary child. During the evaluation period the leader asks: "What were you thinking when you saw Janice, Mary?" Mary cannot seem to answer; finally she says: "Well, I guess I thought that she had fallen and wondered whether I should . . . go . . . and . . . and . . ." The leader stops the meandering conversation gently and suggests, "Mary, thoughts in your head are like words you might say to yourself. You know what it feels like to talk to yourself, don't you? Well, those are thoughts. Now, talk to yourself, out loud for a moment, as you see Janice approaching. . . ."

Almost at once the ideas flow. "Oh . . . poor Janice . . . her knee's bleeding . . . Gosh! . . . I should have watched her! . . . Poor little thing! Come here, Janice . . . Let sister fix it! . . .

[1] Other specific ideas for sense exercises are suggested at the end of this chapter.

There, now, don't cry any more!" And as she spoke the thoughts, Mary moved forward, leaned down tenderly, and lifted up an imaginary Janice. This definite help in thinking the thoughts was very much needed. Now she had found the "key" and from now on she felt secure about "thinking the thoughts"; she was also convinced that it was the thoughts that made her body move and her face react.

This kind of experience also presents the opportunity to discuss a very important theory: One must never tell his body what to do—his thoughts will indicate the movement that is real and right. Never must he say, "Now I'll act afraid," or "Now I'll look as though I am angry." The minute one thinks these directional thoughts, he loses the thoughts that his character is thinking, and the whole picture is spoiled. One leader has developed an interesting and convincing method of explaining this point. Her argument goes like this:

> You see, our brains are funny things; they work very well if we don't get them mixed up BUT if we're not careful . . . they just get confused and nothing sensible comes out. We must remember that each little brain has only room for one person's thoughts at a time . . . So if we're thinking, like Jill, who has lost her dog, "Oh dear, I've got to find him . . . I love him so! What'll I do if he doesn't come home . . ." and then suddenly we think, like ourselves . . . "Now I've got to try to look sad and worried!" . . . then our poor brain gets all mixed up and the messages it sends to our arms and legs and faces are confused, so we don't believe in Jill at all.

This idea of thinking one set of thoughts at a time caused amusement, but also seemed to suddenly clarify and emphasize the point: Do not tell the body what to do.

Each child should be made to understand that everyone doesn't think in exactly the same pattern when he is afraid, sad, angry, or happy. He will feel more comfortable if he also realizes that everybody does not react to the thought patterns in the same way, and that as long as the reactions are honest and truthful and motivated by his character's thoughts, they will be quite acceptable. Some of the following questions are sure to arise: Why do some people finish quickly, while others take a long time? Why are some movements much bigger than others? Why do some faces show so much and others so little? These questions can prove to be a golden opportunity for the leader. This is the moment to talk about how some little bodies have been so taught to stay straight and still that it is hard to let them go when the thought messages come to them. He must try to explain how important it is, nevertheless, for all of us to learn to communicate thoughts and feelings, so that our mothers and fathers and friends can know when we're happy, and sad, and afraid. "How can mother help you when you're in trouble, comfort you when you're sad, or protect you when you're afraid or in danger, if you don't let her know how you feel and what you think?" a leader said to one group of extremely inhibited children. And from that time on it seemed logical, somehow, for them to let their thoughts and feelings come through. Up to that moment they had been suppressed by their conditioning; now there was a reason to let go! Some whose tight, awkward bodies had appeared to be bound by invisible chains seemed, in a relatively short time, to move with freedom and easy coordination. How strong must have been the sense of relaxation and well-being, as they were loosed of those inhibiting bonds!

Work in the area of mood pantomime seems to fall naturally into three divisions: (1) exercises designed to sharpen the senses; (2) the playing of situations controlled by one definite mood, as one's self; and (3) the playing of situations controlled by a single mood, as a completely different personality. Again the assignments should be adaptable for group playing. There will still be a hesitancy on the part of many children to perform alone. If necessary, part of the available space will be assigned to each member of the group, in order to avoid confusion; i.e., an exercise involves six children, each of whom comes into his own living room, sadly, after saying goodbye to Father, and sits down in a chair. A chair should be placed and assigned to each child, and the door indicated, so that he will not be confused or disturbed by another young actor who might suddenly cross his path and ruin his "mind picture" or his thought pattern. A generous time for discussion of the exercise before it is attempted should be allowed. This will encourage questions and will assure the leader that everyone understands the scene, the placement of various objects, and where the dramatization begins. Only when a child understands completely can he feel secure about his work. The critique after each group's attempt is even more important as more complex material is used. The leader must learn to observe everyone, in order to encourage, correct, help, and question, so that each individual will feel accepted and important to the group. Guiding the discussion tactfully in the evaluation period is a real art; every leader must strive to develop this essential skill. At best, it is a difficult, demanding task. Another responsibility of the leader is the opening and closing of each exercise. Because in mood pantomimes we are still in the dramatic play stage, there is no form; no beginning, middle, or end is implied in the scene. Some leaders use a simple statement, quietly made, after the group is standing in the part of the room where the pantomime will start: "Now, when we're all ready, and have the picture in our minds, let's begin!" Then he waits! One will begin to move, then another, and then, perhaps, the rest. If a closing is not implied in the scene itself[2] then the leader may have to remind the group at the outset that each is to stay where his own scene finishes; or, at an appropriate moment, when all seem to have completed their movement, he can say quietly, "Curtain." The one word will signify the falling of the curtain on this particular episode.

Should most of the group show a readiness to try some exercises that require a greater amount of creativity and imagination, several of the following ideas might be used:

1. Walk home from school with a report card in your pocket. Let us see how you feel about this report card. Is it an especially good one? Is it disappointing? Do you feel guilty about taking it home?

Each of six children who perform the first time can be assigned a partner. The partner will watch the player and will try to guess the situation. The groups then reverse the playing pattern.

2. It's the beginning of a school day. Each of you (he selects a group of six) will decide how you feel this morning. Are you sad, happy, angry, afraid? . . . How do you feel? Why do you feel as you do? Has something happened at home, or on the way to school? Come into the classroom, hang up a jacket or a hat on the rack (this must be designated), and then sit down. (A place is pointed out for each child, numbers 1–6.) Your partners, who will watch carefully will see if they can guess how you feel, and maybe even what happened. Don't forget to think every thought!
3. Sit in a window seat and watch the rain pouring down the window pane. Are you happy, angry, sad, disappointed, afraid . . . ? How do you feel? There are many reasons for feeling differently about the rain.

THE USE OF MUSIC

During the two or three meetings devoted to mood pantomime, spend some time working with original background music, if the services of a capable musician can be secured. As has already been stated in Chapter 2, music has no equal in stimulating quick emotional response. Original background music may be used in

[2] In the scene in which the boy comes home from the railroad station and sits down, unhappily, in the living room, an ending is implied. Even if some sit down sooner than others, all can wait until the last has finished. There will be no confusion.

two ways: (1) to intensify the mood stated in a given situation; (2) to imply the mood not stated in a given situation. Both methods are successful and will offer interesting variety to the program. For example, the leader may suggest that some boys and girls who have been cooking a picnic supper, in a pine grove on the side of a mountain, are suddenly caught in a severe summer storm. Frightened and blinded by the heavy rain, they are trying to make their way down the dark, wet trail. The creative pianist, upon hearing the assignment, will at once begin his storm music, which pictures wind at hurricane strength, crashing thunder, falling branches, and sharp flashes of lightning. The sound immediately increases the flow of thought and feeling; bodies begin to shrink, move cautiously and anxiously—responses come with natural spontaneity.

On another occasion, the leader may say, "Now, we are going to pretend that we are coming home from school one afternoon, but we won't decide how we feel as we go along until we hear the music; that will tell us. But we must listen carefully to catch the mood before we begin." The signal is given to the pianist and the music starts—gay exciting notes played in a major key, in fast, rising rhythms. After a few seconds, one or two bodies lift, heads go up, and soon happy smiles appear. Before long, all the children are in motion, running, skipping, and waving to their colleagues in joyous abandon. The music stops, concluding the exercise, and the leader at once begins his questions. "How did you feel, Johnny, as you went home from school?" "Great!" says Johnny. "It was Friday and I couldn't wait to get home and go down to the beach for the weekend." "I don't blame you!" And the leader laughs sympathetically. "There's nothing so exciting as the end of a week at school with a trip to the beach to look forward to. I think we will all agree that the music you heard was certainly happy music. And what about you, Susan? What made you happy?" "Well, mine was different. I had just gotten my report card and found that I had an eighty in my history . . . and . . . well . . . I had sort of thought I might fail." "That's really something to be happy about; and it would make mother and daddy happy, too, I know." The leader continues to question each youngster in turn, making sure that always the child's imagining has been definite and specific. If a particular child's pantomime has seemed vague, her response to the leader's question will probably be something like this: "I was . . . I was . . . just happy." It must then be made clear to her that there is always a reason for joy and that, next time, she must create her situation more accurately.

The latter application of background music is the more difficult and can be used successfully only with a group that has developed a certain facility in creating an imaginary situation, aided only by a sense stimulus.

SUMMARY

The transition from activity to mood pantomime is easily accomplished by pointing out how the changes that occur in posture, walk, body movements, and facial expression are related to the changes in one's thoughts and feelings. The cause and effect become obvious as the class analyzes the differences in the body reactions of a boy who is sad or happy; one believes his reactions as the child learns the second "key" to the door of make-believe— to "think the thoughts" of the character he is playing. Since all thoughts and feelings enter through the senses, this is the time for special work on sense exercises. The rest of the work in mood pantomime includes playing a situation controlled by a single mood either as one's self or as another personality. It is advisable to use groups rather than to require individual work; despite the fact that six or more may pantomime at the same time, each is working on his own. A careful discussion should precede the first playing of each assignment and a critique period should follow. Great emphasis should be placed on thinking the thoughts of the character from the beginning to the end of the improvisation. Original background music can be used profitably to quicken emotional response and deepen the mood for creativity.

EXERCISES

The child can play the following situations as himself, or as another character. For example, in the first trial of Exercise 1, the little girl will express her own reactions. The second time she will pretend that she is a very poor child who has only one dress fit to wear. The boy doing Exercise 4 as another character may pretend that the school picnic was to have been his first outing after a two-month illness. His disappointment upon seeing the rain will be different from that of the boy who has been leading a normal existence. The leader can use all the other exercises for practice work in both types of pantomime.

8–10-Year-Old Group
1. Come in to show mother the rip in your new dress caused by a rough board in the neighbor's fence.
2. Cross a muddy field on stepping stones while wearing your Sunday-best shoes.

MOOD PANTOMIME

3. Search in the high grass for a valuable ring you have lost.
4. Watch the rain beating on the window pane on the day that the school picnic was planned.
5. Steal into the living room to surprise grandfather.
6. After half an hour, you are still waiting on the corner where mother was to call for you. It is growing darker by the minute.
7. Start to put away your toys that baby brother has scattered all over the living room floor.
8. Pick some flowers for mother's party when you'd rather be going swimming with your friends.
9. Try to clean up the ink spot on the desk that you made when you carelessly forget to put the top on the bottle.
10. Try, for the fourth time, to add up a difficult sum that is part of your arithmetic homework.

11–13-Year-Old Group

1. Come home from school with a very bad report card.
2. Wait on the station platform for the arrival of your favorite uncle whom you haven't seen for three years.
3. Read a letter containing exciting news of a trip your mother has planned for you.
4. Pick up the pieces of mother's valuable vase you have just broken.
5. Pretend that Daddy is taking a large splinter out of your finger.
6. Try to get across a street crowded with traffic.
7. Steal into the kitchen to taste one of cook's freshly baked cookies.
8. Try to put the cloth on the table on a windy day.
9. Try on some of grandmother's funny old-fashioned hats that you have found in the attic.
10. Try to put together a difficult jigsaw puzzle on which you have been working for several hours.

14-Year-Olds and Over

1. Read a letter from your best friend that tells you that she cannot come to visit you.
2. Discover that the new puppy has torn your evening dress that you were going to wear to the party tonight.
3. Try on a new necklace that you have just received for your birthday.
4. Make a list of guests for a wonderful party that you are planning.
5. Try to quiet your mischievous baby sister whom you have been asked to entertain while mother has guests.
6. Make the final preparations in dressing to go out with your favorite friend.
7. Struggle to pick up a stitch you have dropped in the sock you are knitting.
8. Try to tie a new bow tie or comb a new hair-do.

Exercises for Stimulating Sense Reactions
(Adaptable to any age group)

1. Listen to birds singing on a beautiful morning in early spring.
2. Walk past a pastry shop at baking time.
3. Walk through a fish market at the end of a hot day.
4. Pick up, in succession, an ice cube, an angora kitten, a hot pan, a thorny rose.
5. Take a dose of bitter medicine.
6. Feel the heat of the noonday sun in the desert.
7. Bite into a delicious bit of pastry.
8. Hear a strange tapping noise. (You are alone in an old house in the country).
9. Start through the living room to get a cookie. The door to the library is open. Hear mother talking to Aunt Polly. Let us see how you feel about what you hear. Does it make you sad, afraid, angry, happy?
10. Walk into a beautiful forest; hear a strange sound. Is it something pleasant? Frightening? Where does it come from? How do you feel about it?
11. On these three chairs, I shall place three lovely imaginary bowls; there are several little spoons lying beside each one. The contents of all three bowls looks alike and quite good enough to eat. Line up and walk along, leaving a little space between you, and take a taste from each bowl. The first will contain something terribly bitter; the next will be hot and peppery, the third will taste really delicious.

5

CHANGE-OF-MOOD PANTOMIME

When the class is ready to progress to change-of-mood pantomime, it has reached the bridge that leads the way from dramatic play to drama. So far, there has been no suggestion of plot in the exercises, no starting point, stopping point, no limitation of time set by form. Let us take, for example, a situation concerning Peter, who was terribly disappointed as he looked into the empty mail box on his tenth birthday. The kite that his uncle had promised was not there. The mood pantomime could start when Peter stands looking disconsolately from the mail box to the floor boards of the porch, wishing he were small enough to disappear in one of the cracks. His feelings may deepen as time passes; he may slump off stage in disappointment or he may drop down to the floor, his head in his hands . . . but his mood does not change. There is no real story here, no ending! Only if something occurs that changes Peter's mood and provides the stimulus for a completely different reaction, can the elements of drama be born. Perhaps mother will come running down the stairs and onto the porch to show Peter an exciting letter from Uncle Joe, saying that he's driving to town for Peter's birthday, in fact, may arrive at any moment. Peter's mood will change at once. His disappointment will become excited curiosity (will Uncle Joe bring the kite?) and then hope. A few moments later, as the familiar horn of the old car announces uncle's arrival and he comes up the path with a package under his arm, Peter's mood changes again to excited anticipation. When the contents of the box is discovered to be the long-awaited kite, it is joyous fulfillment that takes possession of the boy. Here are four different moods, occurring in quick succession—curiosity, hope, anticipation, joy—each of which is stimulated by a different incident, and which, taken together with the earlier moods of anticipation and disappointment, form a complete miniature drama with a definite climax and a satisfactory ending.

INTRODUCING CHANGE-OF-MOOD PANTOMIME

The first few classes devoted to change-of-mood pantomime must naturally be simpler than the story of Peter. In fact, it is advisable to try at least one group of exercises that involve only a single change of mood. Often the mood pantomime ideas that have been used recently can be enlarged for this purpose. For example:

1. While you are stealing into the kitchen to help yourself to a cookie, steps are heard coming down the hall.
2. While you are trying to put a fresh cloth on the garden table on a windy day, a sudden gust takes it out of your hands and drops it in a mud puddle.
3. Daddy has been struggling to get a painful splinter out of your finger. Finally he succeeds.
4. While you're making final preparations to go on that special date, you hear mother call "Don't hurry, dear. The party's off!"[1]

Five or six could try one of these together; each one would, however, be playing his own situation in his own way, as a single individual. Each would imagine his own sound, sight, or sensation needed to motivate his change of mood, whenever he wished it to come. Obviously every participant's ending would come at a slightly different time. The group would be warned of this and assured that it is to be expected. Each would be urged to remain quite still when he finished to avoid disturbing those who had not yet concluded their scenes.

The evaluation, following these first simple change-of-mood efforts, will offer an excellent opportunity to stress the importance of "thinking the thoughts." Usually, the children who finish the scene first are those who have "acted" rather than waited for their actions to develop naturally as an outgrowth of fluent thought patterns.

In Exercise 2 above, the child who finishes first and stands horrified, holding the imagined muddy cloth in his hand, long before the others, will probably have thoughts that run this way: "Wind! . . . In the mud . . . A mess!" The thought sequences of those who take longer and are more believable are probably as follows: "Oh dear! What's happened . . . the wind . . . it's got it! . . . Oh no! It's in the mud. Mommie's clean cloth, ruined. Oh, dear!" When thoughts are incomplete, the body action, too, is abrupt, jerky, and incredible.

At this stage in the dramatization process, working together as a

[1] These pantomime ideas were originally listed at the end of Chapter 4.

related group of friends or family members may be attempted. This is a new and far more challenging experience. Up to this time, although many have tried the same exercise together, they have not related to one another in any way, nor has the group functioned as a single unit. Each one has depended only upon his own thought patterns to guide his actions. In the new framework, a companion might suddenly come to him for protection, take his hand to show him something. He must spontaneously readjust his thoughts and, consequently, his actions, to respond to this unexpected stimulus. This kind of exercise, involving perhaps five or six people, one can describe as *working in a group as a group;* the earlier practice involved *working in a group, as individuals.*

This change in approach also poses a slight problem for the leader. He must often be responsible for inventing a way to give a sound cue for a change of mood, so that all will hear it and react at the same time. Should the creative musician be present, of course, the problem is solved; a sudden change in musical background used for this purpose is interesting and effective. If the leader must give the signal, he will do so as unobtrusively as possible; he may gently clap his hands, tap the table, or use his foot against the floor. He will be careful to discuss his plan carefully beforehand, so that the sound will be expected and will not break the group's concentrated imagining. For example: A group of young people who have lost the trail in the forest that will return them to their camping site hear a distant voice calling. (At this point the leader claps softly.) They listen, but fear grips them once more as they hear nothing but the wind in the pine trees. Perhaps they had only imagined the voice after all. Then it comes again, closer this time, distinct and clear. (The leader claps louder.) Before very long a light appears (this needs no cue but one child is selected to see the light first), and they can now make out the figure of their senior counselor who has come to fetch them. With great relief, they follow him down the trail.

During this part of the work, a discussion, more detailed than ever, must precede the playing of each scene. Ask questions that will force the children to think aloud, in proper sequence, some of the thoughts that might occur during the changing situation. Part of the discussion preparatory to acting out the "lost children" episode might run as follows:

Leader: What are some of your thoughts as you realize it is getting dark and you can't find the trail back to camp?
Child 1: What'll we do?
Child 2: We're lost!

Child 3: We'll have to spend the night in the woods!
Child 4: I'm scared!
Child 5: We haven't anything to eat!
Child 6: Suppose the rest go off and leave us?
Leader: Yes, all those thoughts might come to us; and as we hunted for the trail, we would keep thinking such thoughts and others like them, over and over, wouldn't we? Now, when we hear the voice for the first time, what do we think?
Child 1: What's that? Sounds like somebody calling.
Child 2: Maybe it's an animal!
Child 3: It might be somebody calling us!
Child 4: I don't think I heard anything!
Child 5: Do you think they're looking for us?
Child 6: They must be worried about us by now!
Leader: That's right, some of us would be hopeful, and some wouldn't believe we had heard the voice at all. . . .

And so the questions continue step by step until the whole scene has been covered and every point clearly talked through.

Definite planning of the setting is another very important part of the preliminary discussion. Each young player must know what his imaginary forest looks like, from which direction the voice will come, and where the hidden entrance to the trail lies. Each must also be clear about exactly where, in the story, the pantomime begins; and if there is to be any differentiation in the characters of the children (i.e., a fearful one, a boaster, an aggressive type, etc.), they must be discussed and assigned well in advance. Unless all of these facts are fully understood by the entire group, confusion in entrances and handling of objects will result.

SELECTION OF MATERIAL

In planning the assignments for any age group, four things must be considered:

1. The material must be appropriate, interesting, and within the experience range of the group participating.
2. It must be dramatic in form, suggest some initial incident, a rise to a climax, and an ending.
3. The episodes must vary in content and method of preparation in order to keep the interest high.
4. Incidents concerning human relationships that offer opportunities for discussion of fine attitudes and philosophies are preferable. (The fact that one of the fundamental goals of the worthwhile drama project is the stimulation of the child's growth along these lines must never be overlooked.)

Everyday life provides a wealth of ideas. Other suggestions can be gathered from newspapers, magazines, children's stories, historic episodes, poems, and songs. The creative, energetic, and wide-awake leader will have no difficulty collecting enough material in the course of a single year to last for a decade. He must spend adequate time in its preparation, however. It must often be changed, lengthened, shortened, and especially adapted for a group's use.

Giving an occasional suggestive, partial assignment often provides interesting variety and offers a real challenge to the children. The leader may say, for example, "Today we are all coming home from school as happy as larks. As we open the door we hear or see something that makes us furious. Suppose each of us decides for himself what that something will be." Such a scene, which obviously must be played by each child individually, will be interpreted in as many ways as there are actors. It offers far greater scope for the creative imagination, as well as an excellent opportunity for the leader to test the children's progress in that direction.

After devoting a period or two to pantomiming episodes involving a single change of mood and one character, several successive meetings may be spent on more complex scenes such as the story of Peter and his disappointment, mentioned at the beginning of this chapter. Several characters may be needed, in which case their relationships to one another and to the whole unit must be thoroughly discussed before the pantomime is attempted. The lists of suggested materials that follow include several single, double, or triple change-of-mood pantomimes for each group. The leader should remember that they merely serve as models for the dozens of similar improvisations that can be developed and that probably would prove even more appropriate if planned with the needs of a specific group in mind. A great deal of thought must be given to the manner of presenting each incident to the class. The story must be told vividly, dramatically, and in great detail. (The examples given have therefore been written in that style.) Ward (1957) makes a special point of this fact: "One storyteller creates something beautiful out of the story, another makes only a commonplace thing . . . when the story has been told and the dramatization begins, the quality of the play the children make will depend to no small extent on how the tale was presented by the teller."

SUMMARY

When the class engages in pantomiming situations involving changes in mood, it begins to bridge the gap between dramatic play and the simplest forms of drama. An episode where three or four changes occur can often take on the aspects of a real plot with a beginning, a climax, and an ending. The first experiences in such work should concern incidents involving only one mood change; these should be performed in a group *working as individuals.* Later, more complex pantomimes with several mood changes can be attempted in a group *working as a group,* acting together as a single unit. Many times a sound cue for the change in thought pattern will be needed. The musician may effectively suggest this transition; or, in his absence, a signal from the director will serve the same purpose. During the preliminary discussion of any episode, encourage the children to think aloud, in proper sequence, some of the thoughts that might occur during the changing situation. Plan the setting in great detail. Material selected for this work should be appropriate, interesting, and within the experience range of the group participating—varied in content and method of presentation—and should portray incidents concerning human relationships that offer opportunities for the discussion of fine attitudes and philosophies. The occasional offering of a partial, suggestive assignment provides interesting variety and widens the scope for the activity of the child's creative imagination. The later classes in this section of the project may be devoted to the playing of more complex scenes in which several related characters are affected by incidents causing three or four mood changes.

EXERCISES

8–10-Year-Old Group

A. Single Mood Change (for the group acting as a unit, or the individual)
   1. You are outside the kitchen window watching Aunt Sue icing the most delicious chocolate cake. She leaves the kitchen to answer the telephone, and there sits the icing bowl . . . a great temptation! After all, she has finished the job, and it would be such fun if you could have a tiny taste. You creep into the kitchen swiftly, run over to the sink, and are all ready to dip a little finger into the bowl when . . . alas . . . you realize that it is not only empty of icing, but also full of water. Aunt Sue, like the good housewife she is, has left it to soak. With great disappointment, you leave the room.
   2. Your are down on the seashore playing in the sand. The sun is shining brightly and there is a pleasant breeze. Suddenly there is a rumble of distant thunder. At first you pay little attention, so interested are you in the sand castle that is almost finished. After a few moments, the thunder comes again, louder. The

CHANGE-OF-MOOD PANTOMIME

sound seems so close that it is frightening. You begin to gather up your playthings, but before you can finish, big raindrops begin to fall. You run off hurriedly to find shelter.
3. As you run happily into your playroom to get your new model airplane set, you stop abruptly. There on the floor is a heap of broken bits. Your little brother has invaded your domain and has torn apart many of the delicate little wooden pieces you have painstakingly put together.
4. Jump out of bed bright and early one morning, remembering with great joy that this is the day of the big school picnic down at the shore. It means games and swimming and cooking hot dogs over the open fire. Such fun! As you run to the window and lift the shade, you see a downpour of rain. They sky is dark with gloomy clouds. Of course, the picnic will be called off. What a disappointment after all these weeks of planning! Sorrowfully, you go back to bed, thinking that you might as well sleep another hour, now that the whole day has been spoiled.
5. Pretend that you are the Knave of Hearts and steal into the royal kitchen sniffing the tarts that are baking. Just as you get to the stove, you hear footsteps and, quick as a mouse, you dart under the great table to hide. Tramp, tramp, tramp come the steps, right up to the door, and then, to your joy, tramp, tramp, tramp down the corridor they go again. When all is silent, you creep over to the stove, open the oven door, and in a flash you have picked up one of the golden brown tarts (with a handkerchief, of course, so you won't burn your fingers) and off you go.

B. Several Changes of Mood
  1. (For the individual.) Pretend for a moment that you are like Cinderella, a poor little child who is ragged and hungry. You have just watched your stepsisters go off to a fine party at the palace. Miserably unhappy and exhausted from your household tasks, you sit down by the fire to rest and finally fall asleep. A far-off sound of tiny tinkling bells wakes you. As you open your eyes, you are amazed at the change all about you. You are dressed in shimmering white satin; the drab little room has become a crystal palace. Nearby, a banquet table is laden with more ice cream and cake than you have ever dreamed of. As you eat, hungrily, the clock strikes twelve. Then, quite suddenly, the room grows dark. It has again become the shabby little cottage that you call home.
  2. (For the individual, or two characters.) You have been waiting for mother at the airport for half an hour. It is growing closer and closer to plane time. The crowd at the departure gate is getting larger by the minute. What will you do if she doesn't come? You have only ten cents, and besides, even if it were enough for bus fare back to the city, you wouldn't have the slightest idea how to find your way to Aunt Grace's. Finally

you think you see a familiar hat in the crowd. "Thank goodness! Mother has come at last!" you think to yourself, wriggling your way in the direction of the hat. You are about to call out when the hat's wearer turns around and—alas—it isn't mother at all! What on earth can you do? Now they are announcing the flight to Pittsburgh—your flight! It's hard to keep back the tears. The engines have been started. Just as you are about to give up, you feel a friendly hand in yours. It's mother rushing you off to catch the plane.

3. (For two characters.) You and your sister are spending a vacation at Granny Beam's. For a whole week it has been stormy and rainy, but this morning the sun is bright. Immediately after breakfast, you have both put on bathing suits and are off to the river's edge to play. As you cross the west porch, you see six of Granny's favorite potted plants, which have been blown over by the strong winds during the night. Several of the pots are broken and some of the prize plants have lost their finest leaves. Perhaps you ought to stop and fix them, for surely Granny can't because of her rheumatism. But the sun is so warm, and it's been so long since you could go down to your favorite spot by the river. You are about to give in to the temptation, but somehow you can't get those plants out of your mind. Granny will be so distressed about them. Finally a little voice whispers in your heart, "You must go back. You cannot be so selfish on such a beautiful day." With a longing glance toward the river, the two of you slowly retrace your steps and set about clearing up the debris. It's not much fun, and no easy job either. Pretty soon Granny's voice calls from the dining room and this is what she says: "I have some news for my two little helpers—very fine news! In just half an hour, Uncle Ted will be here with the big car to take two very good little children for a day at the beach. I am fixing up a lunch for you now!" You are so happy you can hardly keep from shouting. Just think of it! A whole day with Uncle Ted by the ocean! Guess it was a good thing you did stop to fix Granny's plants, after all.

11—13-Year-Old Group

A. Single Mood Change (for the group or individual)
 1. It is exactly two o'clock as you run up the steps of the movie house where your favorite picture is showing. Hurray! You made it just in time. As you reach for your money, your heart seems to stop beating and a big lump that doesn't belong there fills your throat. All you can feel is a hole in the lower left-hand corner of your pocket. The fifty-cent piece is lost! There's nothing to do but go home!
 2. You are out on a hike with your scout troop and have taken a

CHANGE-OF-MOOD PANTOMIME 51

new trail through the woods all alone, just to try it out. It's a beautiful day and so far it's been great fun. Suddenly you hear a strange hissing sound at your feet. There in the path is coiled a great spotted snake.

3. You have been struggling for what seems hours over an arithmetic problem. No matter how many ways you try to solve it, the answer just won't check. Suddenly, as you are adding a column of figures for the fifth time, you find your mistake. Thank goodness! At last you can go to bed in peace.

B. Several Changes of Mood

1. (For the individual.) You have just come hopefully into the room where you will live in a new boarding school. As you look at the barren walls, and feel the not too soft bed, your hope seems somehow to melt away. . . . Then when you take mother's picture out of your suitcase . . . you are so lonesome you are ready to burst into tears. . . . Suddenly a song starts outside in the courtyard. . . . Many children's voices are singing. . . . You hear your own name, Julie, called. . . . Go draw the curtains and open the window. There, below you, are twenty smiling faces, children your own age, singing a welcome song to you. . . . There can be no mistake, it's a welcome to Julie! Wave happily to them . . . and then turn back into the room to finish your unpacking!

2. (For individual or group.) You are very poor, and it is Christmas Eve, a time when boys and girls who are poor can't look forward to many gifts. There surely can't be any presents this year with mother so sick. You come into the house quietly, for mother mustn't see the brown package that you carry under your arm. The little book rack that you have carved for her must be hidden until tomorrow. Even if you know there will be no presents for you, it will be fun to watch mother's face as she opens hers. As you cross to your own little cupboard to hide your surprise, you stop abruptly. You must be dreaming! There on the floor, by the stove, is a big basket filled with packages tied with bright ribbons. On the handle is a shiny red and white card. Is it? . . . yes . . . something is written on it! . . . Your name, you very own name! And under it, in beautiful script, "Best wishes from Santa Claus!"

3. (For the individual.) You are happily collecting the ball, bat, and glove after a fine baseball game in the field next to your house. It's been a great afternoon; your team won by a large score. Then, suddenly, your eye catches sight of the little finger of your right hand. It is empty! The ring Aunt Carolyn gave you is gone! Frantically you start to search. You must have lost it while you were playing ball; it's got to be here and you've just got to find it. How can you ever tell mother that

you were so careless, when she has asked you so many times not to wear it except on very special occasions? You go over and over the field; it just isn't there. You sit down hopelessly on a stone; your head droops in your hands and your eyes sting from tears that just will come, in spite of everything. You reach in your sweater pocket for a handkerchief, and, deep down in the corner, your fingers touch something cold and round. For a moment you hold your breath. Could it be? Yes, it is! . . . It's the ring! As you put it on your finger, especially tightly, you say a quiet little prayer of thanks and run into the house.

4. (For the group.) You are in the classroom studying. The teacher has gone out to deliver a message to the principal. In a few moments you hear music. Yes, it's a military band, and it's coming closer every minute. Looking at one another excitedly, you wonder whether you dare investigate. It doesn't take long to decide, and pretty soon the whole class is crowding about the window. Now you remember; it's the parade in honor of the special circus coming over from the next town. Isn't it mean they're coming so soon and you have to stay in school? At that moment, you hear the sound of teacher's footsteps; she is returning. Quickly you make a dash for your seats again and take up your books and pencils. As teacher enters she goes straight to her desk; perhaps she hasn't guessed how you have been spending the time. You'll be lucky if she hasn't, but you won't be very lucky if you have to miss the parade. Then, suddenly, teacher rises and writes something on the blackboard. You can hardly believe your eyes. This is what you read: "Since the circus has arrived a day early, we will excuse all pupils at the end of this period so that they may attend the parade." Oh, boy, life isn't so bad after all!

14-Year-Olds and Over

A. Single Mood Change
1. (For the individual.) "I have been treated like a two-year-old. It's just not fair! The idea of saying I can't go alone to Central City to Margy's for the week-end! I just won't take it any longer! I'll show them! These are your thoughts as the clock on the mantel strikes midnight and you steal out the side door with your suitcase in one hand and your birthday money clutched in the other. Your puppy is following at your heels. "They'll be sorry, won't they, Tim, when they find I've run away?" As you creep determinedly down the sidewalk, a light flashes on. It comes from mother's room. Dear, uncomplaining mother! She's probably having that dreadful pain in her back again! Forgetting your recent denial of your family, you turn to go get her medicine as you have on so many other occasions. Then, re-

membering that you are running away, you stop. As you stand, unable to move down the path, your eyes fixed on that square of light above you, thoughts come crowding in upon you—memories of kind words, sympathetic arms comforting you when you lost the tennis match last spring, courageous smiles when the doctor told mother she must spend two months in bed. Suddenly you feel very cold, very lonely, and very miserable. What will you do without her? Where will you go? Then, as though drawn by an irresistible force, you turn back. No, you can't go away, no matter what you must give up. Home is more important than anything!

2. (For the group.) You are traveling west by plane, on your way home with three of your schoolmates. About halfway, something goes wrong with two of the motors and the plane makes a crash landing in a deserted spot in the Sierras. Fortunately, no one is badly hurt, but all are suffering from the shock and it is bitter cold. Ten hours pass and no help comes. The food has been completely destroyed; it seems days since you have eaten. Everyone is exhausted, but no one dares to stop moving for fear of freezing to death. Finally a welcome sound breaks the stillness! Yes—it is a motor. As you catch sight of it in the distance, hope rises in your heart. Then, for a moment, it seems to take another direction. It has not heard the message; you will never be discovered—never! Again fear possesses the whole party, a hopeless fear. But before long, the purring sound comes again. Yes, this time there can be no doubt; the plane is headed directly for the little mound on which you stand. After what seems hours, but what actually must have been only a few seconds, it is almost overhead. Now there are flares . . . signals! Help has come at last! (We begin the scene at the point in the story just before we hear the plane approaching.)

3. (For the group.) You are one of a group of wives, brothers, mothers, and children of coal miners, who have been waiting for twelve hours at the top of a shaft where a tragic cave-in has occurred. The air is tense with anxiety, for if the signal from the rescue party does not come soon, it will come too late. The silence is agony for those who wait. Suddenly, the great bell in the square begins to toll . . . once . . . twice . . . then three times. That is the signal you have been waiting for. The trapped miners have all been saved!

B. Several Mood Changes

1. (For group or individual.) You are traveling on foot in the desert, having become separated from the rest of your party by a terrific sandstorm. For two days now you have been struggling along alone, without food or water. Suddenly, you see before you the green of trees, and beneath them, in the cool shadows,

the shimmering surface of a deep pool. You stagger forward as fast as your exhausted feet will carry you, and reach down to plunge your hands into the water. Your fingers close on the hot sand. The pool was only a vision—a mirage! You lie there, half conscious, too helpless to make an effort to go on. You are hardly aware of the sound of footsteps approaching. Suddenly you hear your name called, and turn your head weakly. Your brother is leaning over you; he has come to the rescue just in time!

2. (For the individual.) You are coming home from a swimming party and are very happy as Janet's father stops his car to let you out at the corner. As you turn to run home, Spunky, your little black cocker spaniel, leaps from the porch and starts across the street to meet you. At the same time a big coal truck rounds the corner. There is a squeak of brakes, and then a sharp cry. You cover your eyes because you dare not look! Finally, in desperation, you run toward the truck to investigate; there lies Spunky, alarmingly near the front wheel, very still. You pick him up and, holding him close, run over to sit on the little strip of grass beside the walk. If he would only move; if you could only hear him breathe! Suddenly, the strangest thing happens: Just as though he had wakened peacefully from a long nap, he opens his eyes, looks up at you, yawns, stretches, and begins to lick your hand. In a few moments, he is on his feet, as good as ever. Joyfully, you pick him up and run into the house.

3. (For the individual.) You are spending the stormy night alone in your great-aunt's barnlike house in the country. When the family was called into town unexpectedly, of course you had insisted with great bravado that you didn't mind the least bit. Now it is nearly midnight, and the wind is making eerie noises as it rattles the old building. It isn't very easy to concentrate; your half-finished magazine slips to the floor. Wait . . . what is that? What is that strangely rhythmic scratching sound? Certainly it cannot be the wind. It sounds as though it comes from the attic. As you listen intently, trying to locate it, all is silent. Then the scratching comes again. It is distinct now. Your heart seems to leap into your throat. Yes, there's no mistaking it; that insistent, scratching noise comes from the outside door. Trembling with fear, you move across the room, with great hesitation take the knob in your hand, and slowly, very slowly, pull back the heavy oak door. There, on the threshold, is a pathetically soaked, shivering puppy, whose pleading eyes beg for shelter from the storm.

6

DIALOGUE

When a group has had a healthy, balanced first course of pantomime, it is ready and eager for a variation in diet. The boys and girls will have developed an informal, friendly attitude toward one another, an interest and respect for the project, relaxation from tensions, more active imaginations, and better coordinated bodies. Beginning to work with dialogue should be a natural and easy step forward.

THE APPROACH

This new part of the program must be introduced with care. Children like to know the reasons for everything; they are even more pleased when they can make sufficient discoveries for themselves, to answer their own questions. During the group discussions concerning pantomime they learned, through analyzing and testing, the relationship of posture and body movement to physical and emotional changes. There is an equally fine opportunity to point out the influence of the same factors on voice production. A few simple exercises will prove to the youngsters that quality, energy, and pitch of the voice are determined largely by the physical or emotional state.

Another helpful reminder, as work with the spoken word begins, is the importance of the two "keys" that proved so useful in pantomime. Their application is even more significant to the success of this step. Also to be recalled is the fact that the stimulus for all new feelings and thoughts enters through one of the senses. A simple but dramatic demonstration by the leader may help children to understand speech as a three-step procedure: one (1) sees (hears, smells, touches, tastes), (2) thinks, (3) speaks. Such words as "look" are effective for demonstration purposes. The leader might say: "I'm exploring in a most exciting forest," and at this point he looks up as though spying an unusual, bright-colored bird flying from tree to tree. "Look!" At this point some of the children will almost certainly look up in curiosity. "What did I see? Can you guess? Was it exciting? Had I ever seen such a thing before? Where was it?" These and other similar questions will start a live conversation and group discussion. Together they are soon able to guess the exact nature of the experience; they realize the word "Look!" has told them everything. The need for the three-step procedure is clear; the leader has (1) seen (the bird), (2) thought ("How interesting"), and (3) spoken ("Look!").

The same word "Look!" can be used in a different setting. The leader places two chairs a few feet apart designating the space as "the open door to your bedroom." He asks half the group to line up at one side of the room and be prepared to come down the hall to the bedroom, one at a time. The other members of the class sit on the floor, inside the "bedroom" to act as audience. As each one reaches the open door, he will see something inside the room that was not there before, and say the one word, "Look!" "You must decide what has happened in this room since you left it this morning," says the leader. "If you don't know exactly what it is then you can't make a picture in your mind," and he restates the basic principle once more, "Remember to look, think, and then speak!"

Although the children may not realize it, the leader must be aware that he is asking for solo performance for the first time. Previous exercises have been done as groups; if work with dialogue, however, were started with six children, the obvious result would be chaos! The plan for the "Look!" exercise just described, in which each child speaks as he reaches the open door, will usually present no problem of self-consciousness. By the time half the class has finished and the evaluation has been completed, the second group is eager to try the same scene.

In beginning work with speech, scenes requiring only two or three characters are recommended. Until a facility in improvisation develops, a larger group will find the spontaneous creation of meaningful dialogue confusing. It is a wise leader, however, who expects some small troubles as he embarks on this phase of the project. Even though readiness seems evident and questions like "Can't we talk now?" are frequently asked, the actual sound of one's own voice is often a little terrifying. Some groups that have made excellent progress up this time may seem to suffer a slight relapse, or even come to a stand-still, when dialogue is attempted. But once the shock of the first plunge is over, the water no longer seems frigid; swimming is pleasant and challenging! One should, however, not expect too much! Adults sometimes forget that the child has only been aware of words for a few years; his vocabulary is small and his responses are often monosyllabic.

Some of the single words that can serve as interesting and imaginative practice material are: Hello, Goodbye, Tomorrow, Finally! Mine, Wait, Gone! Many others will come to the creative leader's mind. Children carrying out any one of these assignments must be required to imagine specific circumstances in which the one word would be spoken. This statement merely introduces an idea that is an old friend, but now appears in different dress: there must always be a definite reason for thinking and feeling. The leader may set the stage, as he did in the "Look!" exercise, or each child may imagine his own scene.

One teacher found that the words "Come in!" provided her with material for a valuable beginning speech exercise. She announced that she was coming around the class to call on every child. "Each of you is seated in your living room near the front door," she said. "The door is closed but it has a little glass window in the upper panel, through which you can see quite clearly anyone standing outside. I will knock on your door and you MUST open it and say to me, 'Come in.' But there's one big problem: I don't know who I am, or how you feel about me until I hear you say 'Come in.' By your tone I will know whether I am a boring neighbor, a fierce-looking policeman, the school principal, or your favorite aunt. I'm quite willing to be anyone you want me to be, but you MUST ask me to 'Come in.' Now, you will each decide who will come to your door. When you have made up your mind, put up your hand. I cannot start until everyone is ready." Almost immediately one hand went up, then two, and before long all were eagerly anticipating the fun. The teacher continued. "Fine! Now, when you hear the knock, which I will make audible by knocking my heel on the floor, get up, and look out and see me, think, and then open the door and speak. Only if I'm sure who I am to each one of you can I answer properly as I come into the house." This was an exciting experiment to observe. Concentrated attention and imaginations working overtime testified to the success of the endeavor, which, one must say, makes rather severe demands upon the teacher.

ELEMENTARY PRACTICE SCENES

By this time it is quite safe to try some simple episodes in which only a few spoken words are indicated. Some of the change-of-mood material may be readily adapted for this purpose. Since these incidents have already been discussed by the group, the characters are old friends and the settings are familiar. This is an advantageous situation; preliminary analysis and discussion that one MUST accord a new assignment have already been thoroughly done; attention can then be focused on the new technique of communication through the spoken word.

Several of the exercises at the end of Chapter 5, although suggested for the individual, can be adapted for use by the addition of another character. Exercise A-3 in the first list will serve as a good example. As it is introduced, minds may be refreshed in this manner: "Remember the scene about the little boy who ran happily to his playroom one day and found that his two-year-old brother had scattered the pieces of his model airplane set all over the floor—in fact had broken the parts that he had already assembled?"

There will be a general murmur of assent, and interest in the recalling may stimulate several comments. It is a well-known fact that children like returning to stories and characters that they have already met.

"Well," the leader continues, "there is only one problem. If we want to play this story with conversation, our little boy, whom we can call Donny, must have someone to talk to. People don't usually talk to themselves, do they?" This comment causes general amusement and relaxes the atmosphere in a delightful manner. Someone may offer a solution. "I know—let's have him take his friend, Fred, up to see his airplane!" All agree and the leader continues with specific questions that are planned to get minds working and thoughts coming in an orderly progression.

"What would Donny and Fred talk about as they run together down the hall?"

"Oh, Donny would be boasting about how much work he'd done on the plane and maybe showing off a little bit."

"I guess Fred would say, 'Gee, I'd like to help you finish it, Donny.'"

"Why of course," says the leader, "these are fine ideas. Fred would certainly be curious about the plane and, if he's a good friend, he'd be glad to help build it! But what would Donny say as he reaches the door and looks at the broken pieces?"

"Gee! Look! My plane's busted . . . ! Look!"

"He might say: 'It's ruined . . . and I put half of it together this morning!'"

"Then Fred would be upset too," one younger boy might comment. "I guess he'd say 'Gee . . . how terrible . . . !'"

"I'm sure he would be very sympathetic," the leader agrees. "And now, as the boys go into the room and Donny gets down to pick up the pieces of his toy, he and Fred realize for the first time how much damage has been done!" Before the leader can continue often the ideas come pouring forth from the class. One, verbalized like this, however, must be picked up at once, and corrected.

"Donny'd say that he wished he could get his hands on the guy that done it and that if he could he would beat him up."

This contribution may come from Jim, one of the tougher male members of the group. The leader must jump into the conversation here. "That's a good idea, Jim, but tell it to us again please, pretending that you really ARE Donny and thinking his thoughts. Don't say that he would wish, and so forth . . . just speak the words the way Donny would think them."

At once Jim scowls and doubles up his fists, becoming Donny. "Geez! . . . if I could git my hands on de guy that done it . . . I'd . . . I'd . . . I'd beat him up!"

"Fine!" says the leader. "Thats just the way Donny would say it, with one exception. Anybody want to take a guess about that exception?"

A hand goes up at once and its owner's voice chimes in without even waiting for the usual nod of recognition. "Sure, I know! Jim said 'done' and 'git' instead of 'did' and 'get.' I don't think Donny would use bad English even if he were angry, do you?"

"No, I don't think so," replies the leader, obviously pleased by the quick response to his question, which assures him that the powers of observation and concentrated listening are improving. Cleverly he manages to get Jim to agree that right grammar is more appropriate; and the reminder, because it is well timed, can make a far deeper impression upon the boy than the enforced memorizing of rules concerning past tenses. Another fine lesson has been learned by Jim, and, incidentally, the others—a technique which is the key to success in dialogue building: *Be the character! Think the thoughts in the character's words, never in the objective terms of what you think his thoughts might be!*

More questions follow concerning the ending of the scene. What will the two boys do? Will they try to take revenge on the young culprit or will they try to mend the plane? Several possible suggestions are accepted and a half a dozen pairs of Freds and Donnys offer to play. None of the exact words suggested in the preliminary discussion will be used, but the flow of thoughts will have become so clear that voicing the ideas in their own words will be a simple matter. Although some youngsters are much more eloquent than others at the start, even those who are monosyllabic for the most part will soon show promise. Vocabulary will increase perceptibly, as will fluency of speech. During the evaluation that follows each dramatization, a genuine effort must be made to improve the scene. Ask questions that help establish the fact that dialogue has two purposes: (1) to tell something about the character, and/or (2) to tell more of the story. One might ask: "Did the conversation let us know that Donny and Fred were friends? How could we tell by the way the boys spoke what kind of people they were? How did we feel about the little brother? Maybe it was Donny's fault for not putting his plane out of reach. Could we blame aged two-and-a-half, really? Do we need so much conversation about how dreadful this is . . . or will our story move along better and be more interesting if we go on to another subject?"

If necessary, one should repeat the sequence of ideas that will make the scene tighter, before the second group plays. Always, however, some praise from the leader should start the evaluation off on an affirmative foot. Nothing will produce the inner security that motivates creativity like a feeling of having successfully accomplished a task. According to Jersild: "The satisfaction that a child derives from being able to do something well is an important factor in his growing conception of himself."

"Fine . . . that was splendid. I really believed it!" The leader might begin: "My! I was so interested in the story, I didn't like to see it end!" Perhaps, "Oh dear, I felt so sorry for Donny! Skip made me really see the pieces of that plane!" Such remarks will establish a comfortable atmosphere and set the pattern for affirmative comments from the audience children. Then, later, he will find the way to make constructive criticisms and offer helpful suggestions.

GROUP DIALOGUE SCENES

Scenes in which only three or four players are necessary usually prove highly satisfactory substance for secondary exercises. A greater number of characters usually makes for confused dialogue. A leader might try the "lost children" episode that was described on pages 45–46. By now, everyone in the group will have identified himself with one of the children who has missed the trail back to camp. Possible thoughts will have been spoken aloud; these thoughts will form the basic structure for the dialogue. The setting has been established, and the story, with its element of anxiety rising to the climax, when the voice of the counselor is heard above the wind, is clearly understood. In other words, the groundwork has already been laid. The leader may need to restate some of the thoughts in greater detail, in order to refresh young memories, if the assignment has not been referred to for a week or more. This procedure will furnish a more generous supply of ideas for the conversation. One person must be selected to bear the responsibility for each of the cue speeches in order to keep the plot moving forward. Cue speeches now substitute for the sound cues that the leader provided when the episode was played in pantomime. Child 3 may be chosen to hear the voice the first time, child 1 the second time, child 4 to be the counselor who makes the rescue. During the first few trials, decide who will start the conversation and ask the group for suggestions as to what he might say. The scene might open with, "Hey, Johnny, it's getting late . . . we'd better get back to camp." or "Gee! I'm hungry! We must have been gone for hours." or "I don't like the sound of that wind; it's clouding over, too!" Perhaps none of these suggestions will be used—if not, so much the better. They will have served their purpose, nonetheless, for young minds will have been stimulated and will be better prepared to create the kind of opening dialogue that sets the plot in motion.

Groups ready for more challenging experiences in creative dialogue may try the surprise improvisation.[1] Tell a small group of children only the locale of a scene, the relationship of the individuals involved, and a single line to be spoken by a character entering at the beginning. They will create spontaneously the rest of the conversation, progressively developing the surprise plot. This type of exercise, which makes far greater demands upon the imagination, is both popular and profitable. Bridge, speaking of the far-reaching effects of improvisation, or "the impromptu activity," says:

> Since life and drama itself, consists in a sequence of impromptu situations in which the individual acts with only a minimum foresight, in the impromptu activity, we project the individual into certain situations . . . in which he must act as though the situation were real. He has no time to think or plan what to do (as is the case in life) as a rule. He cannot do other than act-as-a-whole. He must invent his way out of the situation. . . . The actor will do things he has not done before: find new words, new voice, and in general call up into controlled action, hitherto unexpressed phases of his personality. . . . The result of the process is to release hidden stores of psychic and emotional resource and so enrich the experiencing self. And since the subject is under the constant obligation to invent, the creative imagination is consequently stimulated.

Pat, a sensitive, repressed fourteen-year-old girl, experienced this complete release to which Bridge refers in a single improvisation. The scene took place in the early morning, near a mountain top in the Sierras. Pat and her companion, who was in ill health, had been struggling westward in the hope of finding a beautiful valley in

[1] See Sections A and B, Variations for Older Groups, in Exercises at end of Chapter 6.

which to make their home. Pat, waking first, climbed to the top of the nearby hill and saw (in her imagination) lying at her feet the green haven that was their goal. With body uplifted and face shining with excitement she said, "Susan! Look! . . . We've found it!" The shy, introvertive child, in her joyous response to an imaginary stimulus, had released "hidden stores of psychic and emotional resource and so enrich(ed) the experiencing self."

SPEECH IMPROVEMENT

The procedure used in playing the dialogue episode is similar to that which governed the previous classes. The same scene may be played by several groups of volunteers, and a critique should follow each trial. The leader should find an opportunity during this discussion period to inject questions that will arouse in the children a desire to improve voice, diction, and oral English. Only now can real strides be made in that direction, for young people must have a reason for wanting to learn to speak more clearly. They will be bored by speech drills as a thing apart, but will take to them readily if the presentation is made at the right moment in an ingenious fashion.

An incident that occurred in a creative drama class offers convincing proof of the wisdom of making concentrated efforts on speech improvement only when the occasion arises. Anne, aged ten, had a nasal, whiny voice and a careless habit of dropping her "ings." She had listened politely to the leader's frequent hints about correcting the fault, but made no apparent effort in that direction. One day she was playing the part of a queen in the improvisation of a bit of fairy tale. During the evaluation period at the end of the scene, her colleagues frankly expressed their opinions of her interpretation.

"Anne walked just like a queen," said one, "but when she sent the elf to get her cobweb shawl she sounded like a little girl with a tiny, squeaky voice."

"Yes," said another, "I thought a queen's voice ought to be soft and silvery, like music."

"And a queen should say whole words, not pieces of ones, so all her subjects could hear her when she sat on the throne and made speeches," a third child remarked. "Anne would be more like Queen Rosamond if she would say her words like that!"

The leader stepped into the situation at once, eager to avail himself of this opportunity. "What do you think about these suggestions, Anne? Don't you agree with Billy and Jean and Tom that your queen didn't have a very soft and silvery voice, and that her subjects would have found her speeches pretty hard to listen to?"

"Yes," Anne responded sadly. "You know, I wish I did have a queen's voice, 'cause then I could play her more real . . . but . . . I don't know how to make a queen's voice."

This was the very chance for which the leader had been waiting so patiently: The child had actually expressed a desire to improve her voice because she wanted, above all else, to be able to "play the queen more real." The next fifteen minutes were spent more profitably in explaining the technicalities of speech mechanism, in a simple and delightful way. By using analogies familiar to children, likening the resonance chambers to the sound box in a violin or cello, the vocal chords to their strings, and other such comparisons, the subject of voice and speech reproduction was given attention. The children had fun saying words like "singing," and then suddenly stopping the sound by pinching their noses with a make-believe clothespin of thumb and forefinger. They felt for vibration on the tops of their heads when they gave the "m" and "n" sounds the proper value; they made original rhymes with groups of words containing the often mispronounced "ow" or "ou" sound, and the especially mistreated "a" as in "grass." Experimenting with such lines as "the bird flew up, up, up, and away to the far-off hill," and "the stone dropped down, down, down, to the bottom of the empty well," proved to be a satisfactory method of teaching the importance of rising and falling inflections. Each student took delight in trying to relate the pitch of his voice to the action implied in the line. Every member of the class was determined to find the secret of making "a queen's voice, soft and silvery like music." The study evolved naturally, not because the leader demanded it, but because the children became conscious of ugly sounds and were eager to increase their ability to interpret more convincingly the parts they might be asked to play.

Any leader who wants to improve the speech of his group should watch for such an opening and make immediate use of it when it appears. He will set no regular times for drills, but space them appropriately throughout the whole season. Little by little, the youngsters will develop a great pride in their own progress and will begin to realize how much it helps them, not only in the play, but also in their everyday contacts. Another little girl in Anne's class—a reserved, timid child by nature—was reported to have burst into the room one day with great excitement. "Oh, Mr. King, Mr. King," she cried breathlessly, "I got chosen! Did Billy tell you, I got chosen?" It was hard to believe that this confident, bright-eyed child could be the once shy, monosyllabic Peggy. And the transformation had been wrought by such a simple thing. She had been chosen by her classmates to read aloud during the weekly story hour because, when

Peggy read, "the story seemed so real." In this case, the child's speech development had won her the long-sought recognition of her associates, which brought concurrently the self-confidence that she so badly needed.

The author has had great success in correcting unpleasant vowel sounds with original verses done dramatically. She had been working diligently without noticeable progress on the various sounds of the letter "A." Everything had been tried—even the time-honored system of giving a simple, familiar word as an example of each sound, beginning with the long "A" spoken in the front of the mouth with the tongue rolled forward, to the sound requiring a completely open throat: ATE, AT, AFTER, ART, were repeated over and over again. Then one day she began the class with this story:

We're going to play this scene in couples. We will call one character A and the other B. A will do all the speaking but B, who is slightly more fearful, has much to say in pantomime. The time is the seventeenth century. The place is an unnamed country in the middle of Europe. You've been imprisoned unjustly in a great medieval castle. Fortunately, you've become friends with the guard who stands the night watch in a sentry box in the flagstone courtyard. He has promised to help you escape and this is the appointed night. There is great feasting and revelry in the large banquet hall, which extends along one side of the courtyard; on another side lies the prison; a third side is bordered by the now empty sleeping apartments; on the fourth side stands a high wall in which there is a gate. The tower clock has just struck midnight. Boisterous laughter almost drowns out the sounds of the minstrels' song that issues from the banquet hall. You're standing just inside the grill-work gate to the dungeon, the key of which the friendly guard has given you. (B stays in a position ahead of A during the whole scene.)

- A: (Looking back to be sure they're alone) Wait! (conditions are satisfactory) It's late! unlock the gate! (B does so, opens it, and looks back for instructions.)
- A: Go fast. Hurry past. (He indicates the banquet hall at left.) It's a chance, but the last! (B runs half across the courtyard and starts to rap frantically on the sentry box, for which a chair serves.)
- A: (Running to stop him) Tap! Don't rap! We're in a trap! (He looks around fearfully. B, corrected, now taps with one finger . . . three times . . . the original plan for the signal to the guard. The imaginary sentry comes out into view, looks around, points to the big gate which he has unlocked for them. The two proceed hurriedly to the gate, where B suddenly stops. He is afraid of the dark shadows that lie before him in the town.)
- A: (Consoling him) Take heart! If we part, we'll meet at the mart! (They shake hands. B goes out, disappears. A goes through, pulls gate closed carefully, and also disappears.)

This scene caught the attention of the young teenage group immediately. Interest was sustained for an entire forty-five minute period. The fact that they are in reality doing a speech exercise that focused on the pronunciation of the letter "A" never occurred to them. A look at the spoken lines, without the explanatory directions, may be helpful:

1. Wait! It's late! Unlock the gate!
2. Go fast. Hurry past! It's a chance, but the last.
3. Tap, don't rap! We're in a trap!
4. Take heart! If we part, we'll meet at the mart!

Another amusing set of verses that has proved very successful with a younger group uses the vowels $\bar{E}, \bar{I}, \overline{OO}, \bar{O}$. The lines are:

1. Whee! We're free!
2. Oh! The snow!
3. Hi! Let's fly!
4. Ooo! He flew!

A story sequence is difficult to imagine at a glance; the lines seem to have no connection. It goes this way: Two friends, who are usually very restricted and never allowed to adventure, finally run off to explore a mysterious and rather magic land. One has wandered off and is standing on a high cliff at the opening of the scene. The other, who speaks, is down in the valley, standing amid heaps of bright-colored fall leaves. He tosses them above his head in great glee, rejoicing at the new-found freedom. "Whee! We're free!" Then he looks down, presumably to gather more leaves and stops for a moment, shocked. Some magic has turned the leaves into snow! He moans in disappointment! "Oh! The snow!" Then hearing his friend's whistle from above him, he looks up, waves and cries, jokingly:

"Hi! Let's fly!" Much to his amazement, his friend, obeys the orders, and, assisted by more magic, takes off across the sky. In absolute awe and amazement he says, "Ooo! He flew!" This kind of speech practice is eminently successful, and great fun! The possibilities are infinite! Once more, it does demand creativity and resourcefulness on the part of the leader.

SUMMARY

Begin dialogue with a discussion of the effect of the physical and emotional state on the quality, pitch, and energy of the voice. In the early practice, dramatizations should be based on a single word or phrase. At this time emphasize the significance of the three-step procedure necessary in all speech work: (1) see, (2) think, (3) speak. It is often easier to utilize some of the episodes that have previously been developed in pantomime, since the scenes and characters have already been analyzed and discussed. Occasionally an extra character must be added. Later classes can be set aside for work with groups of three or four. The inclusion of a larger number of characters will confuse improvisations, unless the group has had a great deal of experience. Introduce technical speech study when the child feels a need for improving his speech. He will be glad to work on diction if he feels that the expended effort will make his characterization more convincing. Advanced work may include "surprise exercises," "monologue," and "couplet" techniques.

EXERCISES

8–10-Year-Old Group

1. See first list, end of Chapter 5, A-1 (add a friend or sister).
2. See second list, end of Chapter 5, B-1 (add a kitten).
3. See second list, end of Chapter 5, B-2 and B-3.
4. This hot July morning mother does not feel well. She asks you to mow the front yard and hose down the patio. Two of your friends come happily down the road, bathing suits and towels over their arms. They call and ask you to join them for a swim in the lake. For a moment, you are tempted to go along; the sun is hot, and it's not much fun pushing the heavy mower. They try to persuade you to do your work later—that mother won't mind. You start to the house to get your bathing suit and then, remembering that mother has counted on you to finish the jobs before noon, you turn back to your friends and refuse the invitation. They go off without you and you return to your work, satisfied that you have done the right thing.
5. It is April 1 and, incidentally, your birthday. Your big sister has just given you a beautiful box done up in the fanciest of wrappings. You thank her over and over again as you open the surprise package. As you unfold the tissue inside you find . . . NOTHING! The box is empty! Looking up in dismay, you see a broad smile on your sister's face as she says "April Fool, Mary!" You are not only disappointed, but also very angry that such a trick should be played on your birthday, of all times! In great disgust, you start out of the room, but your sister calls you back, saying "Wait a minute, Mary! Don't be in such a hurry. That's not your real present. Look!" She holds in her hands another box exactly like the first, only this one is not empty. It contains a beautiful new pocketbook, just the right color to go with your Easter coat.

11–13-Year-Old Group

1. See list A, end of Chapter 5, for this age group. Exercises 1, 2, 3 are all suitable if a character is added and an appropriate ending discussed.
2. See list B, end of Chapter 5, for this age group. Use Exercise 1 with the addition of a sister, and Exercise 3.
3. Use the "lost children" episode discussed in Chapter 5.
4. Pretend that you are children in a town near a newly established army base. You have been forbidden to use the old playfield, situated on a cliff by the sea, because it is being used for drilling soldiers. One day, when the field is vacant, you and your friends steal up to this wonderful spot for a game of ball. You are having great fun till there is a sound of marching feet approaching. The soldiers have returned unexpectedly! What can you do? How can you get home without being caught and reprimanded, when there is only one road up to the cliff? Suddenly, one of you remembers that there used to be a cave in the side of the hill. After much searching, you discover it, almost hidden by vines. You tumble into it just in time to escape from view. Then you hear the sound of the marching feet growing fainter and fainter. The soldiers have gone! Creeping out cautiously, you find that the road is clear and you can make a dash for home.

14-Year-Olds and Over

1. See list A, end of Chapter 5, for this age group. Exercises 1, 2, 3 can be used. In 1, talk to the dog; in 2, imagine that only a sister or brother is awake. The others are asleep or ill. In 3, limit the waiting group to four people.
2. See list B, end of Chapter 5, for this age group. Use Exercises 1, 2, and 3. In 2, talk to the dog, and in 3, add a sister or brother.
3. It is the day of the big school dance and you are miserable. Imagine Howard's getting the mumps, at sixteen! Ridiculous! Now there is no one to escort you. And your beautiful new blue satin formal! Oh, dear . . . you'll never have a chance to wear it now! The sudden sound of the telephone bell breaks the silence. Your dismal "hello" as you answer gives away your unhappy state of mind. When you hear Bill Parker's voice asking you if he may substitute for Howard and take you to the party, the world looks brighter.
4. It is three o'clock on Mary's sixteenth birthday. Mother is putting the final touches on a sweater she has been making for her; it must be wrapped before she gets home from school. These past two years had been difficult; Mary's father had died suddenly and her mother was forced to take a full-time job. She adores Mary and has spoiled her . . . she just couldn't help it. Now that the

girl is growing up, mother is desperately eager for her to have all the nice things her friends have. She has been working night and day to find means to provide the little extras. Just as the sweater is wrapped and marked, mother hears Mary's footsteps on the porch. She leaves the package on the table and slips in behind the draperies to watch her child's surprise. Mary comes dashing in, sees the package, and rather casually tosses aside the lovely birthday card mother had made with such care. She pulls at the tissue impatiently, and when she sees the sweater, her face looks like a storm cloud. She holds it for a moment, frowning, and then tosses it back into the box angrily, saying, "A sweater! Gosh! She knew I wanted perfume!" And with that, she flounces angrily upstairs. What an ungrateful, spoiled child! Poor mother looks at the box sadly; she holds the sweater for a moment, and then puts it neatly away. She should have remembered. Yes . . . Mary had mentioned it . . . of course! She stops for an instant at the foot of the stairs as she goes toward the kitchen. . . . "Sorry, darling," she whispers to herself. "Don't worry! You shall have your perfume one of these days!"

Variations for the Advanced Groups

  A. Surprise Exercises
    1. Imagine yourself sitting alone in the living room. Suddenly there is a knock on the door. Rise, go to open it, and imagine someone standing there. It may be a beggar, a friend, a stranger—anyone you like. Do whatever the situation calls for and say at least one line of appropriate dialogue. (*Example:* Suppose the newcomer were the neighbor's little girl, who is limping and holding her hand over a deep gash in her knee. You would feel sorry, and want to help. You would approach at once, help her to a chair, and probably say, "Oh, my goodness, Jean, what's happened? Here . . . let me help you! You poor little thing!")
    2. Think of yourselves as a group of four friends. Do not plan your specific relationship, or decide why you are together. Another of your friends joins you and says one line, which he has decided upon; it will come as a complete surprise to you and your companions. He may say, "What'll we do? He's run away!" Let that start your thinking; anyone who has an idea may answer him. Try to make the conversation that follows build the scene to a logical climax. Other lines that might be used by the character making the surprise statement are: "It's not fair to leave me here alone!" . . . "Why didn't you tell me about it?" . . . "I can't find it!" . . . "They've told on us!" . . . "We're completely surrounded!"
  B. Couplets. These several lines may be given to any two individuals without any explanation. They will be permitted to go off together for a specified length of time (three minutes is enough) to create a

dramatic situation which these lines suggest. Only the words given may be used. In this kind of exercise, the creative experience lies in the originality of the scene developed. Characters are identified only by A and B.

  1. *A.* What time is it?   *B.* Eleven o'clock.

            ✻   ✻   ✻   ✻

  2. *A.* You've come back.   *B.* Yes!

            ✻   ✻   ✻   ✻

  3. *A.* Hello!   *B.* Hello!   *A.* You're here!   *B.* Yes.

            ✻   ✻   ✻   ✻

  4. *A.* He's gone.   *B.* Yes!

            ✻   ✻   ✻   ✻

C. Episode for the practice of monologue technique (this can also be used with several characters as a regular dialogue scene): Mother has sent you to the store to do the marketing, and warned you to hurry home. This is only the second time that you have been entrusted with such an errand, and mother is rather exacting. Since she has been sick, she has been a little on edge, and overly critical. You just can's seem to do anything right. The store is crowded with customers. Three times you try to give your order to the man behind the counter; but he also seems to be in a bad humor today, and gruffly bids you to wait your turn. Finally, you get your groceries, and, as you leave the counter, glance at the change you hold in your hand. To your dismay, you are ten cents short. This will never do! Back to the counter you go. "Please, Mr. Mike, won't you add my bill again? I ought to have another ten cents." "No such thing," snaps Mr. Mike. "I've been adding figures for the past ten years and I don't make mistakes!" (In a monologue this remark is imagined. It is included here because it must be told in the original story so that it can be heard realistically in the imagination.) There is no use protesting. You start for the door, wishing there were some way to make him listen. Suddenly your foot touches something soft. It is a change purse, and it is not empty. As you pick it up, you think of the ten cents that you need so badly . . . but only for a moment. Almost at once, you approach a lady who is standing nearby. "Excuse me, but is this your purse?" "Why, it certainly is. I must have dropped it," says a very kind voice. "You're a nice girl to return it to me so promptly." With this statement, the grateful lady opens the purse and hands you a quarter. "Please take this, dear, and buy yourself a treat. Such thoughtful little people ought to be rewarded." You try to refuse, but your new-found friend insists. Finally, expressing your thanks, and clutching your quarter very tight, you hurry home, with the right change, thank goodness, and more!

7

THE SHORT PLAY

The weeks that have been devoted to careful improvisations with dialogue will have laid the necessary foundations for creating the short play. In fact, many of the change-of-mood pantomimes on which the longer improvisations were based contained the fundamental elements of drama. The children, therefore, unconsciously will have been developing a certain awareness of the definite form required by the drama but never important in dramatic play.

CHARACTERISTICS

For clarification purposes, a further analysis of the episode concerning "Peter and His Birthday Gift"[1] will serve adequately. At the very beginning, when he finds the mailbox empty, Peter catches the sympathy and stirs the interest of his audience. He is pitied because he did not find his present. An audience is eager to see whether something will happen that can satisfy his needs and end the story happily for all concerned. There is rising interest as Mother tells him of Uncle Joe's proposed visit; there is a flicker of hope that Uncle Joe will bring the kite, but suspense until the fact is established one way or the other. Even when the package is observed in Uncle's hand a certain doubt remains, and audience curiosity becomes more intense. When Peter finally discovers that the package does contain the makings of a most intricate kite, the problem is solved for the protagonist and the audience is happy over his victory. This little episode includes the basic elements of drama. It has an initial incident (finding the mailbox empty), two rising incidents that build suspense (Mother's news of Uncle's visit and the arrival of Uncle Joe with the package), and a climax (the opening of the package) with little or no denouement.

Through the analysis of several different episodes, children will

[1] See Chapter 5.

THE SHORT PLAY

recognize the fact that those which are most interesting to play and to watch have certain common qualities. The youngsters themselves will soon be able to discover and list, almost without assistance, the minimum requirements for material out of which they can hope to create a successful play. The leader must be well grounded in such knowledge so that he can ask leading questions and offer innumerable stories as samples. He should point out that some, when altered slightly, can become good drama, while others that lack certain basic qualities will never be suitable for play acting. In order that he may make this differentiation in material clear to children, the leader must be sure that he understands the seven characteristics of the story with dramatic possibilities. It must possess:

1. A strong appeal to the emotions.
2. Action that moves and interests.
3. A direct unbroken plot line, rising steadily to a climax.
4. A resolution that leads without delay to a satisfactory ending.
5. Characters that are true-to-life, understandable, and interesting.
6. Incidents that can be conveniently grouped into a few closely-knit scenes.
7. A worthwhile theme or central idea.

SELECTION OF MATERIAL

To make a selection of stories that will play effectively, in whole or in part, three facts must be kept in mind. First, the leader must understand thoroughly the interests of his group, as well as the background and temperament of its individual members. Second, he must not be tempted to use stories that make their chief appeal through beautiful language, one or two colorful characters, or the championing of some noble cause; none of these qualities can be substituted for real plot and the other basic elements of good drama. Third, he must recognize the desire and ability of children to think maturely; their interest can be sustained only when they are dealing with content that offers a mental challenge.

INTEREST LEVELS

It is difficult to draw absolute age lines in judging children's major interests, for there are many eight-year-olds who find more in common with colleagues of six than with those of ten. The lists of exercises that conclude the preceding chapters are made in age groupings that have been based on many years of experimentation.[2] In ex-

[2] The age groups suggested in this volume are eight to ten years, eleven to thirteen years, and fourteen years and over.

plaining interests, therefore, it seems advisable to refer to the same classifications.

The child under seven or eight is eager to discover the world about him. The doctor, the fireman, the milkman interest him most. A trip on a train, plane, or boat, a visit to the zoo, a day at the beach, or some other real experience will be the favorite material for his dramatic play at this age. Animals interest him and assume many human qualities. He usually takes delight in fairly tale characters such as elves, giants, and witches.

The eight-to-ten-year-olds are happiest when their plays deal with the magic of far-off lands, peopled with fairy godmothers, and with dragons to be conquered by noble princes. Toward the end of this period they seek adventure stories concerning more realistic heroes. Such characters as the early pioneers, King Arthur's knights, Robin Hood, Charlemagne, and Roland are in high favor.

The younger half of the eleven-to-thirteen-year-old group still enjoys the excitement of adventurous tales of heroism. At twelve and beyond, a strong idealism and love of the romantic (in the true sense of the word) appears. The satisfying hero must possess a high sense of honor and chivalry; his impeccable behavior toward friends, countrymen, and God must win for him the love and respect of the world. During this tender age, children are beginning to formulate their own basic philosophies of life; they are therefore sensitive and responsive to fine ideals and standards. As the emotions mature in the average thirteen-year-old, a need often arises for play material that offers a vigorous outlet. Ballads and other narratives filled with vivid action and boisterous fun may serve that purpose.

The Older "Teens"

The fourteens and over present a rather special problem. It is extremely important that the leader dealing with this older group realize his fine opportunities as well as his possible pitfalls. Although in a matter of years, these boys and girls are still children, they have reached the point of desiring, more than all else, to disassociate themselves from the family group and establish their own identity as responsible members of the social group.[3] When treated by the leader with the consideration and respect that he would accord his colleagues, young people will respond with great enthusiasm; if dominated or approached with condescension, they will withdraw or be resentful. Since they are just now facing, with great seriousness, this problem of growing up, such subjects as boy-girl relations, marriage, careers, religious principles, and standards of behavior are all of deep

[3] See Appendix E—*Youth Speaks for Itself.*

concern. Although there is often little outward manifestation of these interests, their existence must be recognized. The stories that really intrigue the older teenagers are those that deal with life in all its aspects. A high idealism still controls the emotional makeup, and playmaking material involving fine, strong characters will usually be a happy choice. Stories depicting healthy, friendly relationships between the sexes generally meet with favor, but scenes that call for romantic, sentimental love-making should be avoided. Such subjects, unless treated in a light and humorous vein, can only bring about a self-conscious reaction. The untrained leader who believes that his youngsters are interested solely in the production of broad comedy will be surprised to discover that the tale that depicts a strong conflict and presents a vital, timely problem will generate far more enthusiasm.

INTRODUCTION OF THE STORY

Whether the subject matter on which the class begins its playmaking experience is drawn from a story or from a life episode used in previous improvisations, the need for the leader's careful preparation for the introductory session cannot be overemphasized. Only if he has thoroughly digested every detail of setting, exposition, plot, and characters can he put the story before the students in a way that will arouse immediate interest. If it is told instead of read, it will always seem more alive and spontaneous. Since these first dramatizations will be based on very short stories, this informal method of introduction should present no problem for the leader. Use of the dialogue form will help to create interest. Important incidents should be highlighted in a vivid, dramatic way that will build suspense until the climax is reached.

No one explains the best way to present a story as well as Geraldine Siks. She says: "To share a story creatively a leader first makes the story her own . . . she reads it again for sheer enjoyment . . . edits and analyzes the story's moods . . . and drama elements. . . . She sees it happening, unfolding . . . in a series of vivid pictures. She identifies with the characters. . . . A story must become real and alive to a leader before she can make it live for others."

THE DRAMATIZATION

It is time now for a lively group discussion of the story. By posing skillful questions the leader can emphasize the dramatic content and climax, clarify the relationship of the characters, and point out those who seem superfluous. A decision must be made concerning how the play will begin and where the action will take place. Together the group can plan for the actual appearance of the scenes, the entrances, exits, and properties needed. If the leader has devoted time to advance preparation, it may be difficult for him to refrain from expressing his preconceived ideas in many of these areas. He must remember, however, that the objective is to stimulate the young minds to creative thought rather than to discourage their activity by imposing a ready-made plan.

A story suggested for dramatization by one of the children and presented by him to the rest of the group (it may be original or an excerpt from written material) requires an even more strenuous discussion period. It is important that the young volunteer, as well as his colleagues, understand wherein his story possesses or lacks the elements of good drama, whether it must be discarded, or how it can be adapted and altered. Detailed plans must be made for its beginning, climax, ending, and scene divisions. The major characters must be analyzed and developed. Though this procedure may seem to consume a great deal of time, it will usually prove to be time well spent. There is no better way for children to become discriminating judges of good dramatic form than to put their favorite story to this test.

THE LEADER PREPARES

Before the actual dramatization of any part of the story, the leader must have made mental notes concerning the number of acting units into which the play will fall naturally. An *acting unit*, as the term is used here, does not refer to what one normally interprets as a scene, after which the curtain falls. Any drama contains many more acting units than it does scenes. To clarify, let us use the story of Hansel and Gretel as an example. At the outset Hansel and Gretel may be talking about the family's bad luck, the poverty, their unhappiness, and the stepmother's unkindness, as they tidy up the cottage. The door opens and Stepmother comes in from the village. At once the conversation, now a three-way dialogue, will take a different direction, on a different theme. This begins the second acting unit. Should the father arrive, or the stepmother leave, the tenor of the conversation would change once again, and a third acting unit would begin. It is relatively simple for children to improvise a conversation concerning one subject at a time, but confusion arises when several subjects are attempted in unbroken sequence. Important ideas that move the story forward are forgotten, and the results are unsatisfactory. In the story of "Peter and His Birthday Gift,"[4] there need be only one scene. The porch of Peter's home, somewhere near the mailbox, would make an appropriate setting. There are, however, four acting units: (1) Peter's pantomime alone as he enters in happy anticipation, looks in the mailbox, and finds it empty; (2) Mother's conversation with Peter about the letter from Uncle Joe; (3) Uncle Joe's arrival and the dialogue that concerns the presentation of the gift; (4) the opening of the package. If each unit of this miniature drama were attempted separately and the interest concentrated on the germ of the dialogue needed in that unit, all the ideas presented in the preliminary discussion would likely find their way into the conversation. If, on the other hand, the whole story were to be attempted at once, many of the thoughts important to the movement of the plot would be forgotten; the result would be sketchy, inadequate dialogue.

BEGINNING TO IMPROVISE

Several boys may volunteer to do Peter's opening pantomime (unit 1), and a lively group discussion should follow each playing of the scene. The third and fourth Peters will undoubtedly be more convincing, having profited by the constructive criticism of their colleagues. In like manner, the other units should be interpreted by various members of the group, until every section of the play has been created, at least twice. These informal first trials should never be interrupted; each acting unit should be played from start to finish without suggestions from the leader. Only on very rare occasions will it be necessary to stop the procedure altogether, discuss the material in greater detail, and make a fresh start. Sometimes a group may be attempting to build dialogue without the proper understanding of the story; one or two may not have listened carefully and therefore feel insecure and disturb the others with their silences or their nervous giggling. In this case the leader has no choice; he must say, quietly, "CURTAIN" and stop the playing. Without blaming anyone he can suggest, "We started to play before we were all really sure of what our conversation must include. Let's discuss it again until everyone knows, shall we?" The very same group, on the next attempt, will undoubtedly do a good job! So far, no actual cast will have been selected, but every child will have become familiar with the three characters and will be able to play any or all of them with more or less competence. This whole procedure may take from one

[4] This episode has been purposely used repeatedly for reference because it has been thoroughly analyzed for the reader and has become familiar ground.

to four periods, depending upon the length and difficulty of the story being dramatized.

Even during the critique periods following these simple units, the matter of the movement pattern and the balance of the stage picture should be introduced. Questions can be asked that will call attention to the need for considering how the use of space can deepen the meaning of our story. "Did you like where mother stood when she read Uncle Joe's letter to Peter? Was she hiding Peter's face from some of us? How could we have made this moment more interesting? Would it have been better if Uncle Joe had come in from offstage left instead of offstage right? Yes . . . that's right! Then Peter could have run to meet him without crossing in front of mother! Wasn't it fine for Peter to go down on the step to meet Uncle Joe? Why?"

The group is now ready to select one or two casts for the final presentation, to make plans for extra rehearsal periods, and to arrange for the collecting or making of the necessary properties and scenery units. The amount of time allotted for this work will again depend upon the nature of the material and the formality of the occasion for which it is being prepared. If it is possible for the short play to be repeated, it is always advisable to use two casts. If the scout troop, for example, has been asked to present a short creative play for a three-day conference or a camp get-together, an arrangement might be made for two performances, each to be given with a different cast and stage crew. This plan provides an opportunity for many more children to participate in the project and obviates the leader's ever-present anxiety that one of the characters may suddenly succumb to measles or mumps.

THE LONGER SHORT PLAY

"Peter and His Birthday Gift" represents only the briefest kind of creative playlet that can be developed within the time of several class meetings. The leader will often be called upon to prepare a longer short play, lasting twenty minutes or more. Although the general procedures in trying out acting units, casting, and conducting rehearsals are identical, the leader's preparation and his introduction of the story to the class requires a somewhat different emphasis. A narrative containing the makings of a twenty-minute play will be longer, include more characters and many more incidents, than the episode concerning Peter. Rearranging the story in order to make it more workable material for playmaking is the leader's first job. Parts that make no contribution to the dramatization should be discarded. It may be necessary to add new characters, or dispense with some of those appearing in the original story. Although the basic plot and theme will remain essentially the same, changing the order of certain incidents may facilitate production problems and heighten dramatic values. This task should be completed before the leader makes any presentation to the class. It requires considerable knowledge of playwriting and basic dramatic form; these skills are beyond the capabilities of the average child at this stage. Some authorities suggest telling the story in its original form, working through it with the children, and then by group discussion, arriving at a final pattern in which it is to be presented. It has been the author's experience, however, that the advantages of this method are seldom worth the time, unless the purpose of the project is a class in oral playwriting rather than creative dramatics. No denial can be made of the fact that the process is the most effective way of teaching play structure; it is seldom successful, however, even for that purpose, in a group meeting only once a week. Children cannot be expected to remember details over a seven-day period; a great deal of time is lost, therefore, in review at the beginning of each session, which may even diminish the enthusiasm for the whole project. A class organized in a summer camp or in a school, where it meets every day for a month or more, may be able to develop a play from a story, through group discussion, with marked success.

TREATMENT OF MATERIAL

The leader, in revising his story for the first telling, may jot down notes on plot and dialogue in outline form. He may prefer to write it all out briefly, using dialogue for the most part, in order to have a skeletal manuscript for reference around which to build the final drama. It is often helpful to have a crude first draft on paper, for, as units are developed informally, some of the bits of spontaneous dialogue will bear recording. In other words, although the leader's written guide is seldom used as a script for the little play, it will prove useful as rehearsals progress in directing the continuous flow of the plot line.

The process used for introducing the longer story, discussing and analyzing its background, characters, and setting, must naturally be longer. Seldom will there be an opportunity, in a large group, for each individual to try every acting unit and every character. After one or two sessions devoted to the initial steps, casts can be chosen and rehearsals scheduled. Only the characters involved in a particular scene attend the rehearsals for that unit.

DEVELOPING THE PLAY

Building the longer short play is a far more complex and time-consuming process. When there are numerous acting units, involving many changes of thought and mood, the leader must refer constantly to the original story plan, if the essential plot pattern is to remain intact. Although the children should be free to create dialogue in their own terms, they may need to be reminded from time to time of the omission of ideas pertinent to plot or character development.

SUMMARY

Some of the longer dialogue improvisations that have already been used (based on change-of-mood pantomime material) possess the elements of dramatic structure. During the periods spent on these exercises, the children will have begun to develop some conception of the difference between drama and dramatic play. The simple episode concerning "Peter and His Birthday Gift," which contains a beginning, a climax, and an end, serves as a miniature example of the dramatic form. An analysis of similar incidents will gradually develop an ability to recognize the presence of intrinsic dramatic qualities. The leader himself must be fully cognizant of the seven basic characteristics of suitable play-acting material. He must understand the interests of various age levels and remember that only content offering a mental challenge will call forth a sustained enthusiastic response. The story from which the play will be made must be introduced to the class with great care. If it is related in dialogue form whenever possible, the dramatic moments are highlighted, and a feeling of suspense is created and built to the climax, it will make an immediate appeal. The thorough discussion that follows should include analysis of characters, background, setting, and plot construction.

There are always many more acting units in any play than scenes. These should be improvised one at a time with groups of volunteers. Dialogue involving too many different ideas will be sketchy and thin. After a period of trying out some or all of the acting units, the casts should be selected and final plans made for rehearsal periods.

When preparing the production of a longer short play lasting twenty minutes or more, the leader should think through the alterations necessary in the original story before presenting it to the group. If he can write it briefly in its new form, using direct discourse for the most part, so much the better. This manuscript will serve as a useful plot guide throughout the working period. More time will naturally be required for the analysis, development, and rehearsal periods of the longer short play.

8

THE LONG PLAY

There comes a time when every drama group is called upon to produce a full-length play, lasting from one to one-and-a-half hours, before an invited audience. If the children have been working creatively up to this time, the assignment presents certain complications that require careful consideration.

THE PROBLEM

To produce a long play in the creative drama technique, involving such a quantity of freely improvised dialogue, may seem at first out of the question. The intricacies of plot development, the delineation of numerous interdependent characters, stage business that effectively heightens climactic moments, are all necessary components of good theatre. These impose limitations, however, on free improvisation. Shall the formal method be pressed into service, then, and creative drama forgotten for the moment? Shall the cast memorize word for word from a typed or printed script, and follow the prescribed stage directions of the playwright as interpreted by the director? This is one solution of the problem. Many leaders may feel called upon to accept it as the only solution and dispense with creative work altogether. Others, whose major purpose has been the development of the individual through creative expression, will not attempt the task of producing a long play in the formal manner for public consumption. They will see it only as a backward step, blocking the path toward their ultimate goal.

A SOLUTION

There is a middle course open to the director that permits him to apply the fundamental theories of creative dramatics to the direction and production of the full-length written play. It is the method recommended for the ideal children's drama project, which is a two-way program with a dual objective: (1) developing in its participants, through the group experience in creative drama, sympathetic understanding, resourcefulness, quickened imaginative powers, sound behavior patterns, aesthetic sensitivity, and emotional balance; (2) producing plays for an audience of young people (according to the highest artistic standards), which will educate as they entertain. Winifred Ward (1957) feels that these two practices go hand in hand. She finds "no conflict in idealogy between them; rather do they complement each other. Children's Theatre is primarily for child audiences; creative dramatics is primarily for children who participate." The same view is expressed by Geraldine Siks, who says: "These two forms are in harmony as they provide for enjoyment and child growth. Children's Theatre provides strong impressions. Creative dramatics provides for strong expressions. A child must have both. He must take in and he must give out." Marie Dienesch, a French pioneer in creative drama techniques (*jeu dramatique*), agrees on this point. She comments: "Let us say at once that these two forms are in no way opposed to each other, but so far from being incompatible, they appear to us complementary."[1] The latter half of a project's dual objective can be successfully achieved and also closely related to its forerunner: the creative drama experience. Success is dependent upon the wise selection of production material, implicit within which are situations that are suitable for dialogue improvisation. Plays suffer little from being subjected to this liberal treatment; on the contrary, they often gain a large measure of freshness, spontaneity, and sincerity seldom present in the strictly formal production. Only an actor who believes and is believed in can create the magic moment that will stir young hearts to empathize with a "Heidi" or a "Sara Crewe." Such an actor's movements must be fluid, eloquent, and honestly motivated; his speech must sing its message straight to the child's mind. This ideal performer is rare, but when he does appear, one often discovers in his biographical record a rich background of creative dramatics. One director comments on the work of her actors who have creative dramatics training, as follows: "I feel very strongly about the transition from creative drama to formal drama. I have been happily amazed at the results! Coming, as I do, from a strict professional background, this amounts to a right-about-face for me. Results have been most rewarding."[2]

[1] Marie Dienesch, "Jeu Dramatique et Théatre-Scolaire," *World Theatre Magazine*, 11 (Brussels, Belgium: World Theatre Institute, 1953), 30.
[2] Quoted from a letter to the author, September 6, 1958, from Mary Fluhrer Nighswander, Children's Theatre Director, Davenport, Iowa.

Any tested method of producing a formal play that lives up to the highest standards demanded by an audience, and still provides opportunities for the application of creative dramatics techniques, is worthy of closer examination. This chapter, which is devoted to the analysis of such a method, could more exactly be titled, "The Long Play Produced Creatively."

OBJECTIVES

An audience of children gathers in the theatre, the school gymnasium, or outdoor arena at camp to be entertained, in the true sense of the word (not to be confused with the word "amused," often considered a synonym). Good theatre should be pleasing, indeed, but something deeper than a passing delight; it must go far into the heart of the child where he may hold it, as he goes out again into the real world, a little changed by his imaginative experience. This is implied in the Latin derivation of the word "entertain"; it comes directly from the word "tenere," meaning "to hold." Mark Twain, who considered children's theatre one of the "very, very great inventions of the twentieth century," was convinced of its educational value. He called it the "most effective teacher of morals . . . that the ingenuity of man has yet devised, for the reason that its lessons are not taught wearily by book or dreary homily but by visible and enthusing action; and they go straight to the heart, which is the rightest of right places for them . . . ." (Ward, 1958). Boys and girls have varying interests; the story that delights one child may make little impression on the other, and these interests change from year to year. All children, however, demand certain qualities in plays built for their entertainment. They want action that moves in a direct line to the climax; some appeal to the emotions; characters with which they can identify, who are convincing but not too complex; and a satisfactory ending. Many youngsters between the ages of eight and fourteen (and the majority of children's theatre audiences are composed of this age group) enjoy plays dealing with a worthwhile theme: the championing of a cause, goodness rewarded, or wickedness punished. They want something that they can get their teeth into, and the wise director will give them what they want, for the benefits are many. As Kenneth Graham says (in Siks and Dunnington: *Children's Theatre and Creative Dramatics*): "Good theatre for children should provide a wide variety of experiences wherein children can identify themselves with characters in situations which make concrete the vital phases of life. Children should have many opportunities to learn sympathetic understanding of people and the reasons for commonly accepted moral ideas." Entertaining the audience, then, according to its own standards and requirements, is the first objective that the director must keep in mind.

Consideration must next be given to the play's potential for the development of aesthetic sensitivity through artistic production. Young people today are rushed through life at a pace that prohibits a natural absorption of the beauties of color, form, and sound that lie about them. The director of a children's play has an unusual opportunity to awaken the senses and deepen appreciations. If the highest artistic standards guide the designing of movement, the spoken word, settings, lights, music, and costumes, the actors as well as the children in the audience will have a compelling aesthetic experience that will contribute appreciably to total growth.

The conscientious director has a third objective: He must take into account the quality of the educational experience that he is offering to those participating in the project. Having first considered the values to the audience, and rightly so, he must now turn his attention to the young actors. Many of them will have already increased in stature, intellectually, emotionally, and physically, through their previous creative dramatics experiences. But unless they show some personal growth and development in the process of producing the play, a director must admit a certain failure in meeting responsibility to his own group. The choice of subject matter, time schedules, facilities, and methods of organizing the whole endeavor will determine the proportions of the educational opportunities.

SELECTION OF MATERIAL

Much has already been written in respect to the requirements of good dramatic material. All of the points previously stated apply even more pertinently to the long play to be presented before an audience. Other factors, too, affect the selection of material for the more formal presentation. Whereas the interests and abilities of the participants directed the choice of episodes for creative improvisation, the temper, background, and taste of the potential audience must now exert a strong influence. If, for example, the play is scheduled for presentation before a group of eleven- and twelve-year-olds, it cannot be based solely on nursery rhyme and Mother Goose characters, even though content of that nature might appeal to the cast. In order to satisfy this particular audience, the theme must be vital, the action brisk and exciting, the characters real, adventurous, and heroic! Such stories as Ruskin's *King of the Golden River*, Alden's *Knights of the Silver Shield*, and *Tales of Robin Hood*, or *King Arthur's Knights* would be more appropriate. As Jed Davis says in discussing the children's theatre audience (in Siks and Dunnington: *Children's Theatre and Creative Dramatics*): "While features such as suitability for touring, opportunities to augment the cast, and number of sets may affect the choice to some extent, these matters are really peripheral to the major question: WILL THIS PLAY SATISFY THE AUDIENCE FOR WHICH IT IS INTENDED?"

PRACTICAL CONSIDERATIONS

One cannot overlook any of the circumstances which surround the production of a children's play; many questions must be considered and answered satisfactorily. Where is it to be given? How many performances will be presented and for whom? Will the play tour or play on a single stage? What kind of facilities and equipment will be available? Is there a special occasion or purpose for the production of this play? Who will be the actors? What financial budget and rehearsal time have been allotted? These subjects are so complex and vary so with each individual case, that one can answer them only generally in a volume such as this. Naturally, the physical problems will bear careful consideration. No play can be selected until a director knows the space he will work in and equipment that he will be permitted to use, as well as his budgetary limitations. A production that requires five complicated settings, scheduled for a stage that has no wing space, lighting equipment, or switchboard, on a budget of $100 would present problems impossible of solution. If a play is to travel to several school stages, it must be so selected and designed that the touring will not present too many difficulties. Rehearsal space that is readily available, roomy, quiet, and comfortable is also essential. A play presented for a school celebration, designed to use as many participants as possible and to demonstrate the skills of the music, art, and physical education departments, implies problems that only a wise and experienced director would attempt to solve.

THE CAST

The subject of casting deserves a more detailed treatment; many pitfalls for the new teacher-director lie in this area. First, any attempt to present children's theatre for an audience, especially a paying audience, with child actors, all under fourteen, is doomed to failure. A play may be presented informally or staged by children for their peers, but such a creative play could hardly be termed "children's theatre." One cannot often find a twelve-year-old boy who can so characterize a sixty-five-year-old man that members of the audience can identify and believe. If, on the contrary, there is a wide age range in the young actors participating, the problem becomes simpler. Older teen-agers can often portray adult roles with great conviction. For those roles that are too demanding, it may occasionally be necessary to turn to an alumnus of the group or a cooperative and skillful community actor. The eight- to ten-year-olds can handle the small children's and animals' parts, and the twelve- to fifteen-year-olds will often portray the young princess or her serving women adequately. Even if only two performances of the play are scheduled, a double cast should work on the production. No play is immune from the disastrous effects of the mumps or measles epidemic; a wise director will be prepared for such an emergency. If possible, the script selected should provide for a fairly even distribution of responsibility among half a dozen characters. The play in which one child bears the burden of a long stellar role will be more difficult to present from every point of view. When the four or five longer roles can be assigned to young people who have had previous basic training in creative dramatics, characterizations will be natural and convincing. Children who have not had this preparation tend to give a stilted recitation of lines that they have learned from a script. Nothing will guarantee spontaneity and freshness in working with written dialogue like a foundation of creative drama. Ward (1957) makes this statement:

> Young children, probably up to eleven and twelve years, should have informal drama exclusively; for they tend to recite their lines unless they are well-grounded in the ability to think them out as they say them. Having had plenty of experience in creating dialogue, however, by the time they are older they have formed the habit of thinking through their speeches and can be counted on for a much greater degree of naturalness than if they had not had this background.

CREATIVE DRAMA IN DIRECTING

Another suggestion, in respect to casting which may guide the leader who must use a large group, concerns the use of crowd scenes.[3] His task will be less arduous if there are several sections of the story in which extra groups can appear. Such scenes provide

---

[3] The term "crowd" scene refers to any group of five to seven, such as court ladies, village children, women at the fair, and the like.

a double advantage: they give more young people a chance to participate actively, and they can be directed in a creative manner (without the use of scripts). The same crowd or group will seldom appear on more than one or two occasions throughout the course of the play. They can be rehearsed separately and the problem approached exactly as if it were a creative dramatics improvisation.

Several crowd scenes were cleverly inserted in one production of Dickens' *A Christmas Carol* (see Fig. 8–1). They provided an opportunity for many children to participate and added spontaneity and charm to the dramatization. In the first section of the story, Scrooge, led by the Spirit of Christmas Past, looks, in his dream, into

Fig. 8–1. Carolers open a production of Dickens' A Christmas Carol. (Credit: Gaston Remy.)

his old schoolroom, where he sees himself, a little boy, among his fellow-students. Dickens' original story gives few details, but suggests that when the Christmas holiday came, the children all went happily off to their homes leaving the lonely little Ebenezer to spend his fortnight in a barren school with its sour-faced Master.

Fig. 8–2. A scene from *Rumpelstiltskin*. (Credit: Edward J. Peterson.)

The cast of eight- and nine-year-olds, when called together, listened to a dramatic telling of the story. It was pointed out that there were three obvious subjects implied by the plot, which could be discussed: (1) the joy of the anticipated holiday; (2) the children's sympathy for little Ebenezer, whose family cannot accept him at home; and (3) the arrival of the coach, with its new trappings, which was to take them off to the station. Before the end of the second rehearsal period, each child and his counterpart (a double cast had been selected) had decided upon his own dialogue contribution in the three subject areas.

To avoid confusion, each child was given a number from one to six, thus establishing a speech order. The spontaneity of this scene and the genuine empathy it evoked from the audience were breathtaking. Teachers who observed this clear and successful demonstration were convinced at once that application of the creative drama technique is highly effective within the framework of the formal play. The scene that concerned the Christmas party at the Fezziwigs was treated in the same manner and was equally delightful and quite in keeping with the gay spirit of the occasion.

Although it is often possible to pad a written play with such crowd scenes, the leader should be warned against adding too many characters whose presence makes no contribution to the story. Especially must he resist the temptation to insert a dancing or singing chorus, merely because the talent is available, the play needs lengthening, or an ambitious administrator would like to satisfy a larger number of parents. This practice is dangerous; it frequently stops the flow of action and makes a disastrous break in the plot line. There are certain occasions, however, when a dance or song seems indicated because it is so intrinsic a part of the plot that it helps rather than hinders; in such cases this inclusion will serve to heighten the artistic quality of the whole production.

FORMAL DIRECTING

The leader who assumes the role of the director of a play to be presented to the public must have a working knowledge of directing techniques.[4] Although he will still guide rather than dictate, in order to stimulate creative thinking on the part of his cast, he must know what makes good theatre and strive to uphold the highest possible standards for the sake of the children on both sides of the curtain. Frank Whiting, a brilliant and sensitive director himself, believes (in Siks and Dunnington: *Children's Theatre and Creative Dramatics*) that all would-be directors should be provided with "a rich and stimulating environment, particularly during early childhood . . . an environment that would provide much love, but some hate, much joy but some sorrow, much good but some evil, much security but some fear." He goes on to suggest exposing them to wise and talented human beings and rich exciting experiences in living theatre, feeling that a good director, like a good writer or teacher, must first of all be a very dedicated "total human being."

ORGANIZATION AND PLANNING

Long before rehearsals begin, the director will have studied the facilities, equipment, and budget at his disposal, consulted with a

[4] See Chapter 10, "Techniques for the Director."

trusted stage designer, and mapped out his set plans on paper. These he will discuss with his cast in great detail at the first opportunity. If the background of the story lies in a foreign land or another century, pictures should be gathered and studied together. This will help the whole group to absorb color, costumes, and customs of the period, and will insure authenticity in design and movement. During such preliminary analyses, the leader will accept suggestions from the young people that seem appropriate, and reject, with ample reason given, those that seem impractical. This friendly exchange of ideas develops a warm feeling of sharing in a common project and offers the best possible opportunity for teaching fundamental principals of color, balance, and emphasis in stage design. When a final decision as to the settings and detailed placement of entrances, exits, and furniture properties has been reached, scale drawings and color sketches of the several scenes should be made. The director, a talented student, or a borrowed designer-colleague may take on this task. Of even more benefit are simple scale models, made of paper or cardboard. The time devoted to such detailed preparation will be well spent and is guaranteed to facilitate rehearsals. What was an imaginary environment will have taken on a definite shape; the world of play will have become a tangible reality. The number of "work-calls" needed to complete the settings with young students and volunteers will now be evident. Meeting times and a specific place will be scheduled, and materials purchased so that the project may go forward under a designer-colleague's direction, if such a specialist is available. The date set for the completion of this work will coincide with that set for the final on-stage rehearsals.

Although the young cast need not be in on the secret, the perceptive director will have blocked out the basic movement pattern as he sees it, using his own set of drawings, before the play goes into rehearsal. He should have a complete mental picture of the general flow of the action from the rise of the first curtain to the fall of the last. Much of the success of the play will depend upon the effective groupings and stage business that heighten the intensity of dramatic moments and deepen the meaning of the script itself. Notes to remind him of key action patterns may be written in the margin of his script; he should always be flexible, however, and ready to replace his own directions by imaginative and interesting business created by members of the cast. Many a cross or turn made by a young actor, quite spontaneously, will be far more effective than one developed in advance by the most experienced director. This new idea should be incorporated into the director's notes and become a permanent part of his plan.

REHEARSALS

Every individual concerned in the project—leader, musician, technicians, stagehands, cast—should be given a typed or mimeographed sheet containing a schedule of rehearsals for each unit, dress, and technical rehearsals, performance dates, and any other information that will be helpful. The leader must expect to devote a good deal of thought to the planning of this data; especially must he be sure that each rehearsal unit has been allotted to the proper number of meetings. The dividing of a long play into "rehearsal units" is absolutely essential, in the opinion of the author. A "rehearsal unit" is composed of one or several sections of the playscript in which the same characters appear. It may total as many as fifteen or as few as six typewritten pages. The length of the unit will determine the number of meetings scheduled for it on the rehearsal plan; the smallest unit would require about five meetings and the largest, double that amount. This system, which is apparently little known or practiced, has innumerable advantages. One comes immediately to mind.

Only the members of the cast appearing in a particular rehearsal unit will be asked to attend the meetings for that unit, each of which will probably last one to one-and-a-half hours. The purpose of this procedure is to keep interest alive and the rehearsal pleasantly productive. If the whole cast is called to every rehearsal, there will be many occasions when a dozen or more young people will have no chance to perform. Time seldom permits a complete run-through of the whole play, except at rehearsals scheduled near the performance date. Children who are kept waiting naturally become fidgety and restless; when they are bored they will be noisy and troublesome. The actors on-stage are distracted, the leader becomes irritated, and the result is a rehearsal period that is worthless. The sample rehearsal schedule that follows may serve as a guide to the director.

The _____(name)_____ Theatre
_____(address)_____
January 2,_____

Dear (name of student):

You will play (name of character) in _____(name of play)_____ which will be given at ___(name of theatre)___ on Saturday, February 8, 10:30 a.m., 3 p.m., 8 p.m. You will appear in ___(unit)___ which you will see listed below. If

THE LONG PLAY

you cannot attend on the dates specified for these units, please call the office ___(phone number)___ on ___(day and time)___, so that we may replace you. Because this is a very difficult play which we are preparing in a short time, it is necessary that *all* members of the cast attend rehearsals as designated.

Unit I	Unit II	Unit III
Sun. Jan. 12, 3 p.m.	Sat. Jan. 11, 2 p.m.	Sat. Jan. 11, 3 p.m.
Sun. Jan. 19, 5 p.m.	Mon. Jan. 13, 4 p.m.	Sun. Jan. 19, 4 p.m.
Mon. Jan. 27, 4 p.m.	Mon. Jan. 20, 4 p.m.	Tues. Jan. 21, 4 p.m.
Mon. Feb. 3, 4 p.m.	Tues. Jan. 28, 4 p.m.	Sun. Jan. 26, 4 p.m.
Tues. Feb. 4, 4 p.m.	Wed. Feb. 5, 4 p.m.	Wed. Jan. 29, 4 p.m.

Unit IV	Unit V	Unit VI
Sat. Jan. 11, 4 p.m.	Sun. Jan. 12, 4 p.m.	Sat. Jan. 11, 5 p.m.
Wed. Jan. 15, 4 p.m.	Sun. Jan. 19, 3 p.m.	Sat. Jan. 18, 2 p.m.
Sat. Jan. 18, 3 p.m.	Sat. Jan. 25, 3 p.m.	Sat. Jan. 25, 2 p.m.
Wed. Jan. 22, 4 p.m.	Sun. Jan. 26, 3 p.m.	Sat. Feb. 1, 4 p.m.
Sat. Feb. 1, 3 p.m.	Thurs. Jan. 30, 4 p.m.	Sun. Feb. 2, 3 p.m.

Important Notes

1. A special telling of the story of the play will take place on _____ at _____. Every member of the cast and crew is invited and *urged* to attend.
2. DRESS REHEARSALS, THURSDAY, February 6th and FRIDAY, February 7th from 3 until 6 p.m.
3. All rehearsals except DRESS REHEARSALS will be held at _____.
4. Please report for DRESS REHEARSALS and PERFORMANCES one hour before curtain time.

This is a new script and it will be great fun and a real challenge! Show that you are a member of the ___(theatre name)___ family! Follow directions, cooperate, help to make this the finest production of the season!

Cordially yours,

_____
(Director's signature)

APPLICATION OF CREATIVE TECHNIQUE

Too much importance cannot be attached to the method of conducting the first two or three rehearsals of each unit. When the young people arrive they, of course, will be perfectly familiar with the story, setting, the characters and their relationships. (This preliminary study and analysis will have been accomplished at the meeting when the story was told and the whole cast was present.) On the other hand, they will need refreshing on the content of the particular unit in progress. The first step may be a quick synopsis given by any one of the youngsters who wishes to volunteer. A seated reading, in dialogue form, should follow. The few major characters, to whom the director has given duplicates of the script, will read their own lines. The leader fills in for the crowd and minor characters who work without scripts. A second reading should include only the first few pages. Any youngster without a script who has caught the context of his character's lines is urged to express the thoughts in his own terms.

After discussion to clear up certain blurred or difficult interpretations, the same section of the scene should be repeated. At this point, some of the minor characters will probably have caught the full flavor and most of the content of their dialogue. A temporary setting may now be arranged, available chairs or benches marking off acting areas, and the same section attempted with movement. The leader should explain the general pattern of the action, entrances, exits, and crosses, incorporating any of the practical ideas that may come from the group during the preliminary work. When Johnny says, "I think the entrance of the Black Knight ought to be made up center, 'cause he's important," the director should carefully consider the suggestion. Even though he knows the preceding action will make such an entrance awkward, he may say, "Yes, Johnny, it is important. An upstage center entrance ought to be effective—but I'm not sure that it will work. However—try it if you like—we'll see." He is giving Johnny's suggestion the recognition it deserves, because it followed the principles of good staging. He will let Johnny prove for himself the fact that, in this particular scene, it would be unwise to follow the general rules for the entrances of important characters.

The first cast now takes the stage for a quick walk-through of the section that has been prepared. A few suggestions for dialogue or business may be needed, but the flow of both action and words should be comparatively smooth. During the group evaluation that follows (this procedure, recommended during the earlier creative improvisations, is very important), the young people may offer many comments concerning business, characterization, and dialogue. Some will be accepted, and others rejected.

The second cast will now attempt the same unit. If they have been listening attentively, their interpretation will be smoother and more convincing than that of the first group. Even the major characters will make only occasional references to their scripts, for children who are accustomed to working creatively dislike the restraint imposed by the paper in their hands. They will strive to catch the dialogue pattern quickly, in order to feel freedom in speech and movement.

The leader should treat the next sections in a similar manner, if time permits; if not, he will start to work on them at the beginning of the next rehearsal period. Thus the little scenes are built step-by-step—a true creation in which the whole group has shared. To the leader without creative drama experience, such an approach to playmaking may seem a laudable but impractical theory. How common is the remark, "Oh, yes, I'd like to work creatively, but it takes much too long!" If only this same doubting soul could be persuaded to follow the recommended procedure patiently and conscientiously, he would be amazed to discover that the exact opposite is true!

FINAL REHEARSALS

After five or six rehearsals, attention should be given to polishing. Some of the characterizations may need to be more sharply outlined, the pace quickened as the climax of the scene draws near, changes made in the timing of dramatic pauses. A few unsuitable words, colloquialisms, or bits of modern slang may need to be deleted. It is safe to make such specific technical suggestions during these later rehearsals, for there is little danger now of producing self-conscious movement or dialogue. The young actors have already completely identified themselves with the characters they are portraying. Natural sincerity and confidence, established on a firm foundation, cannot be shaken.

The separate scenes of the play are welded together at two or three technical and dress rehearsals. For these the stage is set, every property in place; the costumes and accessories are in readiness. A unit that may have seemed convincing when rehearsed separately may need some changes in emphasis or movement pattern when it becomes a part of the whole. The same is true of colors in setting and costumes, and the timing of music background or sound effects. It is therefore advisable to schedule at least three final rehearsals on stage, one using sets, props, sound, and lights, and the last two complete with costumes. If the director has made careful plans for these rehearsals, organized his young costume and production committees with forethought, and seen to it that every department has functioned as an integral part of the project, there will be no hectic, last-minute chaos. A few minor catastrophes always occur—the disappearance of the queen's headdress or the loss of an important prop just before curtain time. The sagacious director must take such unforeseen hazards philosophically, and think of them not as tragedies, but rather as challenging tests of his ingenuity and creative imagination.

SUMMARY

When the creative drama group is called upon to present a full-length play, certain changes in method are required. There are three solutions to the problem: one, to abandon the play altogether; two, to revert to the formal method of memorizing lines verbatim; three, to combine the creative and the formal techniques. The latter system is highly recommended. The leader must always remember that the basic objectives in arranging for the public performance are to provide good entertainment, an artistically sound production, and a worthwhile educational experience for the boys, girls, and young adults participating. If a large number of boys and girls of varied ages are to be cast, a story in which there are opportunities for the creative development of carefully inserted "crowd" scenes will simplify many problems. The available stage, equipment, and budget must be studied before play selection is made. The leader who finds himself directing the long play must know the basic techniques of design and direction; he must understand what makes good theatre. Also, in his preparatory study, he will have worked out the general pattern of the important action. Although his task is to guide rather than dominate the young actors, he should be able to visualize the total effect that he is working to achieve. A clearly typed sheet containing the complete rehearsal schedule and any other important information should be in the hands of every individual concerned with the project. The first two rehearsals of each scene deserve special care. The last few rehearsals are devoted to polishing, making adjustments in dialogue, characterization, and timing. There should be at least one technical rehearsal, and two dress rehearsals of the complete play, for the purpose of coordination.

9

EPISODIC PLAY AND PAGEANT

Because they bear such a close resemblance, the episodic play and pageant can be discussed in the same chapter. An analysis of structure will at once demonstrate their usefulness.

USES

Both are full-length productions, based on a single theme but composed of several distinct and separate episodes. The episodic units are little plays complete in themselves, related only through their contribution to the development of the central idea or theme. If the subject "What Christianity Has Done for Africa" is to be developed for a young people's conference, the episodic play form would be an appropriate medium. In five different scenes, each of which could be prepared by a separate group, highlighted incidents reflecting the influence of Christianity could be interpreted. The active interest and services of many volunteers will be solicited in carrying the project through to completion, but with responsibility so well distributed that no one individual will be burdened with too great a task. If rehearsals for all episodes are conducted simultaneously, the production will take only a slightly longer time to prepare than that required for the short play.

During World War II, a large children's theatre unit was very successful in developing a timely theme in episodic play form. The favorite question of young people in the community was "What can we do to help?" The thought that immaturity limited their opportunities for patriotic service disturbed them considerably. "Why not state the question, and try to answer it, in a play," said an imaginative leader one day. The idea was warmly received, and several creative drama classes decided to collaborate. About fifty boys and girls between the ages of eight and fifteen gathered to discuss the ways and means of attacking the problem.

From the many suggestions, the following outline evolved: Queen Liberty, representing the spirit of America, holds an emergency court one day, summoning to her aid the men and women to whom she must entrust the safety of the homeland. Marines, sailors, soldiers, nurses, flyers and many others come in answer to her call. Just as they are in the act of taking the oath of allegiance, two children enter the court, without benefit of formal introduction. Apologizing for their intrusion, they kneel before the great lady, begging that the children of America be enrolled in the ranks of Liberty's service. After a moment of hesitation, Liberty reminds them that hers is a difficult task, which only men and women can undertake. She thanks them for their loyalty and willingness, and dismisses her court.

The pages are about to close the great doors of the palace, when a mysterious figure, clad in shadowy blue and purple, appears on the threshold. She is Memory, recently come from the Halls of History. In a soft firm voice she beseeches Liberty to think back—to remember—before she refuses the children the right to join her ranks. "In days long past," says Memory, "young people have courageously served their homelands. Their deeds have been proudly recorded in the annals of Father Time. Come, friend, come with me to the Halls of the Past. Let us remember together." And so, covered by appropriate background music, the two figures drift off into History, and the prologue ends. The next five episodes concern themselves with human incidents which treat of courageous young people of other days. One deals with David and the Israelites, one with Joan of Arc, and another with the Dutch boy who prevented a flood by stopping the leak in the dike. A fourth tells the victory of the young Galahad, and a fifth the story of the brave Norwegian children whose courage in carrying bricks of gold to safety protects the national treasury from the enemy.

The play based on this outline ran without intermission; the episodes were connected by short dialogues between Memory and Liberty, spoken off-stage over a public address system. The content of these interludes provided natural transitions between scenes, and gave added unity to the total plan. In the epilogue, which again was set in Liberty's court, the children were cordially accepted and given real tasks to perform for their country. A thoroughly satisfying and convincing answer was thus provided for the question stated in the prologue.

There are many groups, particularly those that are large in number and cover a wide age range, to whom this type of dramatization will offer distinct advantages. For the festival night in

EPISODIC PLAY AND PAGEANT

the summer camp, when each cabin or tent must participate, the choice of the pageant-type presentation is a happy one. It is an appropriate pattern for the city-wide project prepared cooperatively by several recreation centers. The pageant structure adapts itself well to the special school celebration.

ESSENTIALS

One of the faults most frequently associated with this type of dramatic presentation is a lack in unity and cohesion. Because the nature of the occasion for such a production often requires the treatment of certain specific material, the dramatization must frequently be original. The novice in playwriting is often unaware that:

1. The unifying theme selected must be interesting and capable of dramatic interpretation. (A teacher may attempt a pageant because he sees, in the dramatic method, an easy way of propagandizing an important lesson or moral issue. He sometimes fails to evaluate the dramatic potentialities of the theme, and finds, too late, that he is building with dead wood.)
2. Only dramatic incidents rich with human content should be chosen for the episodes.
3. The writing of the whole script must have uniformity of style. (If several leaders combine their efforts, one must be appointed to revise and edit; this is the only way to insure integration.)

The play analyzed in the foregoing section is an example of the treatment of a worth-while theme in episodic play form. The questions with which every director should test material before accepting it may seem more significant if applied to this play:

Question 1. Can the theme be clearly stated in one or two sentences?
Answer 1. The theme of the Liberty play is "Can children help their country in time of need, and in what capacity may they serve?"
Question 2. Is the question stated at the outset satisfactorily answered at the end?
Answer 2. After recalling the past courage of many young people, Liberty is persuaded to enlist the aid of American youth.
Question 3. Is each episode a complete dramatic unit, and does each make some contribution to the solution of the problem suggested by the theme?
Answer 3. Each episode was written as a miniature play. (Proof of dramatic quality can result only from a reading of the script.) Each depiction of the brave deeds of other young people helped Liberty to make her final decision.
Question 4. Is some interesting manner provided for connecting the links in the chain, so that the unit of thought will remain unbroken despite the wide differences in episodic content?

Answer 4. The conversations of Liberty and Memory that occur between each episode provide the transition vehicle. The audience unconsciously becomes the companion of the major characters in their search for the needed evidence in the pages of History. Music background also helps to integrate the varying patterns.

DIRECTION

In the event that six leaders can cooperate in an episodic drama like the Liberty play, the undertaking will be relatively simple. The more experienced leader should be the overall director. He should assign to each of his five colleagues one episode and a group of children, assuming the responsibility himself for the prologue and epilogue. Together they prepare the script, plan the settings and the general movement pattern, the background music, costumes, and the light plot. Each leader then proceeds to carry out his own assignment with the designated group. Since episodes range from seven to ten minutes in length, eight rehearsals should suffice for each. If the services of a musician can be secured, he should set to work on the composition of the score as the rehearsals begin. Activities of the costumer, light technician, and designer can be scheduled to proceed concurrently. With careful organization and conscientious cooperation, the whole play should be ready in less than a month, provided at least three rehearsal periods are devoted weekly to each episode. The overall director will assume complete responsibility for the last three coordinating rehearsals. If he has checked regularly with his co-directors, and observed at least one of the rehearsals of each of the five episodes, the final integration process will present no problem.

Much of the dramatic material in a play of this nature lends itself to creative direction. The scenes are always short and concern few characters involved in a simple plot. After the leader has related the story twice in dialogue form, a free improvisation of the first two acting units will closely approximate the plot pattern. A brief discussion will correct the few errors, and the second trial will be very commendable. If several major characters bear most of the responsibility, they may need to refer to the script at the beginning. The creative method is recommended, however, as a general principle of directing pageant episodes.

INTEGRATION

The director gives his attention to the integration of his production along two lines: he works for aesthetic unity through the synchronization of music, color in settings and costumes, and lighting effects; his success in technical or practical integration depends upon intelligent planning for the building of set units, and their manipulation during the performance.

Special care must be given to the artistic elements in unifying the production of the episodic play, because of the peculiar nature of its construction. Although the scenes may be widely separated by limits of time, place, and content, they must appear as parts of a whole pattern. The successful drawing together of the component factors depends largely on the director's skillful use of color, sound, and light.

He will find the integrating power of music almost indispensable. A creative pianist, once he has studied the script of a well-written pageant, will at once "hear" its theme in a musical motif around which he will compose an introductory score. He will thus create the mood for the opening statement of the problem, before the curtain rises. The same motif, treated differently, may occur several times during the course of the production. It will certainly appear at the end, as background to enrich and heighten the joyful solution. Even such fragmentary music will help to tie the threads of thought and mood together. Music can perform another function: It can smooth the transitions between episodes.

In the Liberty play, for example, there is a gap of centuries between the Biblical scene in which David fights Goliath and that in which Joan of Arc appears with her playmates at the Fairy Tree in Domremy. Despite the words of the dialogue between Memory and Liberty, which have been purposely written to carry the thought across this awkward space, the audience may feel the shock of the abrupt change. If the exultant music, however, which steals in as the background of David's victory, modulates into an appropriate theme for the offstage dialogue of the major characters as the lights fade, the audience is carried away at once from the mood of the former scene. Then, a moment before the curtain rises on the "Joan" episode, there is another subtle modulation; a soft pastoral theme steals in unobtrusively to set the mood for the next episode. The music has thus successfully linked the divergent stories; through its emotional appeal, it has created the fast mood changes necessary. The audience, without knowing why, has felt no uncomfortable break, no sudden shock. If the director cannot secure the services of a musician, he may be able to use recordings to heighten certain moods and bridge awkward spaces. In that case, he must be sure that he selects unfamiliar music, without a definite rhythmic pattern, and keeps it subdued; the distraction of the audience when it suddenly hears loud strains of a familiar tune will be greater than that caused by the too abrupt opening of a new episode.

Color in costumes and settings will often act as an integrating medium; if it is used thoughtlessly, it may have the opposite influence. That colors have a psychological effect is well known and should be taken into consideration when plans are being made for settings and costuming. If one scene is playing in sharp tones of red and yellow, and the next opens on drab purples and dark blues, the abrupt mood change will often be disturbing unless it has been carefully bridged by music and lights. Even though the theme of the second episode is heavy and sorrowful, a gentler transition could be made, perhaps, through greens and rich browns. The costumes of characters appearing later in the scene can carry the color plan into the more sombre tones.

The lighting of the episodic play may be the determining factor in the unification process. The color, quantity, and distribution of light are largely responsible for creating the desired atmosphere in any scene; its power to stimulate emotional response can be compared with that of music and color. The charm and romance that emanate from candles on a dining table, or softly shaded lamps in the living room, flee before the hard beams of a glaring white, overhead light. The subtle transition from one episode requiring strong light to the next, which will be played in shadows, merits consideration. If the change is gradual, the audience will be spared the discomfort of the man who walks suddenly from a sunlit beach into a dark cave. It is impossible to achieve the proper effect without the control provided by rheostats or dimmers. A leader who is preparing to present a pageant or episodic play must see to it that rheostats are included in his equipment. If they are not available in the auditorium where the production is to be staged, they should be borrowed or rented. The snapping off and on of lights breaks the mood of the child in the audience. Such interruptions completely nullify all other efforts to give smoothness to the production.

The practical aspects of integrating the pageant are related chiefly to the construction and manipulation of the settings. Any good designer could create artistic and charming backgrounds for the individual episodes, were they to be presented as separate units. The pageant designer's task is much more complex. He must suggest the environment for each section of the play so economically that the change of a few units will suffice. The young scene shifters must manage the change in a few minutes, and often in semidarkness, if the flow of action and idea is to remain unbroken. The intermission demanded by a complicated set change will sometimes destroy the dramatic impact of the whole performance. All settings must be designed with this fact in mind. A minimum number of set pieces, such as platforms, benches, screens, and ground rows, may be used singly or in combination to give variation to the different episodes. Accessible storage space must be provided offstage for the units not needed in certain scenes. The form and color of each piece of scenery must be devised in relationship to the permanent background of drapes, flats, or greenery, and specific thought must be given to those units that will serve in several capacities.

PAGEANT VERSUS EPISODIC PLAY

A statement was made at the beginning of this chapter concerning the close resemblance of the pageant to the episodic play; in some instances the two terms have been used almost synonymously. Since the episodic play has been thoroughly studied, it may be expedient to examine the particular features that pertain to the pageant. As defined by Brown, "A pageant is a story told in dramatic sequence as a spectacle . . . the term is now used to denote almost any moving spectacle . . . each part of which illustrates some part of a central theme." Many of these phrases might well be used in a description of the episodic play. In the implications of the word "spectacle" lies the key to the interpretation. A spectacle suggests large groups, gathered to celebrate a religious or patriotic event, suggests parades, vocal choruses, orchestral music, movement of masses rather than individuals, the sound of voices chanting in unison rather than lines spoken by a single character. These are images conjured up by the word "spectacle"; many of them characterize the pageant form. The basic structure of the pageant is identical with that of the episodic play. Each episode is closely related to the central theme, and there is unity of idea rather than of time or place. The pageant will often require a larger cast than the play, and the scenes will generally be interpreted through effective pantomime rather than speech. Singing and dancing play a larger part, and there is little detailed delineation of character. The episodic play often makes the personal emotional appeal of the drama; the pageant addresses itself especially to the visual and auditory senses. Although some of the same themes may be satisfactorily translated by either medium, those with broader scope, deeper impact, and greater dignity profit by being subjected to the pageant treatment. Favorite subjects are those dealing with the worthy expression of some phase of community life (example: "Better Housing Makes Happier People"), incidents related to a hero or historical event (examples: "St. Francis of Assisi and Charity," or "The Discovery that the World Is Round"), steps in the moral, cultural, or social advance of a community or nation (example: "The Advance in Communication Arts"), or the seasonal celebration (example: "The Meaning of Thanksgiving").

SUMMARY

The pageant and the episodic play are full-length productions based on a single theme, but composed of separate episodic units each of which is a miniature play. The unifying factor is the contribution of each episode to the development of the central idea. The nature of the occasion for which a pageant is to be presented often requires its dramatization by the producing group. The theme selected must be capable of dramatic interpretation; the content of the episodes must have human interest values; the whole script must be uniform in style. The production must be integrated artistically and practically. Aesthetic unity depends upon the synchronization of music, color, and lighting; practical integration depends upon intelligent construction and manipulation of settings.

A pageant differs from an episodic play in that it is more of a spectacle; it utilizes larger groups, tells a story through movement rather than dialogue, incorporates more music, choruses, dancers, and treats themes of broader scope and greater dignity.

10

TECHNIQUES FOR THE DIRECTOR

What kind of personal qualifications and philosophies must the effective children's theatre director possess? What kind of training must he seek? Answers to these and similar questions would require far more space than a single chapter; an entire text could be written on the subject. Research and development in the field of children's theatre from 1950 to 1965 (the first edition of this text was published in 1950) have made great strides and advanced some commendable theories, many of which can be helpful to the modern enthusiast. The number of children's theatre projects springing up all over the world shows a sharp increase; new and significant discoveries are made public every day. In the author's opinion, however, the advice of Dr. Frank M. Whiting, who is director of Theatre Arts at the University of Minnesota, and also an experienced children's theatre director, cannot be surpassed. If space permitted, his entire article, "Recommended Training for Children's Theatre Director" (already quoted in Chapter 8), would be repeated here verbatim. A paraphrase, though extremely inadequate, may provide some milestones along the path. For those would-be directors who are seriously considering children's theatre as their life-work, a careful study of the whole article (in Siks and Dunnington: *Children's Theatre and Creative Dramatics*) is recommended.

Dr. Whiting believes that any children's theatre director must understand that this life is essentially a life of service—that there is little room for egocentricity and pride. No matter how great he considers the art of the theatre and his potential contribution to it, he must consider the art of making theatre for children even greater! He should be prepared to work long hours for the pure love and joy of it, never expecting sympathy or congratulations for his martyrdom. He must have an extraordinary appreciation for dramatic literature, and an even more sensitive understanding of children's literature and child psychology. In addition to all of these attributes,

Dr. Whiting recommends basic theatre directing courses and practical experiences that will develop a feeling for keeping the story line moving with exciting action, a sense of fun, and a passion for teamwork rather than stardom. He genuinely believes that children's theatre deserves, and should assume a position of prestige in today's world. Its fate is surely in the hands of the young teacher-directors who are ready to completely dedicate their love of theatre and their love of children to this cause.

The leader who attempts to produce a children's play for an audience assumes a definite responsibility; he has obligated himself to the invited or paying guests. He must not only select his play with great care, but also apply all the time, energy, and technical knowledge he possesses to its direction. Though his plans for the action, dialogue, and characterizations should always remain flexible, and should be presented to the cast as suggestions rather than orders, he must never lose sight of his ultimate objective—an artistic, convincing entertainment. Young players must never be made to feel inhibited or restricted by suddenly imposed rules of technique; the tactful leader will be able to accomplish miracles by carefully worded questions. A young actor, so guided, usually will create remarkably appropriate action that will be far more convincing than that *commanded* by the director.

SUGGESTIVE DIRECTING

Suppose Johnny is watching at a window, stage right, for his father, who is expected back from a long journey. Mother is sitting on a couch, stage left, quietly knitting. At a certain cue Johnny's line reads, "Mother, he's coming! That's his car! It's Daddy . . . it is! I wonder if he'll know me . . . think he will? Oh, look! The chauffeur's opening the door. See?" The first time Bill, who is playing the role of Johnny, tries the scene he may give the whole speech at the window. The director knows that only action can build the excited anticipation needed to prepare for Father's entrance. Instead of telling Bill when and how to move, he might say, "Isn't Johnny excited when he sees the car, Bill? Do you think he can possibly stand still by the window? Might he not run back to mother, and then dash to the window again for fear he'll miss something?" At once, Bill will catch the spirit of the scene. The second time he will say, at the window, "Mother, he's coming! That's his car! It's Daddy . . . it is!" Then, dashing over and throwing one arm about mother, he will continue, "I wonder if he'll know me . . . think he will?" Making another dive for the window, he will shout, "Oh, look! The chauffeur's opening the door. See?" Then, half turning, he will beckon frantically to his mother, and immediately go back to flatten his nose against the window pane. Even if the director's original plan for this action had been identical, and he had ordered every one of Bill's moves, the results would never have been so spontaneous. Only because pointed questions have stimulated the child's imagination does the scene come to life freely and naturally.

MOTIVATING BUSINESS

The term "stage business" refers to any movement made by the actor, from the vigorous slamming of a door to a subtle lifting of the head. The most important rule in the director's notebook states that all business must be motivated; in other words, there must be a reason for every movement of every character on stage. Some motivations are implied in the story itself. Aunt Em crosses to the table because she must put down her sewing. The maid straightens her cap and apron and goes off stage right to answer the doorbell signifying the arrival of an important guest. The child who first hears the coach approaching in the school scene of the *Christmas Carol* runs to look out the door. These reasons for movement are obvious in the story line; seldom would a young actor need to be directed to do any of these things. Other motivations, not quite so obvious, come from within the character; they are crosses, turns, changes of body position that result directly from a particular character's reaction to a specific stimulus. Jill sits down on the rug before the fire; as she watches the firelight and hears the clock strike twelve, she curls up, stretches, yawns . . . because she is sleepy. Susie flops down in the window seat and watches the downpour; finally she buries her head in her arms and sobs in disappointment. Everything she had looked forward to must be postponed! Jennie stands looking down at her soiled, torn dress. Mother is scolding her severely for wearing it in the yard to climb trees. She knows that mother is right, and gradually her body turns away and seems to shrink to half its size. All of these moves stem from the character's reaction to a specific situation. In general, they will also come naturally from young people who have had previous training in creative drama. Should this not occur, a meaningful question from the director will almost always bring an honest reaction. For example, in the case of the torn dress the director's question might go like this: "How did you feel when mother was explaining how distressed she was over what had happened to the new dress she had made you?" "Ashamed," Jennie will reply. "Yes . . . so would I," says the sympathetic director. "And when we feel ashamed, don't we feel like turning away so no one can see our faces? Suppose you try it that way, Jennie . . ." Almost always this system meets with success.

Occasionally there seems to be a real need for movement on stage and yet no business is indicated for any character for either of the reasons just described. If a conversation is taking place near a door through which a third character must soon enter, something must be done to clear the entrance. The director's resourcefulness and imagination must be called into play. He may suggest that the two finish the conversation on the couch, which is on the other side of the room; he might even have to add a line: "Let's sit down and talk about it. I can think better sitting down!" or something else appropriate. For lack of a better name, one might call this *invented motivation* as compared with *story* or *character* motivation. At any rate, to work for naturalness of a stage movement, one must always feel a logical reason behind it.

One of the most common weaknesses of the play performed by young actors is ineffectual business. Either players who are naturally fidgety are in constant motion that signifies nothing and is extremely distracting, or those who are still somewhat inhibited are so immobile from time to time that they resemble talking statues. The director who takes time to study his play carefully in advance and visualize the basic movement pattern will avoid this dilemma. Jed Davis points out the great need for action in the children's theatre performance. He says (in Siks and Dunnington: *Children's Theatre and Creative Dramatics*): "Children are oriented to action. Both in their own lives and in plays children much prefer doing things to talking about them . . . imaginative business and patterns of blocking should be incorporated to present to a child audience an almost constantly changing state picture." He warns, however, of the danger of adding movement purely for its own sake without adequate motivation. If the director has difficulty as he works in advance of the rehearsals, in making a mental picture of the stage movement, he may resort to the "pin-and-blotter" method. Sketch roughly the scene plan, indicating doors, windows, furniture. Tack this drawing over several thicknesses of blotting paper to an old table or board. With one colored pin to represent each character and with the script beside him, the director reads through the scene. His "pin" people stand where he places them because of their blotter base, and as the lines seem to require action, he can test various moves for their effectiveness. Plotting business in the "pin-and-blotter" manner for a short time helps to develop an ability to visualize it mentally.

In giving suggestions for movement, even to young actors, the director should employ stage terminology. An extensive vocabulary is unnecessary, but the use of a few of the more common words is a practical time-saver. *Downstage* means toward the audience, and *upstage*, away from it; *right* and *left* refer to the actors' right and left. *Offstage* is the portion of the stage out of sight of the audience; the *apron* is the part between the front curtain line and the auditorium. The permanent pleated draperies that often extend around three sides of the school stage, providing a neutral background, are called the *cyclorama,* or *cyc. Properties,* more commonly labeled *props,* refer to small movable parts of the setting, such as furniture, lamps, books, flowers, rugs. The words, *cross, entrance,* and *exit* have literal meanings. A *cross* signifies any move across the stage. The director may say, "Don't you think Johnny would CROSS to the desk DOWN RIGHT when he remembers about the letter?"

PLANNING ENTRANCES AND EXITS

Though the terms themselves need no explanation, the director should give some consideration to the manner in which entrances and exits are performed. The young actor should never be hampered by cramped doorways or onstage properties that necessitate an awkward detour. The director must explain to each child the importance of assuming his role offstage—letting the thoughts and feelings of his character completely control him before he enters the scene. He must understand that his appearance and actions, during those first few moments, will tell the audience more about his mood and purpose than will his first speech. The entrance of an important character should be emphasized by the physical arrangement of the people onstage, as well as the attitude expressed by their bodies and voices. If the area near the entrance is left clear, and the grouping on stage is designed to help direct the eye of the audience to the doorway, the effectiveness of the moment will be increased immeasurably. Staying in character well after the exit is also a good habit to acquire. The boy who is creeping fearfully off to the porch to bring the cat in out of the rain, though he knows it is forbidden, must stay in character until he has cautiously closed the door behind him. Children have a tendency to shed their characters, as a snake does its skin, as soon as they have finished their last line onstage. Effective exits often depend upon still another factor: the way the character makes his final cross to the doorway. A child finds a long cross immediately before an exit difficult and awkward. If it is possible for him to break the last speech—say a part of it, cross a little distance, and then conclude it somewhere in the vicinity of the exit—the action will be more natural.

CREATING THE STAGE PICTURE

Balance

The average stage is seen through a proscenium arch, which frames a constantly changing picture for the audience. Too much stress cannot be placed upon the necessity for following the rules of artistic composition in grouping the characters who create the picture. It must reveal the same balance, interesting contrast, emphasis, and rhythm that characterizes a fine painting. The stage must never have a top-heavy look, caused by many actors on one side outweighing empty space on the other. Balance need not be achieved through even numbers; psychological balance is often more effective. The personality of one character who is in direct conflict with the rest is often strong enough to fill the whole right stage area, while his ten opponents huddle together on the left. However it is achieved, balance is necessary to any good composition.

Contrast

Contrast is equally important in holding the interest of an audience. A group of ten children of relatively the same height, all standing on the stage level, will make an even, horizontal line of heads about five feet above the floor. The pattern is dull and uninteresting. If they happen to be standing in a straight line or a semicircle, the effect is even more deadly. All such regularity must be avoided, if possible. There are two simple solutions to the problem: contrast can be achieved by breaking the form of the stage floor, or by varying the body positions of the characters in the scene. (See Fig. 10-1.) If platforms or boxes of several heights are used in appropriate arrangements, the level, horizontal "head-line" cannot appear. When these are not available, the director must work for variety by placing each member of the group in a different position. If the scene is to represent a living room, and there are several platforms at hand, a two-step rise may lead to the doorway up center, a six-inch hearth may be placed before the fireplace, stage right, and a twenty-four-inch box or chest may simulate a window seat, stage left. This arrangement provides five different levels for the use of the actors: the stage floor itself; the hearth, six inches; the first step to the doorway, eight inches; the second step, sixteen inches; the window seat, twenty-four inches. If the same scene must be handled with-

TECHNIQUES FOR THE DIRECTOR

out platforms, the second method should be employed. At times when the picture is static for several minutes, one character should sit on a chair, one stand, one kneel, one sit on a stool and another on the edge of a table, and perhaps still another on the arm of a sofa.

Fig. 10–1. Interesting grouping achieved through varying positions of characters. (Credit: Gaston Remy.)

Emphasis

The part played by emphasis or accent in any painting, interior decoration, or flower arrangement is considerable. In the stage picture, as in any other composition, there is always a point of interest on which the attention of the observer should be focused. There are four practical methods of highlighting an important character:

1. An actor will seem superior to others in the scene if his position is in direct contrast to theirs. If he stands while the others sit or kneel; if he is on a platform, sitting on a table, or occupying a chair on a dais; if he is crouching while the others stand—he will immediately attract the attention of the audience.
2. Placing one character in a strongly lighted area while the others remain in half shadow will give him dominance over the scene.
3. Any actor who is placed in an upstage center position, while those in the downstage area turn toward him, commands respect. His full face is naturally more compelling than the quarter profile of the other players.
4. Sharp color contrast in costume will never fail to stir interest. A

character in all white, red, or green will be conspicuous in a group clad in neutral shades. And vice versa, a figure dressed in drab garments will stand out in a crowd of richly dressed courtiers.

DEVELOPING CHARACTERIZATION

To help the young actor give a sustained and convincing characterization of his role requires patience, tact, and skill. It is so easy to fall into the error of teaching by imitation. Many a director, in a moment of despair, has said, "Say it like this, Jane. Listen, now, and repeat it after me!" Jane's repetition may be exact, the quality, inflection, and pitch identical, but the words sound hollow and empty. By one hasty remark, the director will have induced an artificiality that will weaken the whole interpretation. Children who have had a thorough grounding in creative drama will be prepared to analyze their characters before attempting to portray them. The director must make every effort to help them gain a more complete understanding by posing significant questions. "What does the King look like? How does he walk? What is it that troubles him? Why does he not go to the Queen for help? Why does he feel that he is to blame for his daughter's mistake?" A dozen other such questions may be necessary to clarify for the young actor the thought patterns, behavior, and motivation of his character. An understanding of the theme of the play—its mood, tempo, and historical background—helps in developing a characterization. The relationship of the people in the story must be thoroughly analyzed.

If time permits, each child may prepare an oral or written biography of the character that he is portraying, imagining his likely past, interests, and experiences. When the lines of a children's story or dramatization do not provide sufficient source material on which to base a thorough characterization, the combined imaginations of students and director must furnish the missing facts.

A sharper delineation of character may be indicated from time to time. The following questions may prove useful in checking on progress:

1. Does the picture of the character, as he is developing, resemble the picture you formed in your preliminary study?
2. Do you think he seems live and convincing?
3. Is he sustained throughout every scene, or are some of your own traits occasionally stealing into the interpretation?
4. Is his relationship to the other characters, and to the whole play, clear at all times?

IMPROVING DIALOGUE

The first demand of the audience is that dialogue be audible and natural. If the children sitting in the tenth row cannot hear the lines, they cannot understand the story and will not enjoy the play. If the voice of the giant in "Jack and the Beanstalk" sounds like that of Freddy, the soda clerk who is playing the role (and is familiar to most of the audience), there will again be dissatisfaction. Even more negative reception will be accorded the giant whose words are spoken like a stilted recitation.

Sufficient preliminary experience in creative improvisation should insure natural dialogue. The young actor who has not memorized lines from a printed page will not fall into the dread habit of merely vocalizing meaningless combinations of vowels and consonants. He will communicate his thoughts simply and sincerely. Any director who finds himself tackling the problem of unnatural dialogue during rehearsals for a long play must shoulder most of the blame. If he had previously insisted upon an adequate number of creative improvisations, he would never have been faced with such a dilemma.

Audibility is another matter. Even some of the youngsters who have improvised freely may not have developed sufficient resonance power to project their voices in a large auditorium. If the director will make a practice of sitting near the back of the room during most of the rehearsals, they will be encouraged to speak out. A few individuals may need private exercises in breathing and diction during the course of the rehearsals. They will usually apply themselves readily to the necessary drills, so eager are they to portray their parts convincingly.

Polishing or pointing dialogue for dramatic effectiveness requires subtlety in technique. The director will work from the start toward developing the basic rhythm of the whole play. Although the young actors may not be able to comprehend the technique of building suspense to the climax by tempo change, they will readily grasp the fact that just before the secret box is discovered, the boys will talk fast and breathlessly. They will instinctively feel that during Beth's goodbye to Jo in *Little Women,* words will come haltingly, in uneven rhythm.

Even young children recognize the significance of emphasis placed on a certain word or phrase. The difference in meaning between "She is ONE of my friends," and "she is one of MY friends," will at once be apparent to them. The theory that the director applies to gain emphasis is similar to that used in accenting the important individual in a group, or the dominant form in a stage setting. Even though the interpretation of a line may be natural and the inflection satisfactory, it may be necessary to point out possibilities for greater effectiveness. An example may be drawn from the story of Sam, a little country boy whose stern and wealthy aunt has come to fetch him. He must accompany her to the city because his mother is ill, and there is no one on the farm to look after him. Sam's line reads, "But I can't go, Auntie . . . I have chores to do . . . the chickens to feed, the cow to milk. I haven't any city clothes to wear, and besides, I . . . I . . . can't leave Mother . . . I can't!" Sam sounds reasonably convincing in the young actor's first interpretation; he seems sincere in his desire to remain on the farm. But the speech lacks force because he makes the same pause between each group of words; each is delivered with the same up-down inflection curve and equal volume. The director points out that Sam's first excuses to Auntie would come quietly and evenly, and that as he feels more desperate to find a way to impress her, he will talk faster and with greater intensity. The sentence, "I haven't any city clothes to wear," takes on a higher pitch and more speed. "And besides," has a staccato note, because he must catch his breath in order to give greater vehemence to the last loud outburst, "I . . . I can't leave Mother . . . I can't!" Immediately the young actor will understand how he can give the proper emphasis to the last phrase, the core of his speech. He is happy in his new interpretation, and the scene has gained appreciably in dramatic effect.

The question of "silent dialogue" is often overlooked. The director who is engrossed in pointing up the actual speeches in a scene may fail to observe the blank spots caused by the characters who are listening—or, as is frequently the case, not listening. During the early rehearsals and discussions of character, children should be reminded that an individual's flow of thought is continuous. Sometimes he voices his ideas, sometimes he speaks them to himself while another person talks, but always he thinks. The ability to listen to another character's words and formulate the natural thoughts that his speech provokes is as important a part of a characterization as the spoken dialogue. In fact, it is more important to the success of the whole scene. When eight people are onstage, only one character can speak at a time; if the other seven are not listening and thinking, there will be seven blank spots in the picture, and only one that is effective. The large percentage of the composition controlled by empty inactivity will be more compelling to the audience than the small portion controlled by spoken dialogue.

The imaginative player with a keen dramatic sense and strong concentration powers will think through the whole scene. Others may need their imaginations stimulated by suggestion. If an episode during which one character has a large share of the dialogue seems to become inactive, the director must stop and ask questions. "How do you feel about what the Mayor is saying? . . . Do you approve, Janet? . . . I can't see your thought! . . . And what about you, Harry? Surely you are worried about the new law being proposed? If it goes through, you will lose your job. As you listen to the Mayor's words, wouldn't you think, 'He can't do that . . . I'll lose my job. This is dreadful!'" A few such hints to individuals in the scene may remind the others that they must think the thoughts of the character from start to finish.

SUMMARY

The leader who directs a play for the public must keep his goal in mind: providing artistic, convincing entertainment. He will direct by suggestion rather than command, never permitting suddenly imposed rules of technique to restrict the flow of the child's imagination. Every piece of "stage business" must be motivated. The first law in the director's notebook should read: NO MOVE WITHOUT A REASON. Employing simple stage terminology will facilitate rehearsals. Entrances must be unhampered by furniture and pointed by the positions and attitudes of the characters onstage. Children must understand the importance of getting into character before an entrance and continuing the characterization well after the exit. Long, awkward crosses before an exit should be avoided if possible. The interesting stage picture always follows the rules of artistic composition. Convincing characterization depends on a thorough understanding of the character, his relationship to the other people in the play, and the projection of his silent, as well as his spoken, dialogue.

11

STAGING THE PLAY

The problem of staging the play is a large one; it includes almost every element of the production except the actors themselves. The director, working for an artistic whole, must consider the setting, costumes, lights, sound, and makeup as contributing parts of a single unit. Even if he is fortunate enough to have adult help in each of these departments, he must, as in the production of a pageant, act as the coordinator. There must be complete agreement as to the central idea of the play and the emphasis in its interpretation. Only a properly balanced integration of all the technical aspects will allow good design to fulfill its function: to create environment that will deepen the mood and meaning of the dramatic presentation.

SETTING

Plans drawn for the setting by the director (or by the designer with the approval of the director) during the preparation period before rehearsals begin must be made with regard for space, equipment, and budget available. Scenery must be practical, attractive, and expressive. If it is economically and sturdily built, simple to handle and store, arranged so that most of the acting area is visible to the audience, and provides a comfortable place for the young actors to work, it is practical. It is attractive if the rules of good composition are applied in the creation of the stage picture. Balance, proportion, variety, contrast, and emphasis must all be taken into consideration. (See Plans for Typical Cottage Set, page 115.) The effect is more pleasing if the two sides of the stage are informally balanced by the architectural units, furniture, and platform masses. The relative heights and weights of the forms used are of great importance. The danger of deadening interest by monotony of line, color, and shape, which has been mentioned in respect to grouping, is also present in set design. Too symmetrical a balance, sameness

Plans for Typical Cottage Set

(Using Set Pieces on a Draped Stage)

(Units Needed)

1 Door   1 or 2 Stools
2 Small Windows   1 Fireplace
1 Table   1 Set of Shelves
1 Bench by the Fire

Plan 1 ~ Wrong ~

Analysis
a. Balance too symmetrical.
b. Acting area cramped.
c. Vision and entrance blocked.

Plan 2 ~ Right ~

Analysis
a. Asymmetrical Balance.
b. Large, free acting area.
c. Clear vision of entrance.

Fig. 11–1. Plans for typical cottage set.

in color tones, and the repeated use of parallel lines and identical forms make for commonplace dullness. On the other hand, an abundance of unrelated clutter will only disturb or distract the audience. The key to successfully achieving contrast in design is the proper use of emphasis. In any scene, there is a center of interest, a focal point; it may be the king's throne, the center doorway, a balcony, or a fireplace. Attention will be concentrated on a particular unit only if the rest of the picture is subordinated to it. An object on a higher level, of sharply contrasting color or form, or more intensely lighted will dominate the stage, provided the background is kept sufficiently unobtrusive.

An expressive setting unpretentiously reinforces the mood and meaning of the play. It should never flaunt itself as a separate feature, claiming the attention that should rightly be centered on the dramatic action. It should function in the manner of a well-trained servant, who speaks only in the case of necessity. The religious play that treats a serious, dignified theme uses heights, masses, vertical lines, a more-or-less symmetrical balance, and rich, deep colors. The fantasy demands curved, indefinite lines, lightness in plastic forms, and soft, pastel colors. The setting of the folk tale works for barren simplicity and stolidity through low, horizontal lines and earthy colors. In every case, the particular duty of the stage design is to reproduce the essence of the dramatic idea pictorially.

The visual background for theatric action may be created in any one of many styles. The director, or designer, after studying the play, decides whether a realistic, suggestive, or formal treatment will be most appropriate. The realistic setting attempts to reproduce the environment photographically; the suggestive design gives an impression of the locale, but does not state it in definite terms; the formal setting makes use of a symmetrically balanced arrangement of plastic forms (arches, steps, columns, platforms) to enclose the acting area, but makes no attempt to simulate the background realistically or suggestively.

For the average children's theatre production, the suggestive method is the most practical. The forest scene can be suggested by a blue backdrop, several tree silhouettes, and a rock or flower ground row. A stage enclosed by permanent draperies can take on the appearance of a throne room, with the addition of a high-backed chair raised on a dais, several rich tapestries, and a decorative bench or stool. One children's theatre group gave a remarkably realistic illusion of a fantastic, underwater episode, with great economy of design. The permanent hangings on three sides of the stage were of black sateen; all the decor was therefore carried out in light shades

STAGING THE PLAY 117

of pink, green, blue, lavender, and yellow, for contrast. On two pipes, or battens, hung in the flies (the ceiling area), parallel to the footlights, dozens of heavy black threads of various lengths were attached. Each of these held a fish, sea serpent, octopus, coral formation, or some other form of aquatic life. Several clusters of pampas grass dyed in shades of green and coral were fastened to wooden blocks and placed on the floor, giving the effect of bright-colored seaweed growing on the bottom of the ocean. Long strips of green

BOX-CURTAIN STAGE

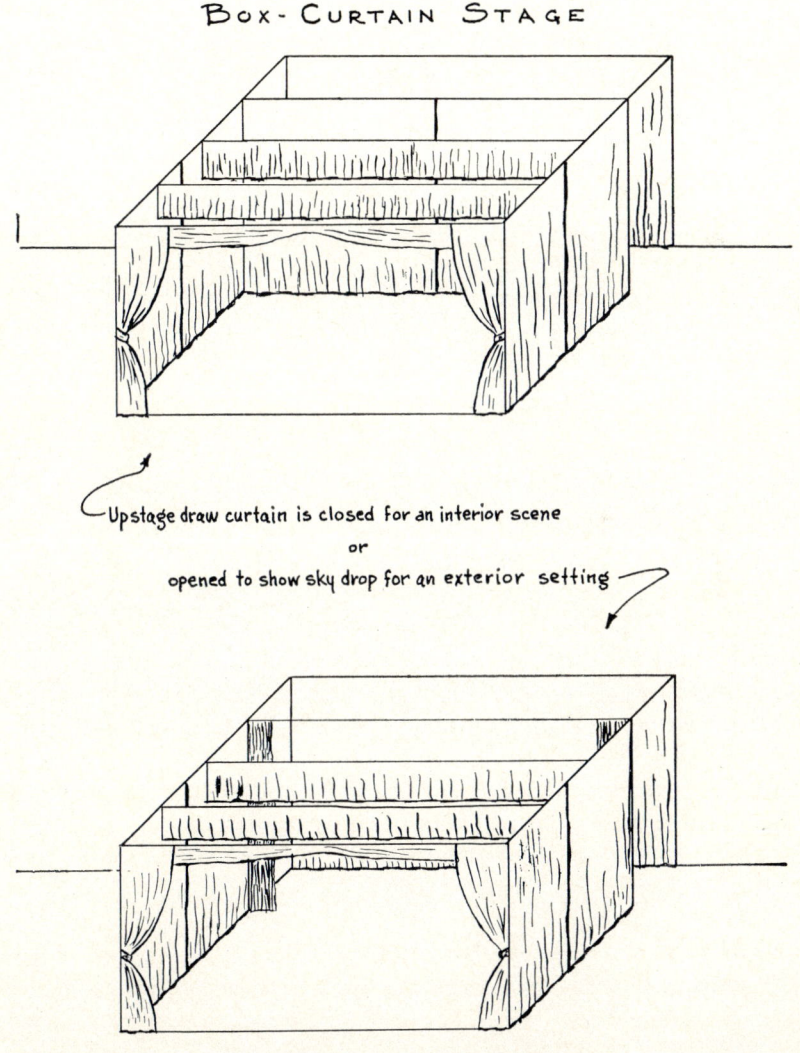

Upstage draw curtain is closed for an interior scene
or
opened to show sky drop for an exterior setting

Fig. 11–2. Box-curtain stage.

and yellow crepe paper tied to varying lengths of black thread hung from the pipes and touched the stage level, simulating long shoots of sea grass struggling toward the surface of the water. The cost of paper, cardboard, water paint, thread, and pampas grass was nominal, and yet the scene, properly lighted and viewed through a scrim curtain (owned by the theatre), was exquisitely beautiful.

Setting the stage with a box set (wooden frames covered with canvas) to represent realistic walls and ceilings of an interior, is not practical for the average children's play. The units are expensive to buy or make, awkward to move, cumbersome to store. The use of a full-length drapery or cyclorama that encircles the entire acting area will be much more feasible. It can be hung on rings from pipes forming three sides of a square. Each pipe will support two sections of drapery, thus providing possible entrances at right, left, and upcenter. The upstage pipe should be placed at least four feet from the back wall. If the back wall is made of plaster and can be painted blue, it will simulate sky for outside scenes, when the upstage sections of the draperies are drawn to left and right. A blue canvas drop hung on the back wall will give the same effect. The audience sight lines must always be considered. The average stage will require several borders, or teasers, hung in such a way that they will mask the overhead space above the stage floor. These strips, made of the material used for the drapes, should be hung six to ten feet apart, and parallel to the act curtain.[1]

The draped stage, which includes only the upstage section of the cyclorama, is also popular. The arrangement necessitates the use of "legs" (narrow draperies hung parallel to the front curtain), or several sets of close-in curtains, to mask the offstage space right and left. Since the legs perform only the masking function, the close-in curtain plan is preferable. (See illustration, page 119.) These extra curtains serve three purposes: (1) when opened, they act as masking pieces; (2) when closed, they provide a shallower stage that may be more appropriate for the playing of certain scenes; (3) they make possible the placing of another setting in the upstage area, while a scene on the close-in curtain stage is in progress.[2]

COLOR

A comprehensive knowledge of color is necessary for the planning of the costumes and the lighting, as well as the setting. Space per-

---

[1] See illustration of permanently draped stage, page 117, Figure 11–2.
[2] See drawing of close-in curtain arrangement, Fig. 11–3, page 119.

STAGING THE PLAY

CLOSE-IN CURTAIN STAGE

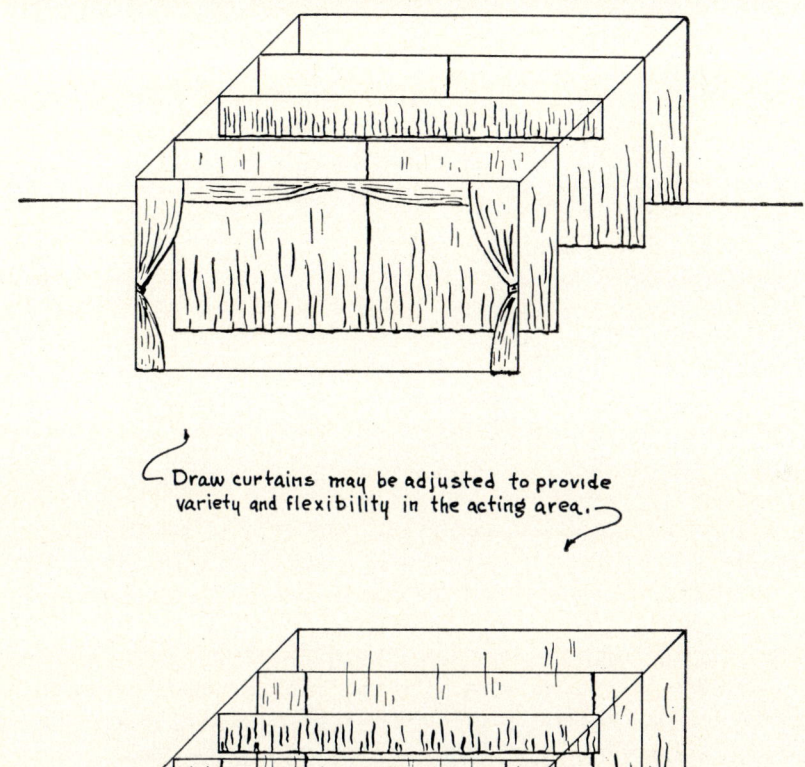

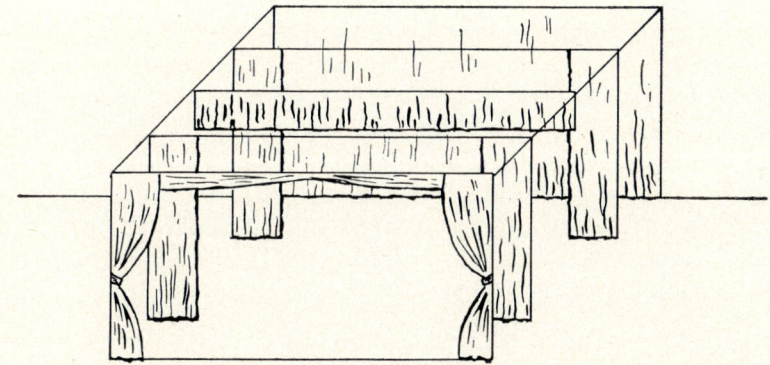

Draw curtains may be adjusted to provide variety and flexibility in the acting area.

Fig. 11–3. Close-in curtain stage.

mits only a few elementary suggestions in that regard, but many books are available to the director that treat the subject in great detail.[3] The basic color scheme for the whole production is determined primarily by the mood of the play. In general, the serious play calls for cold, sombre tones; the comedy for gay, warm shades; the fantasy for soft pastels. Many theories have been expressed concerning the psychological effect of colors; although there is not com-

[3] See Bibliography.

plete agreement as to the nature of the response, it is generally accepted that they do set up some emotional reaction. The following list includes some of the most common color associations:

Blue—formal, true, peaceful
Orange—exhilarating
Gray—depressing, sombre
Brown—stolid, forceful
Black—melancholy, dignified
Green—soothing, restful, fresh
Yellow—cheerful, gay
Red—dangerous, irritating, aggressive
Purple—mournful, regal

If analogous colors (those that appear in sequence in the spectrum) are used in a scene, the addition of a dissonant color (from the opposite end of the spectrum) will give accent and interest to the picture. An emphatic note of yellow, orange, or red will lend force to the setting in which blues and greens predominate; the decor that uses a profusion of yellows and oranges will benefit by a contrasting note of blue or green. The same rule applies to the use of color in costuming and lighting. In any plan, the designer must take into account the effect of the light that the scene requires. The set for an episode that occurs in the evening is subjected to blue and red light, and must be painted with great care. Yellows and greens will look brownish under blue light; blue will look decidedly black under red light. Warm colors in lights, such as red and yellow, intensify warm colors in painted or dyed materials; whereas blues and greens, the cool colors, tend to dull warm colors in materials. A colored light thrown on material of the same shade tends to wash out a great part of the color. (See Color Chart, Fig. 11-7, page 133.)

COSTUMING

The children's play that is presented for an audience should be costumed if possible. Even though the informality of the occasion, a meager budget, or lack of time may tempt the leader to shun this added responsibility, he should not eliminate costumes altogether. A persistent search in any community will usually uncover a gifted, artistic individual who will gladly volunteer to chair a costume committee. The advantages of providing some appropriate attire for the young actors are many. It is a recognized fact that one's behavior is often influenced by apparel; any individual dressed in a new, becoming outfit feels a greater sense of relaxation and self-confidence. In like manner, the child actor, fittingly costumed, will assume his character with greater assurance. He will find it easier to lose his own identity when he no longer looks like himself; behind the curtain that now conceals his personality, he will be able to shed the last troublesome inhibitions. The child in the audience will believe in costumed characters more readily, and for him the play will take on more reality. Another advantage lies in the broadening of educational opportunities. The group study of book illustrations, old paintings, and sketches relative to the period of the play will deepen the interest in the project. Historical knowledge so gained will make a lasting impression on young minds.

As the director plans to costume the play, he must bear three points in mind: the budget, the actor, and the play itself.

Costume and the Budget

With cast list in one hand and expense allowance in the other, the director judiciously apportions the dollars, practicing thrift wherever he can in order to spend generously on featured costumes.

Costume and the Actor

The actor must be authentically dressed. His costume must make an accurate, if simple, statement of the historical period and locale of the play. He must be comfortably and becomingly dressed so that his movements will be confident and free. He must be effectively dressed in colors and lines that will emphasize his dominant traits and underline his relationship to the story.

Costume and the Play

The content and staging of the play are decisive factors in determining the selection of the material and color for costumes. If the set background is to be dark and plain, light colors in varying shades may be used; if it is a light, neutral tone, costumes in strong, deep colors will create a more interesting picture. A knowledge of the light plot and the effect of colors in light on colors in material will assist the director in making his selection. (See Color Chart, Fig. 11–7, page 133.) He will be sure finally that all his costume designs are appropriate to the mood and theme of the play.

Nearly every children's play will be period in nature. If it does not have an actual historical setting, it is likely to be located in a fantastic, never-never land. A study of the dress of any period will reveal the salient features, the predominating colors, and the lines of the characteristic silhouettes. On these three factors the design should be based. Most fairy tales and folk legends adapt themselves to a medieval setting. Even a cursory perusal of book illustrations shows that the princess line, long, flowing sleeves, high-peaked hat, or headdress with flowing veil represents the lady of noble birth. The decorated, belted tunic with wide sleeves, a cloak, tights, and pointed-toed boots make up the attire of the younger gentleman of high estate. The more mature nobleman may wear a long, full robe, richly decorated and belted, with an appropriate headdress. Such simple basic ideas provide the fundamental notes for the imaginative director. (See costume drawing, Fig. 11–4, page 123.) He will add memoranda as to color, material, and decorative patterns; consult his setting and light plan; and then set to work.

Costuming the fantasy will offer a great challenge. There is no authentic model for elves, witches, or gremlins, and the personifications of hope, greed, and the like. Story-book illustrations must be supplemented by the creative imagination of the designer. Again, the silhouette should state the distinguishing characteristics, if possible; it is always the outline of the mass that counts, rather than the detail.

The designer who has made a study of inexpensive materials will find many ingenious methods of using them to advantage. He must recognize those that will hang in soft folds and successfully represent richer fabrics; he will try to avoid those that are too flimsy, or perishable, such as cheese cloth, crepe paper, and paper cambric. He will do well to be consistent in costuming a single production. If dyed muslin is used for some of the characters, and satin or velvet for the others, the incongruity will be apparent. A bolt of unbleached muslin is one of the greatest treasures in the costume closet. It can be purchased reasonably, in several weights and widths. After it is washed, it can be dyed, painted, and even draped, with considerable success. A full skirt of dyed unbleached muslin, the folds of which have been deepened in color with paint, has often been mistaken, at a distance, for rich broadcloth or crepe. Cotton flannel is inexpensive and will also take dye well; it can be used to simulate woolen materials. Canton flannel, which has a little more body, can be secured in many shades and will convincingly replace heavier woolens. Certain less-expensive upholstery materials and sample lengths of felt, which can often be found at a mill-end shop, make effective jerkins, capes, leggings, and jackets. Occasionally, the prices of chintz and cretonne fall within the limits of the modest budget, and both materials are effective on the stage. The rayons, satins, taffetas, many of the acetate, nylon, and dacron combinations, which have appeared on

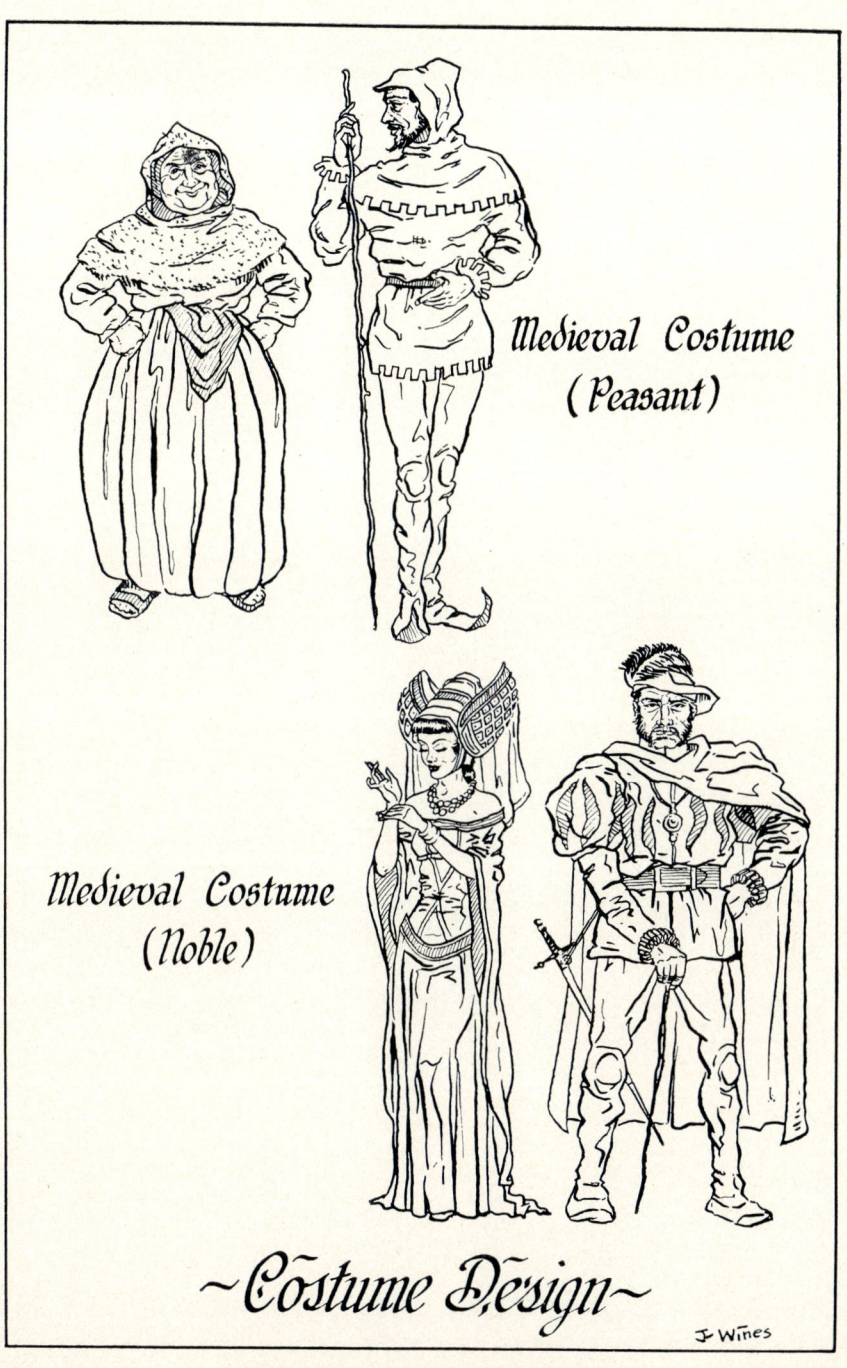

Fig. 11-4. Costume design.

the market in recent years, give a look of richness and texture to the court lady's costume. Burlap, sacking, denims, and some upholstery fabrics are appropriate for peasant tunics. Corduroy and velveteen, although never very reasonable in price, are excellent substitutes for velvet. Well-fitting tights are almost impossible to make, but often permanently-dyed, long cotton underwear can serve the purpose. Best, of course, are the danskins and tights commonly worn by children today: these are not exorbitant in price and the color and size range is large. Shops that supply the dance studios carry full-length leotards, which, though much more expensive, are worth the price for certain costumes. Nylon net and tarlatan can be purchased in a variety of shades and are useful for ballet skirts, ruffs, and the like. Oilcloth, felt, imitation leather, and plastic table coverings are suitable for leggings and boots.

In children's costumes bright colors are preferable to pastel shades. The paler tones fade out under strong light and weaken the stage picture. (Special regard must be given to the lighting of the fantasy where the softer colors are required.) Because of its marked psychological import, the basic costume color for every character should be selected with care, thus deepening the meaning of the character and defining his relationship to the rest of the group. The audience is eager to follow every movement of a prince who mingles in disguise among his villagers. Although he is dressed in peasant clothes, he must wear a color that sets him apart from the rest. The tones worn by the king's courtier who turns out to be a traitor should symbolize his treason. Another decisive factor in establishing the color scheme is the background against which the costumes must play.

MAKEUP

The fundamental purpose of stage makeup is to give greater reality to the actor's characterization, to replace the natural skin color washed out by strong lights, and to help project to an audience some distance away the features of the character portrayed rather than those of the actor hmself. The average play given by a cast of young people seldom requires the use of heavy makeup, for it is usually presented in the intimate atmosphere of a small church hall or school auditorium. The lighting, less powerful than that of a large theatre, does not dissolve so much of the natural skin color, and the proximity of the audience prohibits bold exaggeration. It is unwise, however, to neglect makeup altogether, for it helps the child, as does his costume, to forget himself in creating his character.

1. Straight makeup is used solely to enhance the actor's best features. (Examples: Gretel, Heidi, or Snow White.)
2. Character makeup changes the actor's appearance to suit the role he is playing. (Examples: Heidi's Alm-Uncle, or the wicked Queen in Snow White.)
3. Fantastic makeup suggests the dominant traits of an unreal character. (Examples: witches, elves, mermaids.)

The director considers four points before he begins to design his makeup plan. He thinks first of the size of his theatre; the distance between stage and audience will determine the amount of makeup used. Then he surveys the light plot, realizing that both the placement and intensity of the lights will affect his plan. Overhead lights cast shadows on the downward-sloping planes of the face, while footlights accentuate them. Strong lights, placed close to the actors, drain out face color, and certain special lighting effects in blue and red make startling changes in the makeup. In blue light, rouge looks almost black; in red light, it disappears entirely. The third point, on which the makeup artist must be well informed, is the matter of facial structure. He discovers that shadows and wrinkles appear only in the fleshy part of the face, while the bony structure, which becomes more prominent as age advances, should be highlighted. He also learns that racial characteristics are usually evidenced in face structure, and carefully studies the group which his play involves. The fourth concern is the historical background and general style of the production. The variety and amount of makeup used in *Hiawatha*, for example, would differ widely from that required by a play based on the pilgrims at Plymouth.

The essential articles listed below compose the minimum equipment of the director's makeup kit. With such a supply on hand, and a little ingenuity, he can achieve satisfactory results.[4]

1. Grease paint for foundation color (in sticks or tubes)
   a. Light complexion color   b. Dark complexion color
           c. Tan complexion color
2. Liners for shadows and wrinkles (in sticks)
   a. Blue gray   d. White
   b. Dark crimson   e. Green
   c. Brown   f. Purple
3. Face powders (in colors to blend with grease paints listed)
4. Rouge
   a. Dry rouge (medium)   b. Cream rouge (light)
           c. Cream rouge (dark)

[4] Many directors prefer to use pancake makeup and other modern base materials. The author finds the traditional theatrical stick or tube makeup generally more practical.

5. Powder puffs (inexpensive cotton pads that can be discarded after a single use are advisable)
6. Cold cream
7. Cleansing tissues
8. Applicators, tooth picks, or stomps (for making wrinkles)
9. Crepe hair (for beards and mustaches)
   a. Blonde
   b. Brown
   c. Black
   d. Auburn
   e. Gray
10. Spirit gum (for applying crepe hair)
11. Scissors, comb, hair pins

For character and fantastic makeup, follow the nine steps described below. For straight makeup, omit steps 4, 5, and 6.

1. Apply cold cream to the skin and then remove most of it with cleansing tissue, leaving a light film on the face to receive the grease paint.
2. Mix the proper shade of grease paint in the palm of the hand, which is used as a palette. Dab it on the face and distribute it evenly.
3. Apply cream rouge to cheeks and blend it carefully so that no sharp lines are visible. (In general, the color of youth is high on the cheek, and that of age, low.)
4. Paint in the shadows with red-brown or gray-purple. The two areas that become noticeably hollow with age are the eye sockets and the fleshy parts of the cheeks.
5. Draw wrinkles in dark crimson with applicator or tooth pick, in some or all of the following areas:
   a. The forehead (horizontal parallel lines)
   b. Above the bridge of the nose, on the forehead (vertical parallel lines between the brows)
   c. Below the eye and beyond it (diagonal parallel lines from lower eyelid, sloping downward toward the outer portion of the cheek)
   d. From the outside corner of both nostrils, diagonally down and out
   e. From the corners of the mouth, diagonally down and out
   f. On the neck (horizontal wrinkles following natural lines)
   g. On the chin (lines that give the effect of a double chin)
6. Mark highlights. For every shadowed area and every wrinkle, a highlight should be made with a white liner or a very light grease paint. The bone structure surrounding a shadow should be emphasized by highlighting. The skin on both sides of a wrinkle should be given prominence by a fine highlight line drawn as close as possible to the wrinkle.
7. Apply eye makeup.

STAGING THE PLAY

    a. Blend eye shadow in a becoming shade on the whole upper eyelid.
    b. Draw two dark brown lines on the eyelids close to the lashes, beginning near the center of the eye and meeting at a point about a quarter inch beyond its outside corner.
    c. Darken eyebrows with pencil or dark brown liner color.
8. Shape the lips.
    a. Apply lip rouge to harmonize with the general makeup, shaping the mouth appropriately.
    b. No lip rouge should be used in the old-age makeup. Short horizontal lip wrinkles in deep crimson will help to give an appearance of cracked skin.
9. Powder generously with cotton or soft puff, patting but never rubbing. Gently brush off the excess powder.

The makeup process is now over, unless there is need to touch up cheeks with dry rouge. (Never use cream rouge after powder has been applied.) Eyelashes may be touched up with mascara.

The matter of mustaches, wigs, and beards requires a special word. It is advisable to use wigs sparingly in the play with young actors; really good wigs are seldom available. Unless he expects to spend far more than the budget indicates, the director must be content with wigs that fit badly and are likely to disconcert the actors. If realistic mustaches, beards, and sideburns are indicated, they should be made with crepe hair. This material can be bought in various shades from a theatrical supply house or a costumer. The parts of the face to which the crepe hair is applied must be kept free of grease. Allow a generous coating of spirit gum, or latex, brushed over the area, to set for about fifteen seconds; then press the crepe hair, cut into proper lengths, into place.

Young actors should be taught to remove all makeup with cold cream and cleansing tissue immediately after the performance. If care is taken to instill this habit, the skin will not be harmed by grease paint. A thorough cleansing with hot water and soap completes the process.

LIGHTING

A knowledge of the theory of stage lighting is as important to the children's play director as is that of scene design and costuming. No medium is more effective than light in deepening the impact of a production by stimulating the thoughts and emotions of the audience. (See Fig. 11–5, page 128.)

First consideration must be given to the four major functions of light:

1. Providing visibility. There must be sufficient light to illuminate the acting areas at all times, so that the audience can see without effort; too much light will cause offensive glare. The children's play presents a special problem because of the varying heights of the small actors.
2. Setting mood. The atmosphere and meaning of the play should be conveyed through appropriate lighting effects.
3. Establishing locale. Proper lighting will indicate the place, time of day or year. (It may even indicate the climate.)
4. Marking emphasis. Important characters, acting areas, and climactic movements can be emphasized by color and intensity of light. This treatment gives interesting contrast to the stage picture.

The nature of the play guides the director in deciding upon his lighting style. In general, the more serious the play, the less light is required. Shadowed areas and sharp, cold contrasts in light and dark will intensify the meaning. The gay, buoyant comedy demands bright, warm illumination. In fantasy, use imaginative, atmospheric lighting to help suggest a dream-world.

The stage of a realistic play must be lighted so that it will appear as natural as possible. If the scene represents a forest on

Fig. 11–5. Hiawatha's prayer on the mountain top is lighted with care to deepen the mood. (Credit: Gaston Remy.)

a late summer afternoon, use the warm, rich shades of the setting sun at the rise of the curtain. Lines that indicate the coming of evening call for a gradual change of bluish twilight. Action that takes place in a cottage at night, where lamps or candles light the room and moonlight spills through the window, must be skillfully illuminated. If the stage is too bright, the audience will be confused about the time of day; if it is too dark, the actors will not be visible. The beam of light coming through the window may be mistaken for sunlight if its color is warm amber instead of steel blue. Spotlight beams must intensify the areas affected by the glow of the lamps, in order to give them sufficient contrast to the parts of the stage that would naturally be in shadow. In summary, the director of the realistic play must strive for a natural effect. Light must always seem to come from a credible source, and approximate the color of the light it represents.

The director of the fantasy meets no such problem. He aims to produce artistically the illusion of make-believe. He may use greens and blues, spots and thin beams, exotic color blends, grotesque shadows, silhouettes, and all the other trappings of the land of magic. But even the fantasy's lighting scheme must perform its required function: It must never be just a bag of tricks.

Other factors may modify the tentative plan that the director has based on a study of the play and his knowledge of the four basic requirements of light. The amount of equipment available, and his ingenuity in making use of it, will control his final decision. Although there are many occasions when he must be satisfied with a minimum amount of lighting, he must understand the basic units and be prepared to use them when the opportunity arises.

The following list describes some of these basic units[5]:

1. The *spotlight* is an individual unit, the bulb of which may vary in size from 100 to 1000 watts or more. An adjustable lens distributes the rays to form a small, medium, or large circle of light. "Spots" may be hung onstage, from a beam in the auditorium, in the wings offstage, or on the edge of a balcony in the rear of the house. They are used chiefly for accenting important characters, and acting areas, or creating special effects. (See illustration of basic light units, Fig. 11–6, page 131.)

2. The *floodlight* is usually a single bulb placed in a large reflector without a lens. Bunchlights, or a group of bulbs placed in a

[5] The many new theatrical supply houses have flooded today's market with a dozen different varieties of spotlights, floodlights, switchboards, and dimmers. Each director must study the catalogues carefully and select the pieces of equipment that best serve his purpose.

reflector-lined box, may also serve this purpose; in either case the rays are not focused, but flood the area toward which they are directed. Floodlights may be hung onstage for general illumination, or placed in a strategic position offstage to light a sky-drop. If supported on a heavy iron stand, the floodlight may be used to simulate strong sunlight in a certain part of the stage area. (See C, Fig. 11–6, page 131.)

3. *Border lights* or *strips* are just what the name implies. They are bulbs placed side by side in a metal trough or strip and are frequently hung behind the borders or teasers (the horizontal units used for masking the ceiling in a cyclorama setting). These strips are usually wired in several circuits, each of which may be controlled separately. This provides opportunities for varying color and intensity. The border is one of the most flexible of all lighting units. Several strips may be placed together on the floor, they may stand on end in the wings, or they may be hung so as to light areas behind doors and windows. (See A, Fig. 11–6, page 131.)

4. *Footlights* are similar to strip lights in construction but are permanently installed in the apron of the stage. They, too, are generally wired in several circuits with separate controls. Many modern stages do not include footlights; but sometimes they are necessary to illuminate the faces of small children, whom overhead units cannot light adequately. (See illustration of basic light units, B, Fig. 11–6, page 131.)

5. A *switchboard* is the central unit at which all lights are controlled. The cables of every light, or group of lights acting as a unit, as well as those that govern the auditorium fixtures, lead to the switchboard. This arrangement makes for synchronization and smoothness in effecting light changes. The board should be placed offstage right or left, in a position where the controller can watch the action or conveniently receive signals. Every electrical outlet should have its own silent switch.

6. *Dimmers* (*rheostats*) are mechanical devices that regulate the amount of current flowing through any light or group of lights and have their control handles at the switchboard. They are usually constructed of coiled wire that, by offering more or less resistance to the current passing through it, varies the intensity of the light. A skilled technician can use one dimmer to effect several light changes that do not follow one another in quick succession. The ideal board (which unfortunately is almost never available to the children's play director) provides one dimmer for each circuit. The electrical load that a dimmer will carry varies. The capacity is usually clearly indicated; it should be noted carefully, and never

A. Strip used for overhead lighting (borders)

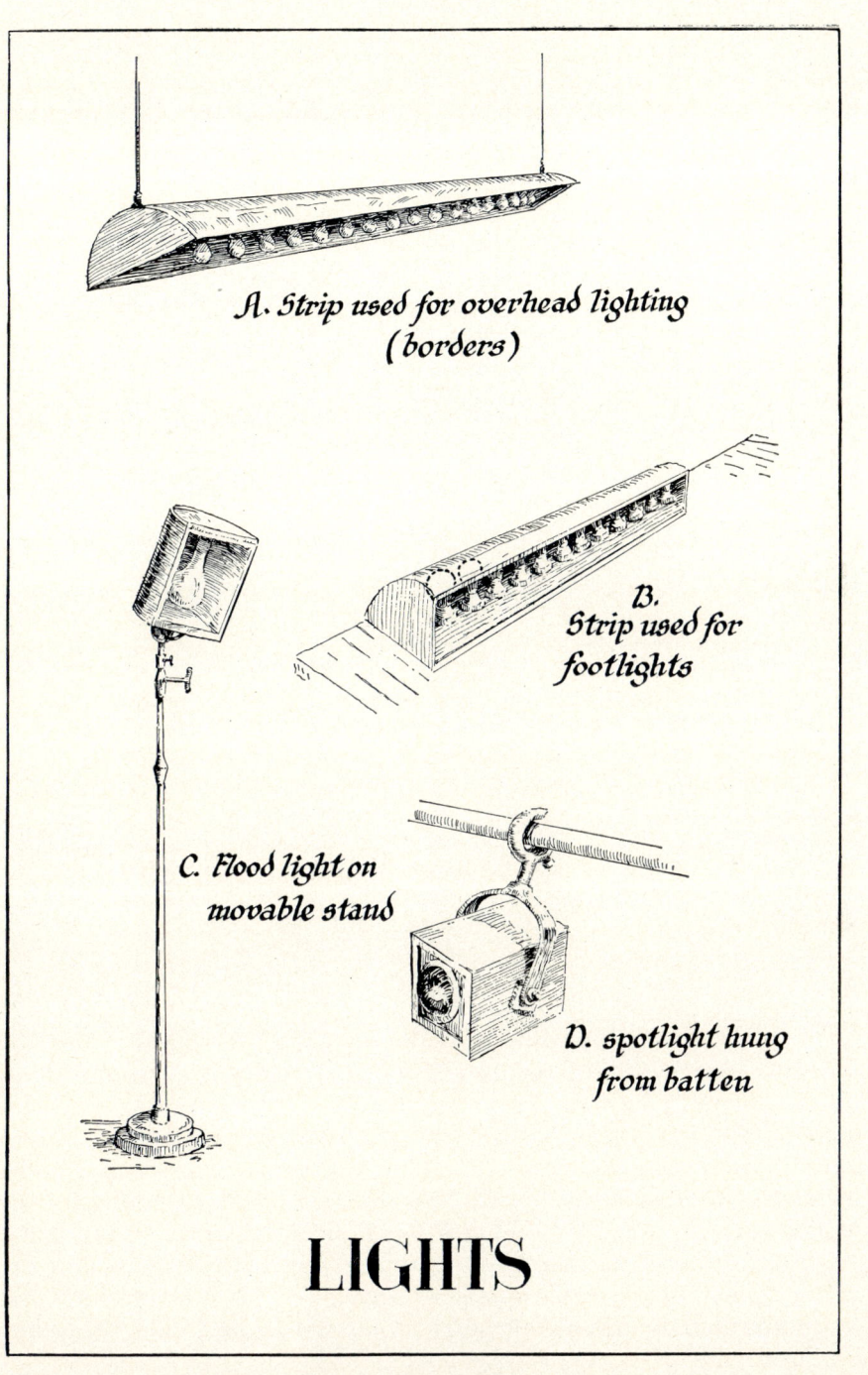

B. Strip used for footlights

C. Flood light on movable stand

D. spotlight hung from batten

LIGHTS

Fig. 11–6. Lights.

exceeded. The total wattage of lights governed by a dimmer should approximate the rating marked on the instrument. Only through this special control device can subtle changes of mood and time of day be effected.

In lighting, as in scene design and costuming, the psychological effect of color has a deep significance.[6] Gelatin is the most satisfactory form of color medium. A sheet 14" x 20" is very inexpensive. These sheets, which come in many different shades, can be cut to fit the removable color frames that slide into the groove in the face of each light container. The darker color gelatins—such as green, red and deep blue—admit little light; straw, amber, light blue, special lavender, and flesh pink have a high degree of penetration.[7] If a director wants to be sure that costume and makeup color will not change materially, he will light with amber, pink, or lavender shades, in combination. (See Color Chart, page 133.)

Here are a few lighting hints for the amateur director:

1. Light the stage sufficiently to make the action visible. A stage too dark or too glaring causes eye strain.
2. Focus attention on the actor, not the set.
3. Give the stage plasticity through contrasts in area lighting; monotonously diffused light flattens out the picture.
4. Treat different areas with light differing in color and intensity.
5. Make light changes gradual in order to avoid disturbing the mood of the audience.
6. Consider scenery, costumes, music, and makeup before making a final light plan.
7. Light the play to emphasize its mood and meaning.

MUSIC

If the play requires music, the musician works closely with the director from the very beginning. Before rehearsals start, he studies the script until he has caught the theme and the mood. He then marks off the sections that seem to need a background score. At a consultation with the director, a tentative plan is set up. The musician is always present at the first rehearsals, listening as the dialogue takes shape, watching the action, catching the spirit of the children's interpretations. As he senses the flow of ideas, and the development of climactic moments, he begins his composition. He must continue to attend rehearsals in order to adapt his score as the

[6] See psychological effect of colors, page 120.
[7] There are several new color media on the market that are more durable than gelatin and far more expensive. Two of the trade names are Roscolene and Cinemoid.

The Effect of Colored Lights Upon Colored Materials

Light Color	BLUE	YELLOW	Material Color— RED	GREEN	LAVENDER	ORANGE
BLUE	Blue	Green	Violet	Bluish Green	Bluish Violet	Brown
YELLOW	Green	Yellow	Orange	Yellowish Green	Yellowish Brown	Light Orange
RED	Violet	Orange	Red	Grayish Red	Purple	Reddish Orange
GREEN	Deep Green	Light Green	Brown	Green	Greenish Brown	Greenish Yellow
AMBER	Dull Blue	Yellow	Red	Brownish Green	Brownish Violet	Orange
ORANGE	Brown	Yellowish Orange	Reddish Orange	Yellowish Green	Light Red	Orange

Fig. 11–7. The effect of colored lights upon colored materials.

pattern of the play unfolds. Not until the movements and interpretation are finally established does the background music take on a permanent form. At least two weeks before the performance, the musician should begin to play at rehearsals. By the time the dress and technical rehearsals take place, the musical score should have become an integral part of the production, weaving subtly in and out, deepening the mood, pointing up significant action, and contributing effectively to the unity of the whole play.

OUTDOOR STAGING

The staging of the outdoor production follows many of the rules that govern the staging of the play presented in an auditorium. The director must consider several special problems, however, that pertain only to the open-air presentation.

The set should be designed to make the best possible use of the natural surroundings. The first task is to focus audience attention on an area surrounded by space rather than one enclosed emphatically by the frame of the proscenium arch. This can be accomplished if the design provides a permanent background (the upstage wall) for the action, in order to attract the vision of the audience to a small area. Without the limitation of an upstage section of greens, screens, or wall, the projection of movement and lines of characters are often less forceful. Screens or greens may also be used as masking pieces, to restrict the width of the stage as the background does its depth. These wings also conceal the properties and actors offstage right and left. The units used in the setting should be few, impressive in form and color so as not to be dwarfed by the surrounding space, and constructed in a manner to permit easy handling in the darkness.

For outdoor staging, the light technician should use about ten times the amount of light required indoors. Placing the light units so that they will either be concealed or be unobtrusive to the audience presents another problem. Since there is no proscenium arch or borders to mask light battens, most of the illumination must come from units placed in trees, on stands, or on platforms situated at the rear or sides of the outdoor theatre.

Costuming, sound effects, and the direction of stage business will need some consideration. The costume designer must be sure that the color and texture of materials are definite and impressive. All music and sound effects will need some amplification, if they are to be effective. The lack of a front curtain will necessitate ingenious manipulation of actors at the beginning and end of each scene.

TRAILER THEATRE

Since 1963, the author has been closely involved with an unusual variety of outdoor staging—the Showmobile. The Children's Theatre Association of Baltimore operates this state-wide service that brings live theatre to Maryland's children during the summer months. The self-contained, fully equipped theatre is a remodeled thirty-two foot trailer donated by the Fruehauf Corporation located in Baltimore. This generous action, in the spring of 1963, was the first step in the realization of a long-time dream of CTA's director. Through the untiring efforts of the agency's Honorary Advisory Board Chairman, Mrs. H. Guy Campbell, business, industry, service clubs, and civic-minded individuals contributed much-needed equipment or financial aid to pay for the trailer's renovation.

Drawings and photographs of other traveling theatres operating both here and abroad had been collecting dust in the CTA files for some time. These were rediscovered, examined with a new interest; suggestions from this source and the ideas of many imaginative people were combined in practical arrangement by the talented engineer from the Fruehauf Corporation, who generously gave his time to draw up the plans. (See Figs. 11–8 and 11–9, pages 136–37.[8])

Twelve young people, between the ages of fourteen and twenty, carefully selected from the members of CTA's creative drama workshops, were invited to become members of the first Showmobile company. Considered as essential attributes were selflessness, enthusiasm, human understanding, and a sense of humor, as well as skill in one or more of the theatre arts. An adult director and technician, two chaperones, and a costume mistress brought the number of the troup on the road to about seventeen.

Two plays have always been carried in repertoire. The program for 1963 was *Alice in Wonderland* and *Puss in Boots;* for 1964, *Cinderella* and *Hansel and Gretel;* for 1965, *Heidi* and *Pinocchio*.[9] The scripts were prepared especially for this kind of out-of-door touring; fortunately one of the members of CTA's Board of Directors is a former actress and an aspiring playwright. She has been willing to experiment with this new technique, under the director's super-

---

[8] These drawings made by Edward H. Parsons, Baltimore, in 1965. Copies may be purchased from the Children's Theatre Association, Inc., Baltimore, Md.

[9] Manuscripts of these and other plays produced by CTA listed in Appendix **may** be purchased. Royalty fees will be quoted on request.

Fig. 11-8. Plan of the Showmobile

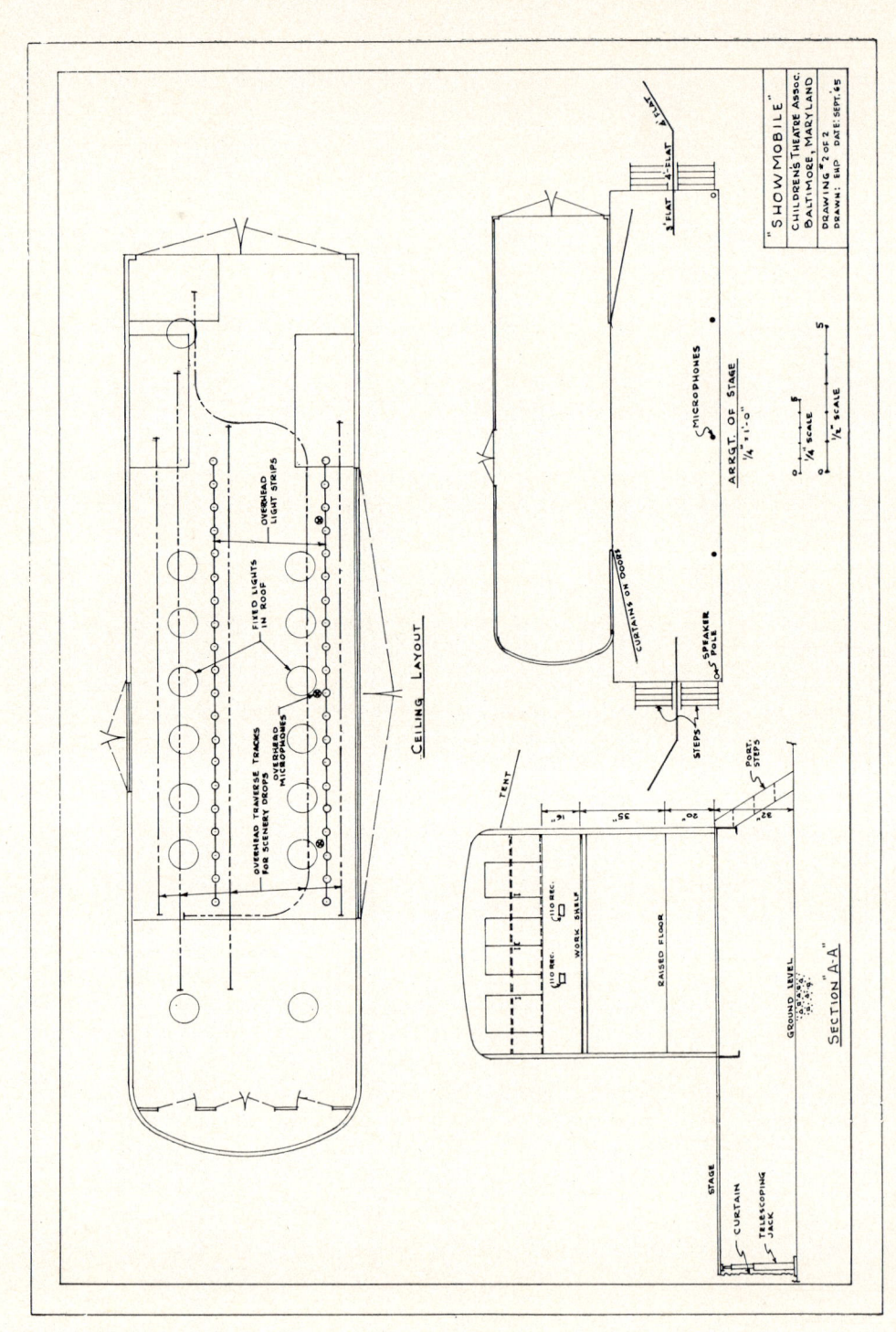

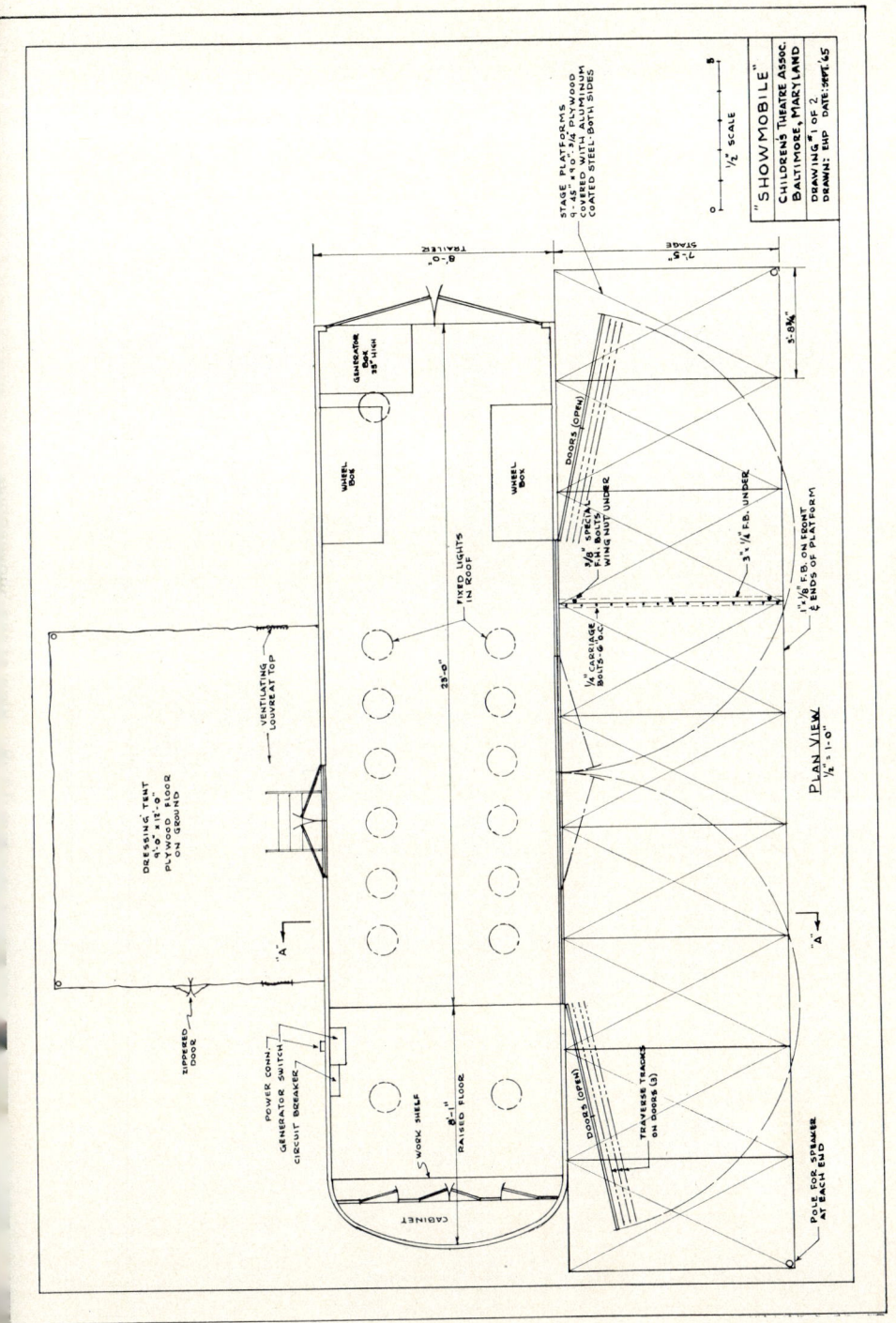

Fig. 11-9. The Showmobile.

vision, and has been extremely successful. Most of the cast accepted a triple-duty assignment: they played a role in both plays, assisted with setting up the platforms and dressing tent, and worked to strike and store sets and costumes for travel. Every member shouldered his assigned task cheerfully, despite the heat and humidity common to Maryland summers. There were few complaints

Fig. 11–10. Staff checks details outside dressing tent of the Showmobile. (Credit: Gaston Remy.)

and no "delinquents." The Showmobile was their project; they were proud of it! Each one realized that he was an important cog in the production wheel; he could not fail. Invaluable were the learning experiences in teamwork, resourceful handling of emergencies, subordination of self to a worthy cause, holding and handling audiences ranging from one hundred to twenty-five hundred, and following self-imposed health rules that all agreed were necessary, if the high standard of performance was to be maintained.

The "trailer-pumpkin," as someone termed it, could be transformed into the "theatre-coach" almost as quickly as a magic wand could be lifted. In thirty to forty minutes, nine platforms forming the "apron" were attached to one long side of the trailer body, lev-

STAGING THE PLAY 139

eled by means of adjustable jacks underneath, and covered with a ground cloth. The side masking flats were then placed. While this was going on, another group put the canvas dressing tent into position, attaching it to the opposite side of the trailer body and lashing it down to weighted pipes carried for this purpose. The dark green tent is accessible from the outside through a neatly zippered

Fig. 11–11. Scene from a Showmobile *Hansel and Gretel.* (Credit: Edward J. Peterson.)

entrance or from inside the trailer, by a small door. The built-in screen windows provide ventilation; a wooden floor, made of three sections neatly fitted together, is especially handy in case of rain. Equipment in the out-of-door dressing room, which was also put into place in a few minutes, included: two tables for props and makeup, a large electric fan, a strip of lights, the costume rack, and six stack-chairs. During this setup period, the technical director and one helper carried four hundred feet of cable to the nearest source of current and attached it. Fans, recorders, and microphones were tested immediately. If for any reason this connection did not prove workable, the flick of a single switch in the trailer cab turned on the generator that was permanently installed in the rear of the trailer. All of this, plus the hanging of the front curtain and the set of backdrops,[10] was accomplished in a little more than a half hour after the tractor had deposited the Showmobile in its designated location.

The cost of such a seven-week summer program is considerable, even though the young actors and stage hands are not paid. A budget of about nine thousand dollars is met by contributions from sponsors drawn from business, industry, recreation councils, the mass media, and shopping center management. A sponsor contributes $225.00 for a single performance; he may select the play and the group of children who will receive the service. If two or more performances are presented in the same area, the charge is prorated.

In 1963 forty performances were played to a total audience of 22,000; the figures for 1964 were forty-six performances and 36,500 children; in 1965, fifty-two performances entertained 48,000 children. Many of these young people would never have seen live theatre to this day had not the Showmobile come to their community. This social agency deserves high praise for initiating and sustaining such a philanthropic, well-organized, and successful community effort in touring children's theatre. Other groups wishing to embark on such a significant youth service would do well to make an observation trip to Baltimore.[11]

STUDENT PARTICIPATION

The whole business of staging the play, indoors, out-of-doors, or in a Showmobile, is of vital concern to the young people participating. They should feel that the production is their project from the time when the original idea is introduced to the striking and storing of sets and properties. They can derive maximum benefit from the undertaking only if they cooperate in backstage, as well as onstage, activities. (See illustrations of young people participating in production and direction, Figs. 11–12 and 11–13, pages 141, 142.) Student assistance and leadership should play a part in every aspect of the endeavor. Although an adult set designer, costume mistress, and light technician may be supervising the three major production departments, the director should always encourage the youngsters to volunteer.

[10] In this kind of theatre one must resort to skillfully painted drops, for the most part, rather than three-dimensional set pieces.
[11] See Figs. 11–10, 11–11, pages 138–39, for *Showmobile* photographs.

STAGING THE PLAY 141

The teenagers in one creative drama project, which presents four plays a year for the public, organize their own working committees annually. The student executive council holds a general assembly, in the fall, of all members of the creative drama classes. At that time, any boy or girl of fourteen or over may express his preference as to service on committees. He may help with stagecraft, lighting, makeup, managing the "house" at performance time, costumes, or painting scenery and posters. The student chairman of each of these units keeps a file of all his volunteers—their names, addresses,

Fig. 11–12. Members of the cast help select and remodel costumes. (Credit: Edward J. Peterson.)

and telephone numbers. When play time approaches, he consults with the adult leader about the work to be done and then calls a meeting of the young assistants. The concerns of his special committee are discussed thoroughly, and ideas are exchanged. A work schedule is then arranged with the adult leader who will plan to be present in a supervisory capacity. The student chairman must see that the schedule is followed and that the jobs are accomplished on time. The leader also must abide by the time sheet and be sure that all materials are in readiness for his young helpers. Each chairman answers first to the adult leader in charge of his special committee, then to the student production manager (who is the

Fig. 11–13. Teenage committee rearranges costume department.

overall committee chairman), and finally to the director of the play. The pattern of this group organization, which was planned by the young people themselves, is practical and workable. Although it may not always function smoothly or coordinate perfectly, it does achieve a purpose by providing opportunity for many children to participate actively. This sharing of responsibility generates a deep sense of satisfaction and pride in the achievement of the common project.

SUMMARY

Only the careful integration of setting, costuming, and lighting will give artistic unity to the production. The setting must be practical, attractive, and expressive. Its practicality depends largely upon the ease with which it can be manipulated; attractiveness results from adhering to the basic rules of artistic composition. It will be expressive if its statement reinforces the mood and meaning of the play. The draped stage, or cyclorama, used in combination with platforms and set pieces, is preferable for the children's production. The psychological effect of color, and changes in colors of fabrics subjected to various light tones, must be carefully considered. Costuming the child actor gives him assurance and helps him to characterize more convincingly. Costumes must be authentic, appropriate to the character, and comfortable to the actor. The director must have a knowledge of lighting units and their uses, as well as an understanding of the theory of stage lighting. Light functions in four ways: It provides visibility, sets the mood, establishes the locale, and marks emphasis. The nature of the play determines the style of the lighting. Color in light can evoke emotional response, accent important moments, and give plasticity to the whole design. A uniquely successful trailer theatre project —the Showmobile—initiated by The Children's Theatre Association in Baltimore, Maryland, is worthy of detailed study. Much of the success of this endeavor, as well as all productions involving young actors, can be attributed to carefully planned teamwork in which the young people, under skilled leadership, become actively involved in all phases of the endeavor.

12

PLAY ACTING AND LIVING

Does the youth leader aim too high when he approaches the drama project as a rehearsal for living? Can any child be so rehearsed for his life role that he will respond adequately to every situation encountered on the world's stage? The obvious answer to the latter question is a negative one; the aspiring leader will, however, also make a negative reply to the former. He is well aware that there is no manner or amount of learning that, if applied to principles of living, will guarantee a Utopian existence. On the other hand, he will enthusiastically adopt any practice that will help him to further the child's personality development. Only if he strives to achieve this goal does he merit the privilege of administering a youth project.

To what higher purpose can an adult's life be devoted than one of assisting, even in a small way, in the building of healthier, happier young people? If the creative drama project provides a successful means of performing such a service, it cannot be disregarded. The leader of such a challenging program finds deep satisfactions in the knowledge that, by helping the individual child to a fuller realization of self, he is contributing to the making of a better society.

The state of society can be improved only through the development of the individuals within it. This is the opinion held by eminent authorities who have been seeking to discover causes of chaos in world order. Some conclude that the root of the trouble lies in the immature state of the human personality. The history of a society composed of well-adjusted, integrated individuals does not record a succession of wars and strikes, mental hospitals crowded beyond capacity, and prisons replete with criminals. Leaders in industry are learning to rely more on the personality factor than on technical proficiency in selecting men to fill important posts. The capable personnel manager today sets a new value on human relations and endeavors to engage key people who are understanding and well balanced. He knows that the successful functioning of his "society," which is composed of the firm's employees, depends finally on the productive interaction of happy individuals.

A writer for the *Baltimore Sun* reported recently a new approach to this idea made by a psychologist speaking at a meeting of the American Psychological Association in Chicago. In the speaker's opinion, something far more drastic was needed than the appeal to the goodwill or morality of human beings, if the problems that beset mankind were to be solved. Use of certain psychotherapeutic skills were recommended. "Many patients, in psychotherapy," he said, "develop a feeling of belonging for the first time in their lives . . . and an attitude of cooperativeness rather than blind subservience or blind rebelliousness." He suggested that, in tackling the prejudices and attitudes that cause trouble among nations and social groups, one might "examine seriously the problem of how to develop love of mankind. We might start by examining those all too few who have this capacity."[1]

The drama leader who hopes to make some small contribution to the shaping of a better society must direct his efforts toward the personality growth of his boys and girls. He will help them believe in themselves and make the most of their own potentialities, through the integration of mind, body, and emotions.

The leader of a drama project has an unusual opportunity to effect the better integration of personality elements, for his subject matter deals with human beings and their relationships. In the process of analyzing and interpreting individuals other than themselves, boys and girls are vicariously experiencing, human understanding is deepening, imaginations are being stimulated, ideas and feelings are being communicated through action. When mind, body, and emotion harmoniously coordinate in expression, growth of the whole "self" is evident.

Most children need this integrating experience if they are to achieve their full stature. Many whom the parent or teacher may not classify as problem children still have tendencies toward exhibitionism, emotional tenseness, timidity, or insensitivity, which inhibits natural growth. Often the creative drama experience can provide these young people with the much-needed opportunities for full self-realization and a sense of the joy of living.

Self-realization is a continuing process; one of the earliest steps involves the beginning of understanding and knowledge of one's

[1] Excerpts from speech by Dr. Harold Greenwald, *Baltimore Sun*, September 5, 1965.

self. Only when one has been willing to realistically examine his natural properties and concepts as a person, discover who he is and what he hopes to become, can he begin to accept himself. Sören Kierkegaard in discussing self-realization says: ". . . so even the richest personality is nothing before he has chosen himself, on the other hand, even what one might call the poorest personality is everything when he has chosen himself; for the great thing is not to be this or that but to be oneself."[2] On self-knowledge and acceptance depends a third development: the ability to understand and accept others. According to Jersild these two processes are closely related: ". . . the process of gaining understanding of others, and the process of self-discovery are interdependent." This acceptance or "love" of one's self and others is fundamental to the good life, the constructive, joyous life, of the individual. When one expresses hostility toward another, it usually follows that he feels rejected by this other. As he tries to make himself more acceptable, and fails, the targets of hostility increase to include his destiny, the world, and himself. This destructive state of being is the exact antithesis of self-realization, which according to Tillich can only occur "when the New Being appears . . . when one feels united with God, the ground and meaning of one's existence . . . then one has the astonishing experience of feeling reunited with one's self . . . in deep self-acceptance. One accepts one's self as something which is eternally important, eternally loved, eternally accepted."[3]

Tillich also gives an illuminating interpretation of the "joy of living" so needed by young people in today's world. Joy is not merely fleeting, temporal happiness, but "the expression of the essential fulfillment . . . joy is nothing else than the awareness of our being fulfilled in our own true being, in our personal center . . . possible only when we unite ourselves with others as we really are."[4] A single incident occurring in one creative drama project can exemplify the joy that comes from inner fulfillment.

Susan and Sally, aged eight, were identical twins. A premature birth, delicate health, and overly solicitous parental care had undoubtedly influenced their behavior at the first creative drama classes. For several weeks they sat close together, often on one chair, although plenty of others were available. They were too timid to volunteer for any individual exercises and reticently entered

---
[2] Sören Kierkegaard, *Either/Or* (Princeton, N.J.: Princeton University Press, 1949b), vol. II, pp. 149–150.
[3] Paul Tillich, *The New Being* (New York: Charles Scribner's Sons, 1955), p. 22.
[4] *Ibid.*, p. 146.

into the group work, often holding hands. On the rare occasions when they participated in general discussions, their contributions were monosyllabic. During the second month, the two little bodies seemed to relax. An occasional smile gave evidence that they had caught the friendly spirit of the group; they no longer felt the need of sharing a seat or holding hands for protection. Within a short time they were taking an active part in class conversations and happily losing their identity in pantomime improvisations. The adjustment was rapid, once the first steps were made. At the end of the season, a report came from one of the other children: Susan and Sally had both been selected for a play at school. The leader was even more delighted when, during the second year, Sally came skipping into the room one Saturday morning bursting with news. "Our scout troop's going to give a play, Mr. Todd," she said, "and Susan and I are going to help put it on. Isn't that exciting?" It was far more exciting to Mr. Todd than Sally could ever realize. Here was a revelation—irrefutable evidence! The experience in creative dramatics had transformed the timid twins into confident, integrated little girls, filled with a new-found joy of living.

The "show-off," too, will find less need for his exhibitionism when he can use play acting as a legitimate outlet for his compelling urge for "love." He soon discovers that "acting up" will not win the esteem of his colleagues that he wants so much, but that sincere acting will. He learns that he is an acceptable member of the group only when he takes his turn along with the rest, instead of demanding constant attention; when he has accepted himself as he is, his hostilities toward the others vanish and, in good time, their resentment of him.

The tense child whose home or school environment has suppressed him unduly is freed by creative drama. He begins to sense his worth as an individual; he is encouraged to express the ideas and feelings that he has tried, for so long, to bottle up inside; he relaxes, he grows, he blossoms!

The heart of the child whose harsh manner or glum, inexpressive countenance has denied him the joys of friendship is stirred and warmed as he begins to understand the characters he is playing, how they think and feel. Gerald's overly protective and demanding mother had been alarmed at his cold, disinterested manner toward the boys in the neighborhood. She came to the creative drama leader one day, near the end of the first term, almost too deeply moved to speak: "I don't know what you've done to him," she exclaimed. "But I do know it's a miracle! The boys are always at our house now, and Gerald is one of them! He's so happy . . . and so kind to his father and me! He acts as though he had a heart for the very first time!" In a way, she was right. For ten years, Gerald's heart had been conditioned never to speak. He was the only child of older, perfectionist parents who were constantly suppressing him: "Don't cry, now" "You mustn't get so angry!" "Nonsense, what's there to be afraid of?" As he struggled to suppress his feelings, he had become numb and sullen. Then, one day in the creative drama class, he felt a satisfying sensation of new life. Before long he was able to express convincingly the feelings of the boys he portrayed in his improvisations; he soon found that he could express his own, in a more normal behavior pattern. His mother was right; Gerald was feeling the warm natural healthy responses of his heart for the first time.

The conscientious leader of a creative dramatics project, cognizant of the serious responsibilities, as well as the privileges and opportunities implied in his work, will take a careful inventory of his own qualifications. Davis describes the qualifications of the ideal play leader as follows: "He must be endowed with compelling gifts, the gentler spirit, high imagination, broad sympathy; and secondarily, he should be imbued with broad education and specific training in minute details and progressive methods." Later on, he mentions the need for: ". . . an understanding of the many complicating factors [of play]—emotional, volitional, intellectual, habitual—all of which enter into and determine types and levels of conduct . . . and an elemental understanding at least of psychiatric problems." Other qualities should supplement these capacities: a sincere love for children, an abounding zest for the subject, sound ethical principles, and an ability to teach by inspirational guidance, rather than by domineering preachments. Good judgment, an objective point of view, emotional maturity, and tolerance are also important requisites. These are the essential qualifications of the well-prepared leader. They show evidence of a total personality development, so vital to the fulfillment of the project's goals. Wittenberg says of the effective group leader: "Personality is more important than skill. This is one reason why what we say is less important than how we say it. Not all of us rate personality as the key factor. If one works with machines, skill will, of course, be the highest requirement, but if one works with people, and particularly with young people, personality is more important."

The experience of the youth leader conducting his first creative drama program can be compared with that of the fortunate inventor. He, like the inventor, will have come upon a great secret. The inventor who contributes to the comfort and happiness of others derives great satisfaction. To the youth leader, the "others" are the young people on whom the future of the world rests; his satisfaction is therefore increased threefold.

The paths that lead toward the ideal goals set by modern education are many. The creative drama project is only one. It lays no claim to being the sole avenue of approach. It is recommended because it has been tried, with results that warrant its position in the vanguard of educational methods. Considerable weight should be added to the recommendation by a careful rereading of the statements and convictions of the boys and girls expressed in the preceding chapter.

May the leader embark upon his thrilling adventure with eager anticipation! If he conscientiously follows the step-by-step procedures, maintains through his own enthusiasm the interest and happiness of the group, and seeks earnestly to augment his power to create and imagine, abundant rewards will crown his efforts. Not least among these are statements like the following, quoted from a grateful ten-year-old's letter.

> Every Saturday morning for the past two years I have awakened early because I have to take the bus down to the Carriage House. After the first few months of going to CTA I was becoming different. I thought more of others than myself. I felt so good in a way I can't explain. It was like some sort of magic hit me. All the same I was getting better. I started to make friends. I even went to rehearsals with some of my friends after school. I even started to meet some of the older folks. It was so wonderful I could hardly believe it. I loved it so much that I went for another year. . . . The same thing happened except better this time. So here I am waiting for another year of it! I simply don't know what I could do without it! R. C., aged 10.

Remuneration that comes over and over in such precious packets cannot be measured. The joy it brings is infinite, for the leader knows that he has discovered in the creative drama technique a means to accomplish his dual objective. Play acting will indeed provide, for the audience, sound entertainment; for the actors, a rehearsal for living!

Appendix A:
SUPPLEMENTARY EXERCISES

The teacher who would stimulate creativity in the members of his class must know each individual, his needs, his interests, and his background. Only after careful study can the teacher develop material which will effectively move these particular children to think and communicate creatively. Materials used successfully for pantomime or dialogue improvisation with one group often bring little or no response from another. If they are not appropriate, or do not fill individual needs, the whole creative drama project may be doomed.

However, the author's memory of the disturbing days when new ideas for class exercises simply refused to materialize is still fresh and vivid. It would seem less than generous not to offer a helping hand when one's files are bulging with interesting class exercises, many of which originated with the children themselves. The aim of this section of the book, therefore, is to share some of this material, with the hope that it may brighten some of those dark days when even the most creative teacher is convinced that his imagination is on permanent holiday.

All of the exercises can be used with children between the ages of eight and twelve. They are presented under five headings: (1) activity pantomime, (2) mood pantomime, (3) change-of-mood pantomime, (4) dialogue improvisations, and (5) experiments in rhythm.

I. ACTIVITY PANTOMIME

1. Let's divide into two long lines, shall we? If we count off by two's, we can do it easily. All the one's will form one team; the two's will line up opposite them as the opposing team. Now, here in front of our lines are two refrigerators, filled with all kinds of good things to eat and drink. I am going to whisper to the leader in each line exactly what he will get from the refrigerator. He will handle it, eat or drink a little on his way back to his team. The second person in line will take the article from the leader; he will turn to face the third person in his line and handle the

APPENDIX A: SUPPLEMENTARY EXERCISES   151

article so that the third person will know exactly what it is. The third person will receive it, and in the same way pass it to the fourth member of the team. So it goes until the article has reached the end of the line. This seems a little like a relay race and so it is; but the objective is clarity . . . not speed. We want to see which team can so clearly picture what they are handling that, when the last in line receives it he can tell us that his article was the same as the one his leader took from the refrigerator. (This exercise can be played several times. The leader takes his place at the end of the line and the second man becomes the leader and selects something else from the refrigerator.)

2. Now, we're all sitting here on the beach on a lovely sunny day. (The class members scatter around the room and select places on the floor to sit down.) We each have a bucket and a shovel. Let's fill the bucket with the damp sand, pack it down carefully, turn the bucket over quickly, and then carefully slip it up and off. There before us will be some lovely little sand towers. If we look about us, perhaps we can find some little shells that will look like tiny windows in the side walls of our towers.

3. Five or six of us are now going to cross to that store counter! (The leader indicates the position of the imaginary store counter.) There we will see lots of little ring boxes lined up. You have been told that you may select one ring for yourself. Pick up the little box, turn back toward us, and let us see you open the box. Remember the top is attached by little hinges so it just falls back—it does not come off. Take out your lovely ring, put the box down on the floor, try the ring on your finger, admire it, take it off again, pick up the box, and put the ring back in. Then when you have closed the box, select someone from the audience and give him the ring. He will try to do exactly what you did. This is sort of like a game of "follow the leader."

4. There on an imaginary table beside you is the birthday card you have just signed for your best friend. The envelope lies beside it, already stamped, as well as the ball point pen to use for addressing the card. Pick up the card, put it in the envelope, seal the envelope, and address it to your friend.

5. On the same imaginary table there are three lovely roses and a small bud vase filled with water. Pick up each rose separately and put it in the vase.

6. Today we will imagine we're out in a clearing where there are logs of wood, about two feet long, being readied for shipment on a nearby river. We will stand in three long lines; there are imaginary moving belts running along, waist-high, on both sides of us. These are to help carry the logs down to the water's edge. As the logs are rolled to our feet, we pick them up, one at a time, and place them on the moving belts. Pick up the first one and place it on the belt at the right, the second goes on the belt at the left and so on until I say, "That's all!"

7. We will do this exercise in groups of six. Here on this side of the room is a long bookcase. Let's stand in front of the bookcase. We will

each be looking for a special book. Take the book from the shelf, turn to a definite page, find the word you want, close the book, put it back on the shelf. Be sure you see your book, its color, its binding, feel its weight in your hand.

8. Again we can use groups of six. Imagine that you are coming into your hallway where there is a rack for coats. Go to the rack, take a jacket off the hook, put it on, button it . . . three buttons in the front . . . and walk on down the hall.

9. This is your sister's fourth birthday. You have brought the cake to the table, which you may imagine before you. Mother has given you the four pink candles and told you to place them and light them. Be careful with the little box of matches you have in your sweater pocket.

10. You are standing by the kitchen sink. There on the window sill over the sink are four little plants in flower pots. They do need watering! The watering pot is standing on the drain board of the sink. Pick it up, turn on the faucet, fill the watering can, and water your little plants. Don't forget to turn the water off.

II. MOOD PANTOMIME

1. This exercise has to do with giving. One can feel very differently about giving. Here are four different characters in four different "giving" situations. We'll divide the class in half, and each half will try two of the characters.

   a. A little boy is giving his sick puppy to the man who has been sent by the veterinarian to take him to the hospital.
   b. A very poor little girl, who has no money to buy a gift for her father's birthday, has made him one instead. She is putting it carefully beside his place at the breakfast table.
   c. A boy or girl is giving daddy a report card containing several failures. Daddy has asked to see the report.
   d. A young boy has been caught playing with his older brother's model airplane. The older brother, furious, has just said "O.K.! Give it back!" The younger brother, fearfully, obeys; he is ashamed of his action and frightened about his brother's response.

2. Let's pretend that these six chairs that stand here in a row are the seats of a bus that is loading to go to town. Now, let's have six people who will get on this bus, and six others who will act as their partners and observe them. We want to see what mood you are in as you board the bus. Are you feeling angry, afraid, mischievous, sad? How do you feel, and what happened to make you feel this way? As soon as anyone is ready, please raise your hand. (The leader selects the first six to be passengers, the next six to act as their partners, establishes the position of the bus and its door, and then starts the exercise.)

3. Here before us is a lovely big apple orchard. You are going into the orchard to pick three apples. But I shall give you a chance to choose

APPENDIX A: SUPPLEMENTARY EXERCISES

one of three ways you might feel as you pick the apples. You decide and raise your hands when you have made up your mind. We will work with four at a time. The rest of us will try to guess which situation you have chosen.

- a. Mother has just promised to make your favorite apple tarts if you'll go pick a few apples for her. What happy news this is!
- b. This is miserable business, having mother ask you to pick apples when you're almost at the end of your favorite mystery story. Just because daddy's bringing a guest home for dinner, you have to leave your book at the most exciting time.
- c. This orchard really is deserted. It belonged to a rich man who used to live here; he was a real miser and kept all his orchards and gardens locked up. Even now, when the gate is open you hesitate to sneak in for apples. But your little brothers are ill and need the fruit, and there just isn't any money to buy it, so gather your courage and go in to pick three apples.

4. Today we will sit on the floor in a big circle. We are going to see how we feel when we see different things here in the center of the circle, one after the other. I will tell you what they are.

- a. Your own little puppy limping toward you, slowly, holding his front paw in the air. He has been hurt.
- b. This time your kitten will be coming toward you proudly shaking in his mouth your lovely new silk scarf or tie. She has pulled it off the bed and torn it to bits.
- c. Now, you see the strangest creature, one that perhaps doesn't really exist. It's half spider and half beetle and seems to have an enormous number of legs. It's a frightening thing!

You'll start with your eyes closed and after each scene you'll close them again. When I say "Look" open your eyes again. Ready?

5. It is rather fun to see how fast we can change from one dramatic situation to another. We will use the whole length of the room for this exercise and will divide into groups of five. We can walk five abreast here, without crowding. The movement will be controlled by one mood, as you walk one length of the room. There you will turn and imagine yourself in the second situation, which involves a different mood. After this walk, also the full length of the room, your turn will change your mood again; and as you travel the length of the room for the fourth time, you will again feel differently. Here are the four situations:

- a. You're returning home from the hospital where you have visited a very sick little friend. You feel very sorry for him and very sympathetic, for you found him in great pain.
- b. This is the corridor into the assembly hall of a new boarding school to which you came yesterday. You don't know a single soul here; it is a kind of frightening experience.
- c. You have heard a friend of yours saying some most unkind and untrue things about you. You are furious!

d. Mother has some friends for tea. One of these neighbors is always exclaiming over you, commenting on how much you've grown and generally embarrassing you. Try to walk very quietly past the living room door and into your room without being seen.

6. This is a joyful day . . . your birthday! And what made it even more exciting was mother's announcement at breakfast. "Nancy dear, this is the day you've been waiting for! You can open your piggy bank if you like to, count your savings, and take it all along with us when we go shopping. You may buy whatever you like for your own special birthday present." When the story begins, you are just entering the library. Go to the bookshelf, where you keep your piggy bank; move with it to the table or a convenient spot on the rug. Dump out the contents, and find, to your delight, that you have fifty cents more than you thought. Pocket the money, put the piggy bank away, and dash downstairs to meet mother. (NOTE: If there is enough space, five or six children can play this scene at once. Each will have his own separate playing area designated beforehand.)

7. It's interesting to examine a single action, like creeping, for instance. Did you realize that always it's the reason why you're creeping that puts you into a specific mood, and changes the form and the rhythm of your movement? That's true, but to prove it today, let's all form a big circle and we'll creep around clockwise, in three different ways:

a. When we start we'll be creeping up on Uncle John, to surprise him.
b. Then we'll be creeping down a long hall, trying to get out to meet some friends, without big brother hearing us.
c. Then we'll try to get out of a dark forest along a path, which we hope is the right one, but which may prove to lead us around in circles.

I will clap my hands once, to change your mood and situation each time.

8. Here's a single action, one which we have all performed many times: mailing a letter in a mailbox. But I'd like to know how you feel when you mail this letter. To whom have you written a letter? How do you think it will be received? Are you really anxious to mail it or do you almost wish, now, that you hadn't written it? I will give you three minutes to decide upon your own reasons for writing your letter. There, along the side of the room are five mail boxes . . . (indicate box 1, 2, 3, 4, 5). Here opposite are your five houses. We will number off by fives and you will know where you are at the beginning of the scene and where you go to mail your letter. (NOTE: If there are four groups of five each, A, B, C, D, each member of A can have a partner in B group and the same plan can be used for C and D. Then the partner will always have the first chance to guess his partner's mood as he mailed the letter.)

9. This time we will work with four people. Each will be carrying something the length of the room. I shall describe these four characters, and you may decide which one you want to play.

a. A poor little peasant child is trudging through the forest on a bitter cold day. He has been collecting twigs and sticks to keep the open fire going

APPENDIX A: SUPPLEMENTARY EXERCISES 155

in the draughty little cabin he calls home. His little sister is ill, and he must do his part to help her get well.
   b. The servant of a rich medieval duke is carrying a jug of water from the well in the courtyard, up to the palace. He (she) is proud, dignified, feels the importance of his position.
   c. You, as yourself, are carrying your very sick little puppy to the vets.
   d. You, as yourself, are carrying a crushed garden snake on a stick to throw him into the trash can. You cannot leave him lying in the path.

10. Sometimes moods and feelings come from tastes and smells. This time you will all pass along by these three chairs. On each is a bowl and a little pile of spoons. The contents of the bowls look exactly alike, in fact quite appealing. Taste each . . . as you go by. The first is terribly sour, the second is peppery hot, and the last is simply delicious.

III. CHANGE-OF-MOOD PANTOMIME

1. It's your birthday, and not a single soul remembered! Mother is ill in the hospital, so of course she couldn't think about it. Daddy had already gone to work, earlier than usual this morning, and when you came down to breakfast, your sister had started for school. There wasn't even a birthday card on the table . . . nothing! The teacher, whom you had known for three years, had forgotten; not a single one of your good friends at school remembered either. Our scene begins when you are walking home from school, feeling very sorry for yourself. Push open the little white gate at the end of the walk and start up the path to your porch. Suddenly you stop, surprised. What's that on the doorstep? It's a large basket with a note on top. Rushing up to investigate, you see, to your surprise, that the note has your name on it. Open it to discover a lovely birthday card on which is written: "Happy birthday, dear! You see, I didn't forget after all! See you later! Love—Dad." So he did remember! How could you have thought such mean things about such a wonderful dad? Just at this moment a strange sound comes from the basket; there's something purring or whining—almost human, and certainly alive. You lean down and cautiously lift the top of the basket. There, inside, is the sweetest little black puppy, the very one you've been watching in the pet shop window for weeks! So that's where dad was early this morning— buying your birthday present! Pick up the puppy, happily, and go in the house. (NOTE: This scene can be played by four or five children at a time, if each is assigned his separate playing area.)

2. This little scene we will play in pairs. We will have three pairs working at once; each will have a separate "forest" area. Yes, that's where we are today, in a lovely glade in a forest. We're like Hansel and Gretel! We were taken here by father, so we could gather berries while he went off to chop wood. It's a lovely day, and we're joyful over the plentiful supply of wild strawberries; our empty tummies feel better every moment. Then, suddenly, the comforting sound of father's axe stops. We listen, expecting it to start again any moment, but the silence is only

broken by the cry of a hawk overhead. Realizing that the sun has gone down and it's getting dark, we look for the path, by which we reached the little glade. On every side the forest looks shadowed and threateningly heavy with underbrush. We can't find the path anywhere. We are frightened, terribly frightened! We know there's no use trying to get home now; it's much too dark. Finally, on a little spot filled with pine needles and quite protected by drooping branches of an evergreen, we curl up close together to keep warm, first saying a special little prayer that God will send His angels to watch over us.

3. You and your brother are visiting an aunt and uncle at their lovely big house in the country. You are here this evening for an hour or so alone, because Aunt Grace has gone to the station to meet Uncle Harry. Your brother is asleep when our scene opens. You are in the next bed, sitting up, reading. You haven't really minded being alone at all! But then suddenly, there is a strange sound. Is it a door opening? Yes . . . and after it closes quietly, you hear steps. They seem to be coming closer. Now, they're coming down this very hall. Frightened you flick off the bed light and slide down under the covers, hardly daring to breathe. The steps seem to pause outside the door; then the knob turns and the door opens, quietly. Peaking out from under the sheet, you can't believe what you see! There, clearly visible in the light from the hall lamp, is Uncle Harry. He is looking in to see if you are all right. In a moment you hear his soft words to Aunt Grace, who must be behind him: "They're fine . . . both sound asleep," he whispers. How silly of you to be afraid. He probably came home on an earlier train. Relieved, and tired now, you settle down for the night.

4. Your first thought as you run in from school is to head for the club room where you left your new puppy in his basket. We will start the scene as you dash into the room and over to the spot where the basket stands. To your horror, the basket is empty. You search frantically, everywhere. Finally you hear a strange little squeaking sound and follow it to the low shelves where mother had some canned goods stored. Sure enough, as you move one of the quart jars, there is Tippy huddled fearfully, and not quite sure how he can get out to safety. He must have crawled on the shelf to investigate, because like all little boys he was curious. This time his curiosity got him into trouble! Relieved to see that he isn't harmed, you pick him up carefully and put him in his basket.

5. You're just getting over the chicken pox! How bored you are! You've read everything in sight, played every game so many times, and even your favorite TV programs seem dull after ten days. Then . . . suddenly life seems brighter. . . . There is a sharp sound of brakes outside and then you hear your mother's voice greeting your favorite aunt who has just driven down from New York for a surprise visit. Run to the window to look . . . Yes, there she is! Wave an enthusiastic greeting and run down to the door to meet her, hoping sincerely that she's not afraid of chicken pox!

6. This is a little Christmas story about two little poor children who sleep in a tiny attic room in which there is a casement window that opens onto the roof. (Explain here the functioning of a casement window.) It's Christmas Eve and the two little ones have gone to bed early, hoping for, but not really expecting, a visit from Santa Claus. We're each going to pretend to be that Santa Claus; and we can play the scene with four Santas at a time. Santa will sneak over the roof, peer in at the sleeping children, put down his pack, quietly open the window, creep into the room over the low sill, pulling his pack in after him. Cautiously he moves up toward the little beds. Suddenly one of the children sighs, almost as though he is waking. Santa hides quickly at the foot of the bed, and then when all is quiet, he proceeds with his work. He smiles with satisfaction as he selects from his pack a lovely present for each child. (Before you begin, you must make up your minds what you will take from Santa's pack.) He puts the presents on the beds carefully, picks up his pack, and sneaks back to the open window. He climbs out, pulls his pack after him, closes the window, after a happy wave to the sleeping children, and goes on to visit his other little friends.

7. This is the biggest day of the year in the small town where you live . . . the day the circus comes to town. Even though your family has moved to a farm now, two miles outside the village, you are not complaining a bit about the long walk into the square. No indeed, the miles will fly by as long as there's the circus to look forward to. Our scene begins when you're almost there, clutching your fifty-cent piece in your hand, and already imagining acrobats on high rings, and seals that balance balls and climb ladders. Suddenly all this changes, as you turn into the square where the big tent always stands. It's empty . . . nothing's there at all except a large sign that reads, "Sorry—no circus this year." You can hardly believe it! But there's no mistaking the meaning of those dreadful black letters. Sadly, and with a heavy heart, turn around and start home again.

8. Mamma Grace was of indefinite age; none ever dared guess. She was like "the old woman who lived in the shoe," in a way, because she owned all the children in the town, or so it seemed. They were always gathering at her bakery shop or in her tiny garden on summer evenings to hear her fascinating stories or to tell her their troubles. She was every child's friend. Each Saturday morning Mamma Grace set up her stall in the open market at the Fair; it was filled with fresh-baked buns and cakes and little pies. And before noon, there were lines of little ones with their pennies and nickels, making purchases. One Saturday morning, Chris, the youngest of a big family, was hungrier than usual. He was so empty that he hadn't even been able to sleep. He never complained because he knew his father did his best to feed them all . . . but today, somehow, he was beside himself. He walked down to the open market . . . not because he had even a penny in his pocket, but because he couldn't resist just looking at the good things to eat. Maybe he thought he might

imagine he had tasted some of them and would feel better. As he came to Mamma Grace's stall, where the delicious cinnamon buns lay, trays of them, he looked longingly. There was no one there, in fact there was no one anywhere at this early hour. He didn't see Mamma Grace, who was bent low behind the stall unpacking a box of doughnuts. All of a sudden he did something he'd never done before; he couldn't help himself. He snatched a big bun from the counter and started off down the street. Mamma Grace's eyes were sad, as she watched, but she didn't move, because she saw to her delight that Chris was stopping . . . yes . . . now he was turning around and coming straight back to the stall. Carefully, he placed the bun back on the tray . . . As he started off again, Mamma Grace rose from her hiding place. She looked after the boy with love and thankfulness. She just knew her Chris couldn't steal! (NOTE: This exercise can be played in pairs, Mamma Grace and Chris, or with several Chris characters and Mamma Grace imagined. It can also be used later for a dialogue exercise with Mamma Grace calling Chris to say "good morning" and offer him a bun.)

9. The following scene can be played in pairs—pairs of sisters, pairs of brothers, or a sister and a brother. We will call our younger sister Jill, and our older brother Jack. Jill has had rheumatic fever and for many weeks has had to remain quiet in bed or on the couch. This has been disturbing to her especially during these months before mother's birthday, when she hoped to do a lot of "baby sitting" so she could make enough money to buy her part of the present she and Jack had planned for mother. One afternoon, the very day before the celebration Jill, who is now able to walk about a little, decides to check her bank to see exactly how much she has saved; she's almost forgotten. She brings the little bank over to her bed, sits down and dumps the contents out. There are only a few coins unfortunately, fifty-three cents to be exact, not nearly enough to buy the earrings to go with Jack's pearls. Oh dear! Tomorrow will be so dreadful . . . when she has no present to give to mother! Sadly she puts the change back into the bank . . . and puts it on the bedside table. She lies down, burying her head in the pillow. A little sob escapes her as she falls asleep. She doesn't know that Jack, all this time, has been standing in the doorway watching. He has just come home from his afternoon job at Mr. Dick's drugstore. He feels so sorry for Jill. Poor Jill! Then suddenly, Jack gets an idea. He looks closely to be sure Jill is asleep, and then cautiously creeps toward the bed. From his pocket he takes a dollar bill, the one he just earned; he folds it and sticks it into the little slit in Jill's bank. Then joyfully he creeps out of the room. My, won't Jill be happy when she wakes up!

10. Here is another little scene which concerns money you have saved in a bank. This little bank you have hidden away carefully behind one of the books on the library book shelves. This is the safest place, because of that mischievous little brother Jerry! There's no telling what he might do if he were to find your piggy bank! Now, this is the day you've decided

APPENDIX A: SUPPLEMENTARY EXERCISES 159

to go to the library, get your bank, dump its contents on the table, count the change, and go to buy some gifts. You may decide which of the three following ways you will end the scene:

   a. Find the bank, and discover it contains more money than you had ex-expected.
   b. Find the bank and discover that it is entirely empty.
   c. Look for the bank and discover that it is not there!

IV. DIALOGUE

1. This is a story about several rather selfish little people. Good friends they were, too, but they were all so wrapped up in themselves that one must prophesy a short life for their friendship. We will call these friends Jean, Chris, Louise, and Jonathon. One day, a Saturday, something happened to these four young people that taught one of them a fine lesson. This was the day when they always went to the movies together and usually had enough left of their allowances to buy some of their favorite buns at the town bakery on the way. Our scene begins when the four children come along, chattering gaily about the movies, and disappear into the bakery shop. Along the street comes Lois, a ragged little girl, the oldest of a family of five, though she herself is just barely eleven years old. She is on her way to the druggists to buy some medicine for her mother, who is ill. Even though she knows there is never a penny for her to spend in the bakery shop, Lois loves to look in the window imagining how the luscious cakes and pies would taste. She is still standing there when the others come out munching on their buns and chattering happily. Suddenly Louise, who is last, drops her fifty-cent piece, her movie money. The three others disappear around the corner, as Louise stoops to hunt for her coin. As she kneels down she notices Lois for the first time. At this moment Lois is carefully picking up a little crumb of bun that happened to fall on the grass near her foot. Louise was shocked! Could this poor little girl really be so hungry? Just at this moment Jean calls her from around the corner. "Hurry, Louise, we'll miss the beginning of the picture!" Louise can find no words to reply . . . she is fingering her fifty-cent piece. Finally she calls: "You go along . . . I'll see you later . . ." and she adds quietly . . . "Maybe!" . . . As Lois starts down the street toward the druggist's, Louise makes a big decision. She runs into the bakery, and a few moments later comes out with a bag of buns in her hand. As she hurries off to catch Lois, she seems to have wings on her feet. Yes, Louise will miss the movie, but she has never felt as happy inside as she does at this moment!

2. This is a story we like to call *Peter Puckle's Predicament* and indeed poor Peter was in a serious predicament. Shall we talk a moment about what that strange word means? (An interesting discussion can be motivated by this word.) In the first place, Peter was a great fellow; everyone was fond of him! With his schoolmates he was a special favorite because

he was the best catcher their "little league" team had ever had. But Peter *was* absent-minded, there's no denying that! And this was always getting him into trouble. On his eleventh birthday, Peter received a magnificent set of tools as a gift from his grandfather. Very grown-up tools they were, too! Mother thought that they should be put away until Peter was older but Peter begged, and he was usually pretty persuasive; this time his promise to be extra careful of them won mother over immediately. And, of course, Peter had every intention of keeping his promise but somehow— Well, I'm getting ahead of my story.

One day, not long after his birthday, Peter was out in the yard, preparing to use the tools to make a ship model. Just as he got them all lined up on the bench, his friend Jimmy called from next door, "Hey, Peter, come here, quick! I've got it . . . the new bike . . . Look!" Naturally Peter, who had been almost as excited about this bike as Jimmy, jumped the hedge and in a few minutes was riding joyfully behind Jimmy down Main Street. Almost before they reached the square a big thunderstorm came up and the boys had to run for shelter. After all, this brand new bike just couldn't get wet! The tools, forgotten, lay in great puddles on the bench and on the muddy ground beneath.

Next morning Peter's mother went down to bring in the bottles of milk. It was Saturday, and the sun was shining. But there was anything but sunshine in her heart as she saw the condition of Peter's once beautiful tools. They were covered with ugly rust! She called, "Peter, come down here at once!" But Peter was so busy getting ready for the big game scheduled for today that all he did was mumble something about being down presently. Finally, when mother called the second time, Peter rushed down carrying his bat and glove saying impatiently, "What is it Mom . . . ? Don't you know I've got to be down at the ball field to practice? Gosh . . . we . . ." Suddenly as his eyes followed the direction of his mother's gesture, he stopped in the middle of a sentence. There, a few feet beyond the door, lay his tools, his pride and joy! "Gee, Mom, that's terrible!" He walked sadly over to examine the ruins . . . dropping his bat and glove against the porch. He picked up one after the other of those once shiny tools, now all muddy and covered with rust. Mother was almost sorry for Peter at this moment; he looked so miserable! But she told him quietly and firmly that he must clean up the tools, this morning, before he did one other thing! He tried to protest, but all of his talk about the big game, and how much he was needed as the pitcher, was of no avail. She stood her ground, and went into the house to get the oil can, sandpaper, and a cloth. "Now," she said, "I'm going down to Mrs. Grady's for the eggs, and I want this job done before I get back. Do you understand, Peter?" Peter had to agree, there was nothing else to do, but he set to work sulkily as she walked down the path, and felt terribly sorry for himself. What would he ever say to the rest of the team? What would they think of him now?

He was soon to find out, for in a few moments he heard a heated conversation coming from the direction of the ball field. "Where in the world could Peter have gone?" "He promised to be there early to practice!" "Gee! I hope nothin's happened to him!" And at this moment several of his friends (and/or their sisters) came into view. When they spotted him, they ran toward the fence, and their questions flew thick and fast. Peter never took his eyes off the ground. He just shook his head in a negative fashion and mumbled that he couldn't play. In real panic, they surrounded him trying to get the whole story. Finally, he told them his problem, explained his predicament. They did all they could to persuade him to play; they complained that they couldn't tackle that champion team without him. "What of it, if you don't do the tools, this morning? Your mother's out, we saw her . . . You can come with us, right now!" said the captain of the team and Peter, for just a moment, was tempted. "But I promised Mom I'd clean the tools and I just can't disappoint her again, fellows. I can't!" Peter moaned. By this time they were impatient; some were so angry with Peter that they suggested that they'd have to find another pitcher for the team and replace Peter permanently. With an unmistakable disgust and repeated threats, the group left the yard. Poor Peter started to run after them, so heart-broken was he at their cruel remarks. Then he stopped; something inside him simply would not let him go to the ball field. He walked back to his bench and set to work more vigorously than ever.

Soon his mother came through the gate—so quietly that Peter didn't even notice. For a moment she watched him working diligently; she shook her head, in sympathy. She had met the children on their way to the field and knew what they must have said to poor wayward Peter. Quickly she went in through the back door, to leave her eggs, and then just as quickly came out in the yard to approach Peter. "My, those two look fine, Peter, the saw and the screw driver . . . not a bit of rust on them. You've done a great job!" "Thanks," said Peter, without looking up. And then came the wonderful surprise. "Peter, there'll be just about time, if you hurry, to make the ball field before the first inning starts . . . Suppose you run along now, and let me finish the other three tools . . . How about it?" Peter was so stunned, he couldn't find a word to say. Finally he shouted breathlessly, "Gee, Mom . . . d'ya mean it? . . . Gee!" He ran for his glove and bat . . . grabbed her around the waist shouting his thanks, ran through the gate, and in seconds he had disappeared. Mrs. Puckle approached the gate and waved to the departing figure . . . saying to herself . . . "Poor Peter, I wonder if he's learned his lesson this time?"

3. This is an interesting dialogue exercise to be played in pairs. The characters we may call *A* and *B*. Each character has a single statement to make in a specific situation. The pairs will go off together to talk about the assignment for two minutes; then we will play the scenes. We, who watch, should be able to tell the exact relationship between the two people.

A comes to *B*'s house and knocks on the door. When *B* opens the door, *A* says "Hello" (or "Hi!").

B says to *A:* "Come in" (or "Come on in!").

4. There is a little poem about an Elf man that is familiar to many young people. This little elf, according to the poem, lived in a secret spot "down where the lilies blow." A little mortal child finally discovered his hiding place. As she wandered deep, deep into the forest she found a little pool and there, sitting on a lily pad, splashing his tiny fingers in the clear water, sat the elf. This is the way the conversation goes:

Child: So, little Elf man, that's where you live—down where the lilies blow! Could I just ask why you're so small, and why you never grow?

Elf: (Rising to his full height in anger) You're very very rude, you know. At least I hope you do! I'm just as big for me, you see, as you are big for you! (And to punctuate his reply, he dips his fingers into the water and splashes the rude mortal child to teach her a lesson. She shamefacedly turns and retreats by the same path, leaving the little elf to his quiet pool and his lily pad raft.)

NOTE: Several pairs can try this dialogue exercise. They may want to repeat it, reversing the characters; those who have played the mortal child usually are anxious to attempt the characterization of the Elf.

5. Our story takes place in Hilltop, a small and rather poor village, but a beautiful one. Few tourists found it worth visiting, but the villagers liked it just the way it was. In fact, they were very disturbed when a Mr. Carrington, a rich gentleman from the big city, a hundred miles away, restored the old manor house on the hill, which had been empty for years, and came to live in it. Everybody said that he was hard and stern and mean. He lived all alone in the big house, and there were strange stories told about why he wanted to come to Hilltop to hide away from the world. Even after he had been there for six months, he had been seen by few and met none of the villagers. The manor grounds did look beautiful, however. The gardens were filled with flowers and the apple trees in the old orchard were heavy with fruit.

One day in late summer, news went about that Mr. Carrington had gone back to the city for a month. Although no one had actually seen him leave, this was the report. A group of children, returning from a swimming party one afternoon, decided to take the long road past the manor house. The apple orchard was too tempting; they agreed to steal in through the open gate, try just one or two, and take a look around.

Suddenly the delightful atmosphere of adventure was broken by a sharp voice, shouting from an upper window, "Hey! Get out of my garden, you little rascals! Jim . . . Jim, I say, if you can't get rid of those pesky creatures, you'll have to use a shotgun."

Fear froze the children to the spot for the moment and then drove each of them to the nearest bush or hedge for protection. There was a sound of crunching gravel under the feet of Mr. Carrington as he hurried down the path that led to the orchard. Suddenly he stopped to pick up a cap

APPENDIX A: SUPPLEMENTARY EXERCISES 163

that one of the boys, in his haste, had dropped. As he bent down, Mr. Carrington's eyes met those of the intruder, curled under a nearby bush. "Well, what in the world are you doing there, son? Come on out and let me have a look at you." Jerry crawled out, as did the others, knowing that they were caught red-handed. They approached Mr. Carrington silently, speechless with fear. Finally, Jerry, finding his voice, tried to explain their presence, to apologize and ask forgiveness. All looked uneasily in the direction of the gate, guiltily emptying their pockets of the apples they had gathered.

Mr. Carrington suddenly broke into a broad smile as Jim, the gardener, came running down the path. "Well, I'm glad you helped yourselves, boys," he said. "This orchard provides enough apples for the whole village." The children looked at him in amazement. Jim drew himself up with pride as he reached his master. "Well, sir, I got rid of those squirrels, every single one of them, without firing a shot." Mr. Carrington congratulated him and sent him off to bring some bags of apples for the boys to take home. So that was what he had meant! Suddenly they all understood. The squirrels not the children were the "pesky rascals" that must be driven from the garden! The children's relief was obvious; color came back to cheeks, tight lips relaxed in smiles. And Mr. Carrington looked ten years younger! After all, if the village children had accepted him, he could be sure his lonely days were over.

NOTE: This story, for use with elevens and twelves, has proved extremely helpful in making clear the importance of trying to find the good in all people, rather than in letting public opinion sway one in evaluating an individual.

6. The following story has been used successfully with groups of children in this country and abroad. It can be played as a group pantomime as well as a dialogue scene. One child must always be designated to find the bird, one to put him in the nest, and one to chase the cat away. The leader and/or members of the observing group can give the sound cues for (a) the baby bird's chirp, (b) the second, louder chirp, (c) the cat's "Meow," (d) the mother bird's frantic cry, and (e) the mother bird's peaceful song:

One day when we were coming home from a picnic, we passed along an old stone wall. It was broken in several places, and we were curious about it. On the other side was a deserted apple orchard, mostly overgrown with high grass. It must have belonged to that empty, dilapidated old house up on the hill, but strangely enough, there were beautiful red apples on the trees and on the ground. It seemed a long time since lunch, so we decided to stop and gather some apples. While we were picking, Amy said suddenly: "Listen! What was that strange whistling sound?" None of us had heard anything; we thought that she must have imagined it. Then she said again: "Really, there is something; it sounds like a bird's chirp . . . sort of." This time we did hear it, but we looked and looked and couldn't seem to find where it came from.

Then suddenly Jean called: "There it is . . . come here . . . come here." When we reached the spot where she was kneeling in the high grass, we saw it—a tiny baby robin . . . barely able to move . . . and looking very frightened in this big green forest where it had fallen. We didn't know what to do. We shouldn't touch it really, because then, they say, the mother bird won't claim it again. But then something happened that made us decide at once. There was a great big "MEOW" behind us, and we turned to look into the green eyes of a huge black cat, ready to pounce on our little bird. Two of us ran to chase away the cat; we even threw an apple or two to get him out of the way, and the rest looked quickly for the nest. Sure enough, in the branches of the tree above the bird, was a nest quite within reach of Jimmy, who was much the tallest of us all. Carefully he picked up the frightened little thing and lowered it into the nest beside the other two little heads that peeped over the edge.

We were all watching, thankful that we had saved the situation, when another sound made us suddenly look up. It was a sharp frightened cry! It came from the mother bird, as she swooped frantically down, almost to the nest and then as frantically flew up again . . . in big circles. Her shrill cries sounded as if her heart would break. She must have thought we were robbing her nest, stealing one of her babies. How could she know that we were just trying to keep one of them out of danger. "Quick," said Amy to us all, "let's hide! Let's go! It's the mother; we mustn't frighten her so!" And with that we all scurried away and hid behind the stone wall.

In a few minutes we were glad Amy had thought quickly! The mother bird came closer and closer and finally settled down gratefully with her little ones. We could hear their chirps of greeting and her soft answer as she comforted them . . . As quiet as mice we sneaked in, picked up the jackets and bags that we had left in the orchard . . . and crept away . . . down the road! "It's a good thing we went after apples when we did, isn't it?" he said. "Yes, and it's a good thing Amy's curiosity made her listen," said Jean.

7. Because most young children have enjoyed their association with Peter Rabbit and his family, this fictitious incident based on the same characters may prove interesting for use as a dialogue scene:

Yesterday, poor, absent-minded Peter had been late for supper again! Today, Mama Rabbit had stated emphatically that Peter must forego the pleasure of going off to the old fishing hole with his brothers and sisters. Peter had been sulking about this since morning. He grew even more miserable as the others gathered their things together for the trip. Mama Rabbit was helping them and finishing the gingerbread she was about to bake for supper. Finally Peter, in disgust, slipped outside the hollow-tree house with his butterfly book under his arm. He sat down on the ground with the book open in his lap and leaned against the old tree, trying to look as though he didn't care, although he really felt so ashamed about having to be punished again. But then, that's the way with people as well as rabbits; it's so hard to admit we've been wrong and say we're sorry!

When our little play begins, we see Peter coming sadly and grumpily out with his book, sitting down, with his head leaning unhappily upon his two brown paws. We hear Flopsy, Mopsy, and Cotton Tail talking inside the house: "Oh my, I'm glad I got my fishing rod mended in time for today. Tom Squirrel says they're biting fine down at the Big Hole." "Shall I carry the bathing suits, Mopsy?" "Yes, please. Flopsy and I'll carry the lunch basket." In a few minutes they appear with all their togs. When they see Peter, they do feel badly, all of them! They love Peter; he's such fun to have on any excursion—always telling funny stories to make them laugh. Each makes a sympathetic remark to Peter as he goes by, commenting on how much he'll be missed. Peter's replies are largely peeved grunts. They go on down the path and out of sight just as Mama Rabbit comes out with her bonnet and shawl on.

"Peter, for some reason or other I've misplaced the recipe for Gingerbread frosting. I'm going to run over to Mrs. Owl's and ask her for a copy. Now you be sure to take care of the gingerbread. Take it out of the oven in just five minutes, do you hear?" "Yes, ma'am," says Peter meekly. "And do try to be a good boy this time, Peter, and mind what I say!" And almost before Peter can reply, she is off down the road, and Peter buries his head in his butterfly book. Peter always had loved butterflies; whenever he was sad, a trip through the pages of his butterfly book could always cheer him up. Suddenly, a real live butterfly flew right across his page! Peter looked up in amazement; he could hardly believe his eyes. It was the very same kind of butterfly that was painted on this very page. He looked up and he looked down; he compared the real one with the painted one again and again and finally he put the book down determined to try to catch the butterfly just to examine him more closely. It flew from bush to bush, sometimes almost stopping within Peter's reach, then, quite suddenly it would fly off, almost teasing him to follow.

Finally, after he had chased it all around the hollow tree and back to the other side of the door, he stopped suddenly! What was that he smelled? Something was burning!

Of course, the gingerbread! He had forgotten the gingerbread. He dashed into the hollow tree, but he was too late. In a few moments he came out again carrying a smoking pan of charred, unappetizing gingerbread. Just at that very second, Mama Rabbit came hurrying along with her frosting recipe. She stopped, horrified. Poor Peter tried to apologize, tried to explain about the butterfly. But he was so upset that the words wouldn't come. Great big rabbit-tears made little wet furrows down his soft brown cheeks. "I'm sorry, Mama, I'm so sorry!" He sobbed as he dropped the blackened pan and threw his paws around her waist. "I guess I never can do anything right! I'm just a bad, bad Peter Rabbit, that's all!"

Mama Rabbit was touched. She put her big paw around his little shaking body and tried to comfort him. "Now, now, Peter . . . come . . . you're not a bad Rabbit . . . just forgetful, that's all! So come along, we'll make some more gingerbread together and we'll have just time to frost it before the others come home!" Nothing was so good to Peter's ears as the sound of Mrs. Rabbit's soft, forgiving voice. He would have worked all afternoon for her, and gladly. Promising to clean out the burned pan and beat all the eggs and chattering about anything and everything like Minnie Magpie, Peter took Mama Rabbit's hand and went inside to start his work.

8. The following story has been used both as a pantomime for the whole class of fifteen or twenty and as a group dialogue exercise. It is appropriate for the younger age level. It plays best when the children sit in a large circle on the floor, imagining that they are resting after a strenuous game. The leader gives the sound cues in this order: (a) the crackling of the ground, (b) the tinkling of elfin bells, (c) the swish of the leaves floating to the ground, (d) the laughter of the elf, (e) the sound of the elf sliding down the vine, (f) the rustling of the vine as it folds up and disappears. The introductory discussion should emphasize the importance of seeing the vine grow, the little elf climbing up, the falling of the money-leaves, in fact every detail of our strange story. The elf's purpose in playing this trick upon the children should be analyzed. Someone is likely to suggest: "Well, I guess he wanted to show us that if we grab for money that isn't ours, we get fooled. We really didn't have any right to take the money-leaves. They belonged to him." This interpretation has hit upon the underlying theme of the fantasy. After several attempts at playing the story as a pantomime, it is profitable to discuss what each one might say, to help tell the story, instead of depending upon the leader's sound cues. Anyone in the circle can start; he contributes one thought and the person on his left offers the second, and his immediate neighbor the third and so on. The dialogue sequence usually runs like this:

1. Listen . . . what's that sound?
2. There's a big crack in the ground. Look!
3. Something is coming through . . . Oooh! It's a plant . . . it's growing!
4. It's going right up . . . and up and up!
5. And it's getting branches, too . . . like a ladder.
6. It's almost up to the sky . . . when will it stop?
7. Listen! I hear bells! Tiny little bells, they are!
8. It's an elf, with bells on his cap. See, he's coming out of the ground.
9. And he's climbing up the vine.
10. He's got a pack on his back! *Etc.*

One child's contribution will naturally evoke one from the next in the circle; each will have something to contribute until the story is told and the last idea sends them all back to their places to settle down, heads in hands: "Funny, I wonder? . . . I must have been dreaming!"

APPENDIX A: SUPPLEMENTARY EXERCISES 167

The Story:

Once, when we'd been out playing a fast game of ball in a favorite field near our village, the strangest thing happened. It was quite warm that day, and we were so tired and hot after the game, that we all sat about resting . . . half asleep . . . The hum of dragon flies and busy bumble bees stealing from the wild flowers were the only sounds we heard . . . when suddenly there was a strange crackling noise right in the middle of our circle . . . We looked up, startled to see the ground opening . . . and through a small crack came the bright green point of a flower, or bush. At least that's what it looked like! But it kept growing and growing as we watched, and as it grew up, new shoots sprang from the side, like little branches; then up it went and another pair of branches came forth. Would it never stop? It seemed almost to reach the sky now! A tall green ladder it was.

And, then, from the base of the vine came the sound of tiny tinkling bells. And what do you suppose came up through the hole? A little green and brown man . . . not much bigger than my arm, with tiny bells all over his little cap and jacket. He had an impish smile on his face as he looked swiftly about, adjusted the big sack he carried on his shoulder and then, quick as a wink, climbed up the green ladder till he was almost out of sight. We were too surprised to move or to speak; we watched, fascinated.

Suddenly he opened his sack and took out handfuls of lovely gold and silver leaves, which he tossed to the ground. As they floated near, we just had to jump up, for they were not real leaves at all, but little pieces of gold and silver money. Naturally we wanted some; who wouldn't? We scrambled about trying to catch them, and then the strangest thing of all happened. As soon as one of the leaves touched a hand, it disappeared. The first time it happened to me I just dived for another one, pushing Jimmy out of the way to get to it. But the same thing occurred, again and again. We looked at each other disappointed, of course, but also a little frightened, when suddenly loud laughter came from the top of the vine . . . at least it was loud for such a little fellow. Yes, sure enough, the little elf was laughing at us for thinking that we could so easily run off with his magic money. He had played a trick on us; indeed he had!

And then, as we watched him, he suddenly grabbed his pack, which looked as full as ever, slid down the vine, and disappeared, amid his jingling bells, just as swiftly as he had come. And suddenly the vine itself began to move, it began to fold up its branches and grow downward, just like a folding-up telescope, until it had completely disappeared in the ground again.

As we crept closer to see where it had gone, we couldn't believe what we saw. Not a single hole was there, not even one as big as a pin; just smooth meadow earth exactly as it was before. We went back, puzzled, and sat down again to try to figure it out. What in the world had been happening? Were we dreaming . . . was that it?

V. EXPERIMENTS IN RHYTHM

The close relationship of rhythm and creative dramatic expression has been touched upon earlier in this volume. One needs only to look about him to be convinced of the basic role rhythm plays in both nature and human nature. Patent is the evidence in the continuing ebb and flow of the tide, the rising and setting of the sun, the earth's recurring seasons, the beat of the human heart. In artistic communication one finds the rhythm of color, line, sound, or plastic forms. A child expresses his thoughts and feelings through rhythmic movement in space. Even the very young child seems to be controlled by an inner rhythm pattern peculiarly his own. He walks, runs, skips, jumps, and whirls, naturally motivated by his own inner responses.

A perceptive leader will broaden the scope of his creative drama project by making use of this natural response. Rhythm or mood music relaxes tense muscles, improves body coordination, motivates imaginative response, and heightens sensitivity. The author has found three specific ways in which music and/or rhythms, skillfully integrated in the program framework, can be of value.

   a. Creative rhythm or music, used to deepen or change a mood in a dramatic sequence, motivates a more relaxed and meaningful expression of thought and feeling through movement. The success of this kind of activity depends upon the skills of the leader or the availability of a capable creative musician; this point has been discussed in Chapter 2.
   b. A rhythm pattern, introduced by the leader, may tell a story or it may suggest several different sequences, all of which may be accurately expressed by the same rhythmic arrangement.
   c. A simple activity like picking apples, bowling, tossing, and catching a balloon, or playing hide-and-seek may provide themes for movement to a specific set of rhythms.

Rhythm Patterns that Tell a Story

1. 4/4 TIME.

   Situation: (To be played in 4 measures). You have just had an argument with a good friend, and are hoping that he will forgive you. You admit that you are wrong and are asking him to patch up the differences. He refuses to listen.

   1st measure: 11111111 (eighth notes, take you running toward your friend)
   2nd measure: 1--- (extend both arms, pleading with him)
   3rd measure: 1--- (drop your arms, discouraged at his silence)
   4th measure: 1--- (turn away, in despair)

This can be repeated. The leader may suggest that one can always try again. The child will then repeat the same four measures, turning and running toward the friend, on the first measure of eighth notes.

APPENDIX A: SUPPLEMENTARY EXERCISES   169

2. 4/4 TIME.

   Situation: (To be played in 8 measures). Today we will pretend that we're investigating a beautiful and mysterious forest. We've never been here before. As we run happily in among the trees, we are startled by the strange, harsh cry of a bird overhead. We look up to see a huge hawklike eagle swooping down to the spot where we stand, or so it seems. We duck quickly to hide behind a large bush, and then, as the whirr of the wings passes, we peer out to watch the great bird wheel upwards. Creeping out slowly, and then walking swiftly to a clearing where we can see him, we watch the winged creature become no more than a black spot in the distance. Still feeling shaky over the experience, we run out of the forest and back along the trail toward home.

   1st measure: 11111111 (run into the forest, eighth notes)
   2nd measure: 1--- (stop suddenly, startled by the strange bird call)
   3rd measure: 1--- (hide behind the bush, as the hawk swoops down)
   4th measure: 1--- (watch him fly far above the tree tops)
   5th measure: 1-1- (get up carefully and step forward to investigate)
   6th measure: 1111 (walk forward to a clearing where you can see the sky)
   7th measure: 1--- (watch him disappear in clouds)
   8th measure: 11111111 (run out of forest along the same path by which you came)

3. 4/4 TIME.

   Situation: (To be played in eight measures). One morning, when you wake in a big forest where you've been lost the night before, you see before you a strange little candy house, similar to the one we associate with the "Hansel and Gretel" story. Slowly rise and creep forward until you stand beside the house; clear the tiny window pane with your hand and look inside. While you're standing there, fascinated by what you see, a cackling laugh comes from inside the house. Terrified, you turn and then take to your heels and fly out of the forest.

   1st measure: 1-1- (rise to your feet)
   2nd measure: 1-1- (walk two steps forward to investigate)
   3rd measure: 1111 (taking courage, walk to the tiny window)
   4th measure: 1--- (try to look in the window)
   5th measure: 11-- (clean off window pane with your hand, two strokes and hold two counts)
   6th measure: 11-- (same as fourth measure)
   7th measure: 1--- (listen to the fearful laugh)
   8th measure: 11111111 (turn and run out of the forest)

4. 4/4 TIME.

   Situation: (To be played in 8 measures). For a long time you had been hanging on to an old yellow paper said to belong to your great-grandfather. It told of buried treasure, on the island in New England where your family always spends the summer. One day, in July, you decide to explore, following the directions and clues on the old map. You find the spot and you start to dig. Sure enough you do come upon a little chest, and in it are very old coins.

1st measure: 1-1- (dig with small shovel and throw dirt over right shoulder)
2nd measure: 1-1- (dig with small shovel and throw dirt over right shoulder)
3rd measure: 1-1- (dig with small shovel and throw dirt over right shoulder)
4th measure: 1--- (shovel hits something hard; stop in amazement)
5th measure: 1111 (drop down on one knee and dig three times with hands)
6th measure: 1-1- (with right and left hands grab handles of chest)
7th measure: 1--- (lift chest out of ground)
8th measure: 1--- (put chest on ground beside you)

5. 4/4 TIME.

   Situations: (To be played in four measures). There are two sequences here, both of which fit the same rhythm pattern of four measures. The purpose of this kind of exercise is to explain clearly the fact that two completely different circumstances involving different moods can still be expressed by the same rhythmic pattern.
   A. You are trying to secretly slip out of grandmother's house on Hallowe'en to join the rest at a big party in the village.
   B. You are trying to find a ring you put away carefully in your room, some time ago; you've forgotten where you put it.

A.

1st measure: 1--- (start down hall, and listen to be sure no one's coming)
2nd measure: 1-1- (take two more steps, gaining confidence)
3rd measure: 1111 (since no one is about, hurry along, four steps)
4th measure: 1--- (stop to listen; you think you hear footsteps)

NOTE: This can be repeated three more times, and on the last measure of the fourth pattern, eighth notes can be substituted for the whole note. Because you're safe, you run out into the yard.

B.

1st measure: (step into room . . . and stop, trying to think where you put the ring)
2nd measure: 1-1- (slowly approach the desk . . . trying to remember)
3rd measure: 1111 (now go direct to the chest of drawers . . . you're sure it was there)
4th measure: 1--- (pull out the top drawer . . . and there it is!)

Simple Activities Played Rhythmically

1. 3/4 TIME.

   Situation: (To be played in sixteen measures). You are standing out on the beach holding a lovely balloon-like, plastic beach ball. It looks like a great soap bubble; the irridescent colors seem to float about in it as you hold it up in the sunlight.

   1st measure: 1-- (lift ball from sand where it lies near the toe of your right foot)
   2nd measure: 1-- (hold it high and look at it in the sunlight)
   3rd measure: 1-- (toss it diagonally up to the right)
   4th measure: 1-- (watch the wind catch it and carry it across in front of you to deposit it on the sand by your left foot)

(Repeat the exercise to the left, again to the right, and again to the left.)

APPENDIX A: SUPPLEMENTARY EXERCISES

2. 3/4 TIME.

Situation: (Most successfully played in sixteen measures). You are walking along the seashore collecting interesting shells for a design you are making. Some you will keep, some you will toss away again.

1st measure: 111 (walk three steps along the sand)
2nd measure: 1-- (stop to look about you for an interesting shell)
3rd measure: 111 (pick up the shell and examine it)
4th measure: 1-- (drop it in the basket on your arm)

NOTE: This gathering of shells can be done in many different ways using the same rhythmic pattern.

3. 4/4 TIME.

Situation: (Use a minimum of sixteen measures). We are gathering apples from the ground and from the low branches of trees as we walk through the orchard. We can all gather together if we stand in a large circle and move forward in a clockwise direction. The first apple will be picked from the tree and the second from the ground, the third from the tree, and the fourth from the ground. We'll continue until we have enough for our party.

1st measure: 1111 (walk three steps and look up to see apple on tree)
2nd measure: 1-1- (pick apple, look at it, and put it in basket)
3rd measure: 1111 (walk three steps and discover good apple on the ground)
4th measure: 1-1- (pick up apple, look at it, and put it in basket)

NOTE: Repeat as long as it seems to interest the group.

4. 4/4 TIME.

Situation: (Four, eight, or sixteen measures can be used). Playing hop-scotch. We are trying to hop first on one foot and then on two feet in a lined rectangle without touching any lines. There are five horizontal spaces marked off in the rectangle. The first, third, and fifth are divided in to two blocks by a vertical line down the middle. In these we land on both feet. In the single bars we must land on one foot. We start standing on both feet in the first bar; on one foot in each of the small blocks.

1st measure: 1111 (hop on the right foot in second bar, both feet in third bar, right foot in fourth bar, and both feet in fifth bar)
2nd measure: 1--- (hop up and turn completely around and land on both feet in fifth bar)
3rd measure: 1111 (hop on left foot in fourth bar, both feet in third bar, left foot in second bar, and both feet in first bar)
4th measure: 1--- (hop out of the rectangle on the left foot . . . the game is over)

NOTE: This can be repeated any number of times.

Appendix B:
STORIES FOR DRAMATIZATION

Literature and legend provide such a vast supply of stories that could be dramatized for children between the ages of eight and eighteen that the compiling of even a reasonably inclusive list would require many years of research and fill the pages of several volumes. Therefore, the following collection merely suggests a few sources of material which may prove helpful to the leader.

The stories are grouped according to the age levels discussed in other parts of this volume. Those that may be appropriately used for more than one age range are so indicated. In several cases whole books or biographical story cycles are cited because they contain many episodes which can be treated successfully as separate dramatizations. It is not intended that the entire sequence be used as a single play project. When it was impossible to give the many sources of some of the more familiar stories, one or two publications only are mentioned. No source is included for the fairy tale favorites.

A few subjects, suitable for the under-eights, are suggested for the benefit of those leaders who may be in charge of a first- or second-grade class. Although they, too, will work creatively, according to the procedures outlined in Chapters 1 through 6, the selections for their dramatizations must be less complex.

FOR THE UNDER-EIGHTS

THE THREE BEARS — Johnson, E., Sickels, E. R., and Sayers, F. C., *Anthology of Children's Literature,* new rev. ed., Boston: Houghton Mifflin Co., 1960

SIMPLE SIMON
JACK AND JILL
THE QUEEN OF HEARTS
WEE WILLIE WINKIE
LITTLE BOY BLUE
LITTLE MISS MUFFETT

Real Mother Goose, New York: Rand McNally & Co., 1960

APPENDIX B: STORIES FOR DRAMATIZATION

The Three Billy Goats Gruff — Thorne-Thomsen, G., *East O' the Sun—West O' the Moon,* New York: Harper & Row, Inc., 1946

* The Elves and the Shoemaker — Bryant, S. C., *How to Tell Stories to Children,* Boston: Houghton Mifflin Co., 1924

* Snip, Snapp, Snurr and the Red Shoes — Lindman, Maj, Chicago: Albert & Whitman Co., 1932

The Elf and the Dormouse — Brewton, J. E., *Under the Tent of the Sky,* New York: The Macmillan Co., 1937

Little Black Sambo — Huber, M., *Story and Verse for Children,* 3d ed., New York: The Macmillan Co., 1965

(The asterisks indicate material also suitable for the 8- to 10-year-olds.)

FOR THE 8- TO 10-YEAR-OLDS

Rumplestiltskin
Cinderella
The Sleeping Beauty
Snow White
The Frog Prince
Hansel and Gretel
Jack and the Beanstalk

Fables — Aesop's *Fables,* New York: Grosset & Dunlap, 1947

Uncle Remus: His Songs and His Sayings — Harris, J. C., New York: Appleton-Century-Crofts, Inc., 1921

The Voyage of the Wee Red Cap — Sawyer, R., *This Way to Christmas,* New York: Harper & Row, Inc., 1916

Twig — Jones, E. O., New York: The Macmillan Co., 1964

Forest Full of Friends — Alden, R. M., *Why the Chimes Rang and Other Stories,* Indianapolis: Bobbs-Merrill Co., 1945

The Enchanted Shirt (poem) — Untermeyer, L., *This Singing World,* New York: Harcourt, Brace & World, Inc., 1926

The Little Rabbit Who Wanted Red Wings — Harper, W., *Story Hour Favorites,* New York: Appleton-Century-Crofts, Inc., 1918

William and Jane — *Told Under the Blue Umbrella,* New York: The Macmillan Co., 1962

Winnie-the-Pooh — Milne, A. A., New York: E. P. Dutton & Co., 1926

The House at Pooh Corner — Milne, A. A., New York: E. P. Dutton & Co., Inc., 1928

Ameliaranne and the Green Umbrella — Heward, C., and Pearse, S. P., Philadelphia: The Macrae-Smith Co., 1920

FOR THE 11- TO 13-YEAR-OLDS

The Shepherd Who Cried Wolf — *The Fables of Aesop,* New York: The Macmillan Co., 1964

The Three Wishes — Jacobs, J., *More English Folk and Fairy Tales,* New York: G. P. Putnam's Sons, 1894

The Emperor's New Clothes	Anderson, H. C. (bound with Grimm Brothers, *Tales*), New York: Random House, Inc., 1900
The Plain Princess	McGinley, Phyllis, Philadelphia: J. B. Lippincott Co., 1945
The Barring of the Door (poem)	Johnson, E., Sickels, E. R., and Sayers, F. C., *Anthology of Children's Literature*, Boston: Houghton Mifflin Co., 1960
King John and the Abbot of Canterbury	Baldwin, J., *Fifty Famous Stories Retold*, New York: American Book Co., 1928
The Pied Piper	Colum, P., *Children Who Followed the Piper*, New York: The Macmillan Co., 1922
The Leak in the Dike (Little Hero of Haarlem)	Bryant, S. C., *How to Tell Stories to Children*, Boston: Houghton Mifflin Co., 1924
The Stone in the Road	Bailey, C. S., and Lewis, C. M., *For the Children's Hour*, Springfield, Mass.: Milton Bradley Co., 1909
King Robert of Sicily	Crommelin, E. G., *Famous Legends Adapted for Children*, New York: Appleton-Century-Crofts, Inc., 1904–Bryant, S. C., *Best Stories to Tell Children*, Boston: Houghton Mifflin Co., 1912
The Boy Knight of Reims	Lownsbery, Eloise, Boston: Houghton Mifflin Co., 1927
The Magic Fishbone	Dickens, Charles, New York: Warne Frederick & Co., n.d.
The Happy Prince The Star Child The Selfish Giant	Wilde, Oscar, *Fairy Tales*, New York: G. P. Putnam's Sons, 1913
The Twelve Dancing Princesses	*Grimms Fairy Tales*—many publishers, or De La Mare, W., *Tales Told Again*, new ed., New York: Alfred A. Knopf, Inc., 1959
The Adventures of Tom Sawyer	Clemens, Samuel L., New York: Harper & Row, 1917
Pandora (and other Greek myths)	Guerber, H. A., *Myths of Greece and Rome*, New York: American Book Co., 1921
The Merry Adventures of Robin Hood	Pyle, H., New York: Charles Scribner's Sons, 1946
Old Pipes and the Dryad	*The Best Short Stories of Frank R. Stockton*, New York: Charles Scribner's Sons, 1957
Indian Legends	Grinnell, G. B., *Pawnee, Blackfoot and Cheyenne*, New York: Charles Scribner's Sons, 1961; Zitkala-Sa, *Old Indian Legends*, New York: Ginn & Co., 1901
King Alfred and the Cakes	Baldwin, J., *Fifty Famous Stories Retold*, New York: American Book Co., 1928
Joseph and His Brethren David and Goliath The Good Samaritan Ruth and Naomi Esther	Olcott, F. J., *Bible Stories to Read and Tell*, Boston: Houghton Mifflin Co., 1916
The Alhambra	Irving, W., New York: The Macmillan Co., 1953
Stories of Ulysses	Baldwin, J., *Story of the Golden Age*,

APPENDIX B: STORIES FOR DRAMATIZATION

	New York: Charles Scribner's Sons, 1887; Guerber, H. A., *Myths of Greece and Rome,* New York: American Book Co., 1921
STORIES FROM THE ILIAD	Butcher, S. H., and Lang, A., *The Iliad of Homer,* New York: The Macmillan Co., 1947; Church, A. J., *The Iliad and the Odyssey of Homer,* New York: The Macmillan Co., 1964
STORIES OF SIEGFRIED	Baldwin, J., *Story of Siegfried,* New York: Charles Scribner's Sons, 1931
STORIES OF ROLAND	Baldwin, J., *Story of Roland,* New York: Charles Scribner's Sons, 1930

FOR THE 14-YEAR-OLDS AND OVER

Episodes about: JOAN OF ARC	Paine, A. B., *Girl in White Armor,* New York: The Macmillan Co., 1964; Bick, C., *The Bells of Heaven,* New York: Dodd, Mead & Co., 1949
ABRAHAM LINCOLN	Sandburg, Carl, *Abe Lincoln Grows Up,* New York: Harcourt, Brace & World, Inc., 1931
BERNADETTE	Werfel, Franz, *The Song of Bernadette,* New York: The Viking Press, Inc., 1942
ST. FRANCIS OF ASSISI	Baldwin, J., *Fifty Famous People,* New York: American Book Co., 1912; Jewett, S., *God's Troubadour,* New York: Thomas Y. Crowell Co., 1957
FLORENCE NIGHTINGALE	Richards, L. E., *Florence Nightingale,* New York: Appleton-Century-Crofts, Inc., 1909
KING ARTHUR'S KNIGHTS	Pyle, H., *The Story of King Arthur and His Knights,* v. 1, New York: Charles Scribner's Sons, 1933; Pyle, H., *The Story of the Champions of the Round Table,* v. 2, New York: Charles Scribner's Sons, 1933
WHERE LOVE IS, THERE GOD IS ALSO	Smith, E. S., *Christmas Book of Legends and Stories,* New York: Lothrop, Lee & Shepard, 1944
THE BISHOP'S CANDLESTICKS	Hugo, Victor, *Les Misérables,* New York: Dodd, Mead & Co., 1925
THE CONVENT FREE FROM CARE	Tyler, A. C., *Twenty-Four Unusual Stories,* New York: Harcourt Brace & World, Inc., 1921
WINGS	Tyler, A. C., *Twenty-Four Unusual Stories,* New York: Harcourt Brace & World, Inc., 1921
HOW THE GOOD GIFTS WERE USED BY TWO	Pyle, H., *The Wonder Clock,* New York: Harper & Row, Inc., 1887
HOW THE PRINCESS' PRIDE WAS BROKEN	
THE WATER OF LIFE	
THE GODS KNOW	Frost, F., *Legends of United Nations,* New York: McGraw-Hill Book Co., 1943
YS AND HER BELLS	

ANTHOLOGIES

World Tales for Creative Dramatics and Story-Telling — Fitzgerald, Burdette S., Englewood Cliffs, N.J.: Prentice-Hall, Inc., 1962

Stories for Creative Acting — Kase, C. Robert, New York: Samuel French, Inc., 1961

Stories to Dramatize — Ward, Winifred, Anchorage, Ky.: The Children's Theatre Press, 1952

Children's Literature for Dramatization — Siks, Geraldine B., New York: Harper & Row, Inc., 1964

Appendix C:
SHORT PLAYS

THE QUEEN OF HEARTS

THIS small play, *The Queen of Hearts,* is included because it clearly demonstrates the latent dramatic possibilities within a single incident, suggested by a poem or story. A group of young children, working creatively with nursery rhyme and fairy tale characters, will find many opportunities to develop similar dramatizations. *The King's Birthday* (see page 182), in which these and other familiar characters are combined in a more intricate story, would be an appropriate project for the same group to undertake at a later date.

Characters

| THE QUEEN | THE KING | A GUARD |
| A LADY-IN-WAITING | THE KNAVE | |

Scene

The action takes place in the Queen's special kitchen, which she uses on the rare occasions when she bakes delicacies to the King's taste. There is a stove down left, at the corner of which is placed a low stool. A heavy wooden table stands in the center, slightly upstage, and there are two doorways, one in the center of the right wall and another on the left of the upstage wall. (Openings in the cyclorama may be used to suggest doorways.) On the right side of the upstage wall stands a cupboard, the shelves of which hold china, bowls, and tins of flour, sugar, etc. A high-backed chair, regal in design, stands in the down right corner. As the curtain rises, the Queen, standing at the right end of the table, is carefully cutting out little circles of pastry with a long knife. The tart pan rests on the table near her, along with a bowl of strawberries, a large spoon, and a rolling pin. The strap of a dainty apron, which covers her royal gown, has slipped off one shoulder; her crown is tipped slightly in the wrong direction. Her movements are excited and hurried.

QUEEN (*looking anxiously about as she works*): Susan! Lady Susan . . . do hurry, please! It's getting very late!

LADY S. (*offstage*): I'm coming, your Majesty . . . right away, your Majesty! And I found the precious sugar box, too. (*She enters up left, carrying a large tin marked "The King's Sweets." She crosses to above the table, and speaks breathlessly*) See? It's his Majesty's pink sugar lumps . . . the ones you thought were lost!

QUEEN: Oh, thank goodness, Susan . . . thank goodness! But where on earth did you find them? I know I put them right over there on the second shelf, last February. (*She indicates cupboard up right.*) I did, Susan, didn't I?

LADY S.: Oh, yes, your Majesty, you did.

QUEEN: And everybody in the palace knows they're to be used only on top of the King's birthday tarts. The Chancellor knows, the steward knows, the gardener knows, the groom knows, the—

LADY S.: Yes, your Majesty, everybody knows! And everybody knows where you keep them, too. (*She pauses and says, with special meaning*) The Knave especially, your Majesty. And . . . and . . . he has a very sweet tooth, your Majesty.

QUEEN (*suddenly understanding*): That's it, Susan, that's just what happened. The Knave has been sampling the King's sugar lumps! Oh, dear . . . I suppose we shall have to get rid of him, after all.

LADY S.: Oh, I trust not, your Majesty. He's really a very good fellow, you know . . . so jolly and so kind. Couldn't you ask the royal dentist to remove his sweet tooth? Then everything would be all right, your Highness.

QUEEN: Well, perhaps . . . we'll see.—There! Now, I'll put in the strawberries while you test the stove, Susan. His Majesty likes his birthday tea on the dot of four, you know . . . we must not keep him waiting. (*The* QUEEN *hastily fills the tart shells, as* SUSAN *crosses to the stove.*)

LADY S.: Oh, no, your Majesty. Never in ten long years have we been more than twenty seconds late . . . never! (*She opens the oven, puts first one hand in, and then the other, and dashes back to the* QUEEN.) It's just right . . . just exactly right, your Majesty.

QUEEN (*placing the last sugar lump*): There, Susan . . . aren't they beautiful? They're even prettier than last year! . . . Don't you think so?

LADY S. (*clapping her hands*): Oh, they are, your Majesty! Never has anybody in the land made such perfect tarts! No wonder his Highness can't wait for his birthday to come . . . no wonder! (*She starts toward the stove with the pan of tarts.*)

QUEEN (*putting the rolling pin and bowl away on the cupboard shelf*): He's talked about nothing else for days and days, Susan. And now, poor thing, he even dreams about it!

LADY S. (*amused*): Dear me, what a funny thing for a King to dream about . . . strawberry tarts!

QUEEN: Oh, no, Susan . . . it wasn't funny at all. It was a very serious

APPENDIX C: SHORT PLAYS 179

dream he had . . . almost a nightmare. In fact, it gave him a dreadful headache.

LADY S.: A headache? But why, your Majesty?

QUEEN: Well, you see, in his dream, he discovered—just the week before his birthday—that there was only one large strawberry to be had in all his kingdom, and it was guarded by a three-headed dragon. And do you know, he couldn't find a single knight who was brave enough to go fight the monster and bring me the strawberry to make his birthday tarts?

LADY S. (*gravely*): Oh, dear . . . how very sad. No wonder his Majesty's head ached. It makes me want to cry to think of it.

QUEEN: Well, don't cry Susan, 'cause it was only a dream . . . and besides, his Majesty's tarts are in the oven, and in a few minutes he'll be the happiest King in all the world. Come now, we must hurry! I must get my jewels, and straighten my crown. The first thing you know, his Royal Highness will be here before we're ready. (*She starts for the door up left.*)

LADY S. (*following*): Oh, that would never do, your Majesty . . . never!

QUEEN (*as she exits followed by* SUSAN): No indeed . . . it would not do, Susan.

(*The stage is empty for several seconds. Ominous music and a dimming of lights set the mood for the villain's entrance. Cautiously, the* KNAVE *peers in at the door, right. He sniffs and smiles,—he sniffs and smiles again, as he steps into the room.*)

KNAVE (*taking a deep breath, he rubs his tummy and licks his lips*): Ah! Delicious! Delicious! (*He looks about curiously to locate the source of the tempting odor; finally, his sensitive nose directs him to the stove. "Yes, that's it . . . the stove," thinks the* KNAVE. *He crosses quickly to look outside the door up left, and then investigates the door right. He steals across to stage left, takes a great red handkerchief from his belt, and starts to open the over door. For a moment, he thinks he must be strong. He cannot steal from his good master . . . and on his birthday, too! No! . . . that would be high treason. He might even lose his head. But the poor* KNAVE *cannot resist the temptation! His sweet tooth is too much for him! In a flash, he has taken the pan from the oven, closed the door, and run offstage, right. The voices of the* QUEEN *and* SUSAN *are heard offstage, almost at once.*)

QUEEN (*off*): Quickly, Susan, quickly! We have just one minute and forty-two seconds left!

LADY S. (*entering and holding back the curtain for her mistress*): Yes, your Majesty . . . I know, your Majesty.

QUEEN (*crossing to chair down right, she sits and arranges the folds of her gown*): Now, get the tarts from the oven first, Susan. And then you may tell the royal cook to bring the tray of tea. (SUSAN *crosses to the stove*) I think we shall have the blue cloth on the table, and the—

LADY S. (*uttering a sharp cry*): Oh, your Majesty!

QUEEN: Susan! Quiet! Whatever is the matter?

LADY S.: The tarts, your Majesty! They're gone!

QUEEN (*rising*): What? Gone? You stupid girl, you must have lost your wits. (*Crossing to stove*) Why, I saw you put them in the—Oh! They are! They're gone! (*She paces frantically up and down during the rest of the speech*) Susan, what's happened? What'll we do? What'll we ever do? The King's birthday's ruined . . . ruined! (*She drops in the chair down right, in tears*) He'll never forgive me . . . never!

LADY S. (*close to tears, but trying to comfort her mistress*): I'm so sorry, your Majesty . . . I'm so terribly sorry. Let me explain. I'll tell his Highness that . . . (*The* QUEEN *is crying so loudly now that she does not hear the* KING *as he enters, up left.*)

KING: You'll tell his Highness what, you silly girl? What have you done to her Majesty? What is all this crying about?

LADY S.: Well, your Highness. . . . I . . . she . . . I mean, her Majesty . . . (*The* QUEEN's *cries are growing steadily louder.*)

KING: Speak up, will you? Have you lost your tongue?

LADY S. (*weeping*): Not my tongue, your Majesty. It's the tarts that are lost . . . the tarts! (*The* QUEEN *is in agony now.*)

KING: The tarts? My birthday tarts? I don't believe it! Who would dare? (*He crosses to the stove and turns back in rage, as he discovers the proof*) Just wait till I catch the villain who took those tarts . . . just wait! I'll have his head, I will! (*He crosses to the* QUEEN *as* SUSAN *slinks upstage in terror*) Don't trouble, my dear. We'll punish the traitor! We'll have a public execution! We'll make an example of him. If I only knew . . . if I only had some idea who could have done it! (*He paces thoughtfully*) There isn't anyone in this whole country who has such a sweet tooth that he would dare . . .

QUEEN and LADY S. (*suddenly looking at one another*): Sweet tooth!

LADY S.: The Knave!

QUEEN (*rising*): The Knave!

KING: What's that you say? Do you think the Knave did it?

QUEEN (*crossing center*): I don't know, my dear . . . I don't know. But I . . .

LADY S.: It's his sweet tooth, you see, your Majesty. He's always getting into trouble because of it. He can't help it.

KING: Can't help it, can't he? We'll see about that! (*Crosses toward right, near door, claps his hands*) Ho, there . . . guard! (*The* QUEEN *and* SUSAN *whisper together at left.* GUARD *enters.*)

GUARD (*entering*): Yes, your Majesty?

KING: Have you seen the Knave of Hearts about?

GUARD: The Knave? Why, come to think of it, I have, your Majesty. He's been walking up and down in the long hall, looking very sad . . . very sad, indeed. Every now and then a great tear falls from his eye upon the stone floor. It's making a dreadful mess for the pages to clean up, your Highness. But the Knave won't speak, won't go to his room, won't stop crying. (*Confidentially*) Sire, I fear that he is suffering from some unknown illness. (*The* QUEEN *and* SUSAN *are touched by the sad story.*)

KING (*laughing*): Unknown illness, eh? It may be unknown to you, my friend, but not to me! Bring the villain here at once.

GUARD: Yes, your Majesty . . . I'll try. (*Exit.*)

KING: Suffering! He hasn't begun to suffer! Wait till he visits the torture chamber—then he'll have a right to weep!

QUEEN: Oh no, my dear, no! I can't bear it! The poor Knave . . . he's so kind and so . . .

KING: Kind? Kind to steal my birthday tarts? I don't call that kind! He's ruined my tea, and he shall suffer for it. (*The* GUARD *enters, followed by the* KNAVE, *who looks pathetic*) Kneel before me, villain.

KNAVE (*kneeling*): Your Majesty, do with me what you will. I cannot ask for mercy. It was I who stole your birthday tarts . . . I alone am guilty.

KING: So . . . you admit it, eh? You wretch! . . . traitor! I'll have your head . . . I'll—

QUEEN: Wait, my love, wait! Please let me have a word with him. (*She steps in center, and the* KING *paces down right*) Rise, Knave, and look at me. (*The* KNAVE *stands*) You have done a wicked thing, you know . . . a very wicked thing.

KNAVE: Yes, your Majesty . . . I know.

QUEEN: Where are my strawberry tarts? Where are they now?

KNAVE (*slowly*): In the cook's ice box, your Majesty.

LADY S. (*slowly*): They're saved!

QUEEN: You didn't eat them, then . . . not one?

KNAVE: No, your Majesty . . . not one.

QUEEN (*crossing to the* KING): There, you see, my dear? The day's not ruined, after all. The tarts are safe!

KING (*still angry*): That makes no difference! He's got to be punished just the same! He stole those tarts, and he's got to be punished.

QUEEN: But, my dear! The poor thing! Look at him! He's very sorry, and it was just—

LADY S.: It was just his sweet tooth, your Majesty. He can't help that, can he?

QUEEN: That's it! The tooth! That's the very thing! (*Very seriously, to the* KING) Yes, my dear, you are right. He shall be punished. You shall send for the royal dentist at once, and the Knave shall have his sweet tooth removed. (*To the* KNAVE) Will you be satisfied, dear Knave, to give yourself up to the royal dentist?

KNAVE (*joyfully*): Oh, yes, your Highness . . . gladly . . . gladly!

QUEEN (*to the* KING): There . . . you see, my dear? The Knave will be punished, we'll have our tarts and tea . . . only ten minutes late, too . . . and your birthday will be a happy one, after all.

KING: Very well, my dear . . . very well. Go fetch the tarts and tea, Susan.

LADY S.: Yes, your Highness. (*Exit up left.*)

KING: Take this mischief maker to the dentist, guard.

GUARD: Yes, your Majesty. (*Exit with the* KNAVE, *right.*)

KING (*crossing to the* QUEEN, *and taking her hand*): You're a very clever Queen, my love. You should be ruling, instead of me. I ought to have known before, that one sweet tooth in the country is enough . . . and that one belongs to me.

Curtain

Production Notes. Such a short play as *The Queen of Hearts* seldom will be staged with complete setting, costuming, and lighting. The leader who plans to present it as a public performance is referred to the notes on the production of *The King's Birthday* which follows. Two of the lighting suggestions made therein are applicable to the staging of *The Queen of Hearts:* the dimming of the stage during the Knave's entrance, and the intensifying of light to emphasize the happy conclusion.

A Longer Short Play:
THE KING'S BIRTHDAY[1]

Characters

KING COLE
THE QUEEN OF HEARTS, his wife
THE FOUR PRINCESSES MUFFET, their children
MISTRESS NAN, the nurse
THE FOUR SPIDERS
TWO SERVANTS
THE FIDDLERS THREE
A LADY-IN-WAITING
SIMPLE SIMON
MRS. SIMON, his mother
THE PIEMAN

Scene

The scene is laid in the birthday throne room of the King, which is used only for this annual celebration. A throne is placed on the platform down right, and a small table stands to the right of it. Slightly above center, left, is the royal stove; above it is a shelf, which holds the bowls for the Princesses' curds and whey. Four large silver spider webs stand in a row, about three feet below the upstage wall. Two stairways, to the right and left of the main platform, lead to the upper level playing area and entrances on the apron. The closed curtains of the main stage provide a background for the whole scene. At rise, the silver of the webs glistens in

---

[1] *The King's Birthday* was written to be staged as a curtain raiser. The action takes place on a large platform (placed in the auditorium floor against the stage), stairways to right and left of the platform, and the apron of the stage.

APPENDIX C: SHORT PLAYS 183

the blue light of an empty stage. There is strange, ominous music playing, its theme suggesting the villain's approach. Soon the spiders, entering on the upper level, two from the right and two from the left, creep down the steps. They go to the center slightly up, to admire their webs.

   1st Spider: Well, the webs we spun last night are still here.
   2nd Spider: They certainly are. What do you know about that?
   3rd Spider (*looking at calendar which hangs on back of* King's *throne*):

Fig. C–1. Scene from *The King's Birthday*.

And look . . . it's the King's birthday, too! Wow! Won't Mistress Nan be angry?
   4th Spider: Do you suppose she'll sweep us away before the King comes down?
   1st Spider: Goodness! I hope not! I'd like to watch the goings on.
   2nd Spider: Yeah! If we stick around we might get a taste of the Queen's tarts and the curds and whey.
   3rd Spider: You mean the strawberry tarts she makes for the old man's birthday?
   4th Spider: Yep! Every year she makes the same kind and they say they're the best in the kingdom. (*The laughter of the* Princesses *is heard*

offstage) Say, here come the Princesses. They don't like us . . . we'd better hide in our webs. Come on, brothers! (*They hide in their webs as* Mistress Nan *and the* Princesses *enter on the upper level from stage right.*)

1st Princess: Please, Mistress Nan, let's play one more game.

Mistress Nan: Not another one. No, indeed!

2nd Princess: Oh, please, let us. We don't want to go inside.

Mistress Nan: I tell you, children, I haven't time.

3rd Princess: You know father never gets up early on his birthday.

4th Princess: Besides, what have you got to do in such a hurry?

Mistress Nan: Do? Good gracious, I have to sweep and dust this throne room. You know the birthday throne room hasn't been used since this time last year, and it's probably a fright.

1st Princess: Well, we'll help you if you'll give us some curds and whey. We never get enough at the party.

2nd Princess: 'Deed we will, Mistress Nan, 'cause we just love curds and whey!

Mistress Nan: All right then, come along, all of you. Here's a dust-cloth for everybody. (*She takes the cloths from her sash, where they have been hanging, and the group moves across upper level and downstairs left to the platform.* Mistress Nan, *who is leading the way, stops amazed as she reaches the lower level*) Good gracious! Look at these cobwebs! Those wicked spiders have been up to mischief again! Whatever will we do?

3rd Princess: That's easy. We'll each dust one of them away. Come on, sisters. (*They all approach webs timidly while* Mistress Nan *sets to work to sweep downstage below the throne. As the* Princesses *approach the webs the spiders jump out and frighten them. All this movement is pantomimed rhythmically to music.*)

Mistress Nan: Do hurry, children, or it will be too late. The King'll be here any moment now.

4th Princess: But we're frightened of those great big spiders!

1st Princess: They look as though they'd like to eat us up!

2nd Princess: And they have such wicked eyes!

Mistress Nan: Nonsense, you silly girls . . . here . . . let me do it! (*She starts to lift her broom to destroy the webs once and for all when the royal trumpet sounds.*)

3rd Princess: Oh dear, there's father now! (*A jolly laugh offstage identifies* King Cole.)

Mistress Nan: Yes, that's King Cole's laugh, all right. Well, it's too late now, that's all there is to it. It's too late to do anything.

4th Princess: Oh, never mind. Maybe he won't notice. (*The* Princesses *tuck their dustcloths into their belts and* Mistress Nan *stands her broom in the corner by the stove. They form a group on the lower level left, as the* King *enters on upper level right. His Majesty, with great dignity, goes down the right stairs and stands before his throne.*)

APPENDIX C: SHORT PLAYS

KING: Well, well, well, and how are the Princesses Muffet this morning? Eh?

ALL (*as they curtsey low*): Very well, thank you, Your Majesty. And may we wish you a Happy Birthday, Sire?

KING: Thank you, my children, and you too, Mistress Nan. So you didn't forget your old father's birthday! Well, well, well! (*He takes his place on the throne.*)

1ST PRINCESS: Oh, no, father, I brought you some tobacco for your pipe. (*She presents it with a little curtsey and returns to her place.*)

2ND PRINCESS: And here are some cleaners to clean it with. (*She makes her offering smilingly.*)

3RD PRINCESS: I brought you some spices for your bowl of punch. (*She is proud to present him with such an original gift.*)

4TH PRINCESS: And I have a new song for your Fiddlers Three to play. (*She presents the* KING *with a tiny roll of music.*)

KING: Thank you, dear children. These are very useful gifts indeed. Now, Mistress Nan, I think they should be rewarded with some extra portions of curds and whey, don't you?

MISTRESS NAN: As you wish, Your Majesty.

ALL: Oh, goody! Thank you, father! How wonderful! Father, thanks! (MISTRESS NAN *now gives a bowl and spoon to each* PRINCESS, *taking it from the shelf over the stove, and the little girls go to sit on the stairs left to enjoy their feast.*)

KING: Now, Mistress, go summon my servant with the bowl of punch. I must try out Elizabeth's new spices. That will start the day off right, you know!

MISTRESS NAN: Yes, Your Majesty, at once, sir. (*She curtseys and goes up steps right, and off.*)

KING: Well, well, well, funny thing about these birthdays . . . (*he stretches*) I feel younger every year.

1ST PRINCESS: And you look younger, too, father.

2ND PRINCESS: And handsomer, I think.

KING: Do I indeed? Well, well, well!

SERVANT (*entering on upper level and coming down steps right to throne*): Yes, Your Majesty? Your punch, m'lord. (*He sets the punch bowl on the table to right of throne.*)

KING: Ah . . . splendid . . . now, take that package of spice and put two pinches in the punch.

SERVANT (*looking doubtfully at the various packages*): But how am I to tell which is the spice, Your Majesty?

KING: Smell it, idiot! That's what your nose is for!

SERVANT (*following instructions, selects right package and adds spice to bowl*): Yes, sir, so it is, sir!

KING (*tasting the cup which the servant pours for him*): Ah! Delicious! Just exactly right! (*During this dialogue, the spiders have been crawling, with threatening gestures, toward the* PRINCESSES. *At this point, they are so frightened, they scream*) See here . . . what's this? (*As he observes spiders*) Why, you cruel beasts! How dare you frighten my little girls? Come, kneel before me! (*The spiders obey, humbly*) You know I've ordered you out of my kingdom a dozen times! You thought you'd hide in my birthday throne room, did you? Well, this time, King Cole shall punish you as you deserve. In the dungeons you shall spin your webs, where they will do some good. There you shall spend the rest of your lives, catching the flies that disturb the kingdom. Go! (*To sombre music, the spiders go meekly up steps right, and out*) Go with them, sirrah (*to the servant*). And you, Princesses, dry your tears and take your bowls to Mistress Nan and she will fill them full again.

Princesses (*as they run up steps left to exit*): Oh thank you, father, thank you.

King: And send my servant with my pipe!

1st Princess: Yes, Sire, at once. (*Exit* Princesses *on upper level left. The* King *sips his punch, enjoying every mouthful, until the* Queen *appears, on upper level left, followed by her* Lady *carrying the tray of unbaked tarts.*)

King: Ah, there you are, my dear, I wondered if you had overslept! (Queen *comes down steps left and bows before* King.)

Queen: Ah no, Sire. I come to wish you the happiest of birthdays, and to say as soon as Lady Anne bakes the tarts, your birthday gift from the Queen of Hearts will be complete.

King: Dear Queen of Hearts. . . . I tell you I have the most loyal Queen in all the world! Let me have a look at those tarts! (Anne *brings them over for inspection*) Yes, indeed, as beautiful as ever, and my own Queen's handiwork. (*The servant with the pipe has entered during this speech, right on the upper level, and is coming down steps right*) Well, you go on with your baking and I shall have my pipe. Ho, sirrah!

Servant (*presenting pipe*): Your pipe, Your Majesty! (*The* King *smokes contentedly as the* Queen *and* Anne *busy themselves at stove.*)

King: Filled with my tobacco?

Servant: Yes, Your Majesty, from the package here on the table.

King: That's right. . . . Mmmmmm! Fine tobacco! That will be all, sir. (*The servant bows and exits up steps right, and off.*)

Queen: Anne, my dear, are you sure the stove's quite hot enough?

Anne: Oh yes, mistress, quite! See how it sizzles! That means it's hot. (*She tries it with her finger to prove the statement.*)

Queen: Then, put them in. (Anne *obeys*) That's it! (*To the* King) Now, Your Majesty, if you'll excuse me, I'll go off to get my jewels, while the tarts bake, and when I return, we shall have a splendid feast.

King: Very well, my dear, but hurry. I can hardly wait! (*The* Queen *and* Anne *go up steps right and exit on upper level. Before many minutes the* King *begins to nod and falls asleep. The lights dim and the knave enters on upper level right. He sniffs curiously, and following his nose, proceeds to creep across upper level, right to left, down steps left.*

APPENDIX C: SHORT PLAYS 187

Cautiously he finds his way to the stove, steals the tarts, and running up steps left, exits at upper level left. The QUEEN *now enters, on upper level right, hurriedly followed by* ANNE. *They come down the right steps.*)

QUEEN: We must hurry, Anne, before the tarts get too brown.

ANNE: Shh! Your Majesty! The King is asleep!

QUEEN: Let's go on tiptoe then, and have them all ready to eat when he wakes! (ANNE *crosses left to oven, and opens stove door.*)

ANNE: Oh goodness! Goodness me! How dreadful!

QUEEN: What is it, Anne? What's the matter?

ANNE: Oh, Your Majesty, the tarts are gone!

QUEEN (*running to look*): Gone? But they can't be! (*As she sees the empty oven.*) But they are! My lovely tarts are gone! Whatever will I do? (*She cries so loudly that she wakes the* KING.)

KING: What's all this noise! What's happened here? (*He rises*) What? Crying, my love? What in the world has happened?

ANNE: It's the Queen's tarts, Your Majesty. They've disappeared.

QUEEN: And now I have no birthday gift for you, m'lord. Your birthday's ruined. (*She cries out more desperately than before.*)

KING: Dear me, this is dreadful! Let me see what can be done . . . (*He paces as he thinks*) Some knave has stolen them for sure, and yet, if we should find him now, it would do no good. He would probably have eaten every one. (*The* QUEEN *cries louder. At this moment* SIMPLE SIMON *and his mother come up the center aisle from the rear of the auditorium.* SIMON *is whistling, and sucking on a lollypop*) Wait, I'll ask these passersby. See here, good woman, have you met the knave who stole my tarts, along the road?

MRS. SIMON: Oh no, Your Majesty. We have met no one for many miles . . . Have you lost some tarts?

KING: Yes, the Queen's birthday tarts have been stolen from the oven, and we'll have no tarts for the feast today.

MRS. SIMON: Dear me, that is too bad! I wish that I could help, Sire!

SIMPLE SIMON: Well, nobody asked me . . . but maybe I could help.

MRS. SIMON: Hush, Simon. Don't you know you're speaking to the King? Hold your tongue.

SIMPLE SIMON: Well, he wants some tarts, doesn't he . . . and I can get him some.

KING: What's that you say, boy?

SIMPLE SIMON: I said I could get you some tarts, Sire, and I can.

KING: But how . . . tell us how?

SIMPLE SIMON: Well, you see, when mother and I were coming from the fair, just now, I met a Pieman coming this way, a very nice Pieman too, he was. He had a whole tray of freshly baked tarts, the best I ever tasted, and I'm sure he'd be proud to give them to his King. Shall I fetch him?

KING: Of course, go fetch him, boy. (*As* SIMPLE SIMON *goes to the rear of auditorium calling for the* PIEMAN, *the* KING *goes to comfort the*

QUEEN) There, there, my dear, dry your tears. The birthday will be a happy one after all. Come Princesses, come Fiddlers Three, make music and let us all be gay again. We're going to have some new tarts for the King's Birthday! (*The* PRINCESSES *and* MISTRESS NAN *enter right on upper level, and the* FIDDLERS *left.* SIMPLE SIMON *leads the* PIEMAN *up center aisle.*)

SIMPLE SIMON: Here he is, Your Majesty, with tarts fit for a King.

KING: Splendid . . . splendid! You, sir, shall be made assistant to the Royal Baker, sir!

PIEMAN (*bowing low*): I am honored, Your Majesty, to serve the royal table.

KING: And now let us all go to the birthday feast. You, Simon, and your mother, shall be our honored guests. Play, fiddlers, play!

(*To the music of the fiddlers the procession starts off, up the steps left. The* KING *and* QUEEN *lead, next the* LADY-IN-WAITING, *the* PRINCESSES, MISTRESS NAN, SIMON *and his mother. The* PIEMAN *brings up the rear, holding proudly over his hear the tray of tarts which has brought him fame. As the last one disappears stage left (upper level), the fiddlers, who have been standing center stage, face left and follow the others off, playing as they go.*)

Curtain

Costuming the Play. For the sake of simplicity in creation and attractiveness in design, the medieval style is suggested for general costuming. Tunics and tights will serve for the gentlemen (the King may have a train and a crown in addition); the ladies will wear princess-line dresses with flowing sleeves, and medieval headdresses. The spider costumes may be made like children's sleeping suits, from unbleached muslin, dyed, or some similar heavy material. If these are painted (and a water paint mixed with powder glue will suffice), with yellow and black stripes and dots in fantastic design, they will give a sinister effect. The heads should be covered with tight-fitting caps of the same material as the costumes. Black antennae may be made of twisted heavy wire. Simple Simon, his mother, and the Pieman will be suitably dressed in medieval peasant costumes.

Settings and Properties. If *The King's Birthday* is used as a curtain raiser, it must be so set that when it is over, the young stage hands may quickly remove any objects that might obstruct the vision of the audience during the major play. For that reason, the property list includes only bare essentials. The position of platform and stairs was described in the note on page 264. The spider webs can be simply constructed, but must stand firmly, and be easy for the spiders to carry off, when they are sentenced to the dungeon. A slit, wide enough to hold an upright lathe about four feet high, is made in the center of four blocks of wood, 6″ x 8″ x 2″. At a point one foot from the top of this upright strip, two other lathes can be crossed to form an X. This will be the frame on which lines

APPENDIX C: SHORT PLAYS

of rope may be knotted in an irregular, hexagonal shape to form the web. If the whole unit is given several coats of silver paint, the finished product should bear a startling resemblance to its filmy prototype.

The small properties (hand props) should be placed offstage in the wings, except for the Princesses' bowls and spoons. These stand on the shelf over the stove, at the opening of the play. Simple Simon and the Pieman must be responsible for their own props, because of their entrance from the rear of the auditorium.

Offstage left: A muffin ring, containing tarts or cookies, for the Lady-in-Waiting to bring onstage.

Offstage right: A broom for Mistress Nan and four dustcloths for the Princesses.

The Princesses' presents for the King.

The King's pipe, punch bowl, ladle, and cup.

For the fiddlers, their fiddles, or simulated fiddles.

NOTE. If a complete, draped stage is used for the performance, it can be more elaborately set. A carpeted dais may hold the throne, the table, and an extra chair for the Queen; a stool for the Lady-in-Waiting may occupy a place on the floor, to the left of the dais. A long banquet table, set far upstage, bearing fruits and delicacies for the coming feast, and backed by a decorative tapestry, would add to the pictorial effect. Right and left entrances, both up and downstage, may be needed to give variety. The entrance of Simple Simon, his mother, and the Pieman from the auditorium would require a stairway leading to the stage level.

Lighting. Elaborate lighting is never needed in plays for young children, but some thought should be given to the achievement of interesting effects that will establish the mood. Two acting areas should be stressed in this particular play: one surrounding the King's throne, and the other near the stove. Although the total playing space will be lighted, the important areas should have a special accent.

Plan 1—Curtain Raiser Production

Eight spotlights, hung from a bridge in the auditorium, will suffice.

A. Three spots, connected in a single circuit, carrying amber or straw gelatin, will be so directed as to cover the whole scene.
B. Two spots, each on a separate circuit, colored in lavender or pink, will be carefully focused, each on one of the two accented areas.
C. Three spots, operating on the same circuit, carrying blue gelatin, will cover the entire playing space.

As the auditorium lights dim out, group C comes up, creating the appropriate mood for the villainous spiders' entrance. When the Princesses appear, group A comes up gradually, as C dim down. During the action concerning the King and Queen, the two accent spots (B) come up. As the King falls asleep, group A fades, as does the throne area accent spot. Group C comes up full, and the stove area accent spot dims to half color. This change creates the ominous mood for the stealing of the tarts, and centers audience attention on the stove. Group A comes up gradually as the Queen returns, and the King wakes. Full intensity of light is used to emphasize the happy conclusion.

Plan 2—Full Stage Production

Five spotlights, hung just inside the proscenium arch, and two light strips, one placed behind each teaser, will be required.

- A. Three spots, connected in a single circuit and carrying straw or amber gelatin, will cover the general area, right, center, and left. (Cf. A in Plan 1.)
- B. Two spots, each on a separate circuit, colored with lavender or pink, will be carefully focused, each on one of the two accented areas. (Cf. B in Plan 1.)
- C. Two circuits in each of the strips, connected so as to be controlled as a unit, will carry blue gelatin, and provide the mysterious effect where necessary. (Cf. C in Plan 1.)
- D. One circuit in each of the strips, connected so as to be controlled as a unit, will carry amber or straw gelatin, and will help the A spots to give the general illumination needed when the stage is in full light. (See Plan 1 for full description of light changes.)

Appendix D:
THE LONG PLAY

CHILD OF THE SKY
(An original play based on Oscar Wilde's *Star Child*[1])

Characters

STELLA, The Star Child
PAPA CARL, Woodcutter
MAMA OLGA, His wife
JAN　⎱ Woodcutter's children
ELENA ⎰
PETER　　　⎫
ANYA　　　 ⎬ Village children
CHRISTINE ⎭
RABBIT
MOLE
SQUIRREL
RED BIRD
BLUE BIRD
BABY RED BIRD
OLD WOMAN, Stella's mother
TWO SOLDIERS FROM CITY
GUARDS (may be played by soldiers)
NOBLELADY
PEASANTS, Villagers
BOLOKOFF, the Magician
POKO, Magician's servant
MAN BEGGAR, Stella's real father
NINA　 ⎱ Gardener's children
STEFAN ⎰
FOUR CHILDREN IN THE FOREST
SPIRIT OF THE WELL
PAGE

[1] By permission of Mr. Vyvyan Holland, copyright owner.

ACT I

The action takes place outside the Woodcutter's cottage in Karakov. At stage left, down, we see the doorway of the simple dwelling, outside which stands a rustic bench. At stage right, fairly far down is a well, on the edge of which sits a bucket and a dipper. Upstage a few feet before the blue sky-drop are several ground rows representing low bushes, or an uneven hedge. They are placed so that entrances may be made from up right and left, behind these ground rows, or below them. (See Act I plans, page 193.) As curtain rises, JAN *and* ELENA, *the Woodcutter's children are sitting by the well, right, weaving a flower crown for* STELLA, *their much admired foster-sister.*

ELENA (*taking flower from* JAN): I don't think that is very fresh, Jan.

JAN: Of course it is, Elena. I just picked it down by the brook.

ELENA: But one of the petals is mashed—and you know how particular Stella is about her flower crowns. She'll just throw it away unless it is perfect.

JAN: Well, I don't blame her a bit. Any girl that is as beautiful as our step-sister deserves the best of everything.

ELENA: I wonder sometimes how anyone could be so beautiful.

JAN: It must be true, what Father says . . . she must have fallen from the stars, because she looks like an angel.

(*Voices of* PETER, ANYA *and* CHRISTINE *offstage call, "Stella . . . Stella . . . we're ready for the journey."*)

CHRISTINE (*as three children enter*): Hello, Jan . . . we're ready . . . we're ready to take Stella for a ride.

ANYA: But where is she?

PETER: We've got the cart down at the foot of the path.

CHRISTINE: It's all trimmed with flowers—too.

ELENA: She'll be here in a moment . . . she's combing her hair.

CHRISTINE: What a beautiful crown you have made, Elena. Do you think Stella will like it this time?

JAN: I hope so. I gathered the flowers for it before sunrise. They are fresher when you pick them in the dew, you know.

ANYA: She'll really look like a queen in that, Jan. (STELLA *appears in doorway.*)

STELLA (*from doorway*): I hope I don't need a silly flower crown to make me look like a queen, Anya.

ELENA: Of course not, Stella, of course you don't.

ANYA: We are ready to take you for a ride, Stella.

PETER: The cart's right at the foot of the path.

JAN: We'll carry you if you like, Stella, so you won't spoil your shoes.

STELLA: No, thank you . . . I wore my old ones purposely.

ELENA: Do try your crown, Stella. I think it will just match the flowers in your dress.

CHRISTINE: Let me put it on you.

Fig. D–1. Set plans for *Child of the Sky*.

ANYA: No . . . let me.

STELLA (*pushing her away*): Thank you, no. I'd rather do it myself. You might muss my hair. (STELLA *takes crown, goes down right and sits on edge of well. She admires herself in the water as she arranges the crown. The others stand about in admiration.*)

ELENA: It is beautiful, Stella.

CHRISTINE: You look prettier than ever.

JAN: Indeed you do!

MOTHER (*calling from indoors*): Stella . . . Stella dear.

STELLA (*impatiently*): Oh dear, what does she want now? (*Pause*) Yes, Mother Olga, what is it?

MOTHER (*appearing in doorway*): Stella, will you go over to Aunt Elise's and take this bit of broth I made for her? She is so ill, and she would be so thankful for a glimpse of you.

STELLA (*to center, defiantly*): Why must you always ask me to do errands for you, Mother? Such jobs are for servants, anyway. Besides, it makes me sick to look at crippled old people.

MOTHER: But Stella . . . your old auntie hasn't long to live, and there is so little we can do to cheer her.

STELLA: When people get old and sick and ugly, they ought to die. There's no room in the world for ugliness.

MOTHER (*unhappily*): I sometimes wish your eyes could see the beauty that lies in the heart, my child, instead of in the face. If you could only remember how Papa Carl and I helped you when you were left alone and desolate, you would not be so cruel to those who need your pity.

STELLA (*impatiently*): Oh dear . . . let's not go over all that again. I'm tired of hearing it. Come on, everybody. (*All exit up right except* JAN.)

JAN (*up center*): Don't scold Stella, Mother . . . please. We can't bear it when her eyes are full of tears. I'll take the broth to Aunt Elise.

MOTHER: Always protecting her, aren't you, Jan? Let's hope that one day she'll be worthy of your love. Well . . . run along now, and tell the others not to go too far. See, there's your father now, and he'll be wanting supper soon.

JAN: We'll hurry, Mother Olga. (*He moves up center as Father enters up right*) Hello, Father.

FATHER: Well, boy . . . where are you off to in such a hurry?

JAN: Just to Aunt Elise's, I'll be back before you know it. (*Exit.*)

FATHER: Good boy, Jan . . . always so cheerful and such a help to us all.

MOTHER: Yes, we have reason to be proud of him, Carl . . . and of Elena too. I only wish I could say the same for Stella.

FATHER (*sadly*): Yes. It's strange to see that beautiful child growing harder of heart every day. I remember so well the morning I found her in the forest, wrapped in the golden cloak sprinkled with stars. The beautiful, innocent face of an angel, she had then.

MOTHER: Well, she's anything but an angel now, I'll tell you. Do you

APPENDIX D: THE LONG PLAY

know, the holy Father told me today that he had found her jeering at a crippled beggar by the church, and urging the rest of the village children to throw stones at him.

FATHER: It makes me so ashamed to hear such tales . . . and yet, we've tried so hard. We've done all we could for the little foundling. Surrounded her with love all her life . . . and this is what she gives us in return.

Fig. D–2. Scene from Act I, *Child of the Sky*. (Credit: Gaston Remy.)

MOTHER: What surprises me most is the power she has over all the other children. They practically worship her. And yet, she despises them really . . . boasts constantly that she was born of the stars, while they have ordinary common parents. And still they love her and do her bidding like servants. Our Jan is the most devoted of the lot!

FATHER (*sighing*): I don't know what we can do, my dear. We can't turn her out. Somehow, I feel that one day we will know the mystery of her birth, and why the Lord gave her into our care. There must be some reason for it, Olga. I suppose we must be patient. (*He goes in.*)

MOTHER (*following him indoors*): Yes, Carl . . . I suppose we must. But sometimes I think I can't hold my temper another moment.

(*A tired old beggar woman enters up left and comes down right to well . . . As she stoops to drink, voices of children are heard off right. She hides down right on the far side of the well. The children (except* STELLA) *come running in; they are playing "Hide-and-seek." They each find a place to hide and then call to* STELLA *that they are ready.* STELLA *enters right and starts to hunt.*)

STELLA: I can find you all in two minutes . . . see if I can't. There's Anya . . . I spy Anya!

ANYA (*coming out of hiding*): I'm getting too big to hide in such a little place . . . that's why you found me.

STELLA: And there—there's Christine—and Peter!

CHRISTINE: You're always so much quicker than the rest of us, Stella!

STELLA (*looking back of well and seeing* OLD WOMAN): Well, look who's here! Who gave you permission to join our game, you ugly old hag?

OLD WOMAN: 'Deed, I wish I *were* young enough to play with you, children, but I am old and tired. I just stopped a moment to rest.

STELLA: Well, you'll have to go find some other place to rest . . . we'll not have beggars disturbing our game . . . will we?

PETER: Indeed we will not.

CHRISTINE: Stella doesn't like ugly things.

ELENA: You'll have to go away.

OLD WOMAN: But I am so tired and hungry, children. I have traveled a long way today. I have had nothing to eat or drink.

STELLA: What business is it of ours? We have nothing for you. Now, get out! (*She picks up stone and walks threateningly toward* OLD WOMAN *as others collect stones.*)

OLD WOMAN: Very well, I will go . . . but I am sorry to see such a beautiful little girl with no kindness in her heart. I'll . . .

STELLA: We've heard enough of your silly chattering. Get out! (*She throws stone*) There . . . take that!

CHILDREN (*throwing stones*): And that! And that! (OLD WOMAN *exits up left.*)

STELLA (*laughing*): We'll make you forget your rheumatism! Look at the ugly old thing, she's almost running! I'll bet we can hit her again.

FATHER (*coming out of the house*): What's all this noise about? Stella . . . drop that stone. What wrong has that poor old woman done you that you should treat her thus? Aren't you ashamed?

STELLA (*defiantly*): And who are you to dare scold me for what I do? I'm not your daughter, anyway, and I don't have to do your bidding! (*To children*) Come on, let's finish our game down by the brook. (*She and children run off right.*)

FATHER: You hard, unfeeling child . . . you'll pay for this! (*He goes to look up right and goes to* OLD WOMAN) Ah, there you are, my good woman. Here . . . let me help you. (*He leads* OLD WOMAN *on stage, goes toward well*) Let me get you something to eat and drink. Olga! Quickly . . . bring a cup of wine and some bread. (*To* OLD WOMAN *who is sitting on edge of well*) Please forgive our Stella's rude behavior. She is a very strange child . . . a foundling whom we have tried to bring up as one of our own.

OLD WOMAN (*sitting*): She is such a beautiful little girl, but so proud and cruel . . . I can't understand it.

MOTHER (*appearing in doorway*): Oh dear . . . has Stella been doing harm again?

FATHER (*sadly*): Yes, Olga, she and the other children were throwing stones at this good woman, driving her down the road.

MOTHER: Dear me, what's to become of us? I'll declare . . . a curse has been upon us for ten years now . . . ever since the evil day you found her in the Vronska Forest, Carl!

OLD WOMAN (*startled*): The Vronska Forest? Ten years ago you found this child in the Vronska Forest?

FATHER: Let me see . . . yes, it was ten years ago, almost to the very day.

OLD WOMAN (*excited*): And what signs did you find about her? Was there—was there a chain of amber about her neck, and was she wrapped in a golden cloak embroidered with silver stars?

MOTHER: Why . . . yes . . . yes, she was.

FATHER: But how could you know this?

OLD WOMAN (*in tears*): I can't believe it . . . at last. I'm so happy . . . I . . . I . . . could I see the cloak and the chain?

FATHER: Certainly. Go, Olga, quickly—bring the cloak and amber chain.

MOTHER (*going into house*): Yes, I have it safe, still where we've always kept it.

FATHER: Here my good woman. Drink a little—it will strengthen you!

OLD WOMAN (*still weeping with joy*): After all these years of wandering and hoping!

MOTHER (*returning with box*): Here they are—the cloak and amber chain!

OLD WOMAN (*holding cloak against her heart*): It's true! It's my own little one I lost in the forest. I have wandered over the whole kingdom in search of her! I had given up all hope of ever finding her alive!

FATHER: Stella is your child?

OLD WOMAN: Yes, my friend, this is the very cloak I wrapped her in.

MOTHER: But it looks like a queen's veil . . . it seemed much too beautiful for a mortal to wear. We thought she must have fallen from the sky . . . a fallen star, perhaps. That's why we named her Stella.

OLD WOMAN: I'm glad you called her Stella. It's a lovely name. She is like a star . . . shining and bright. And to think that I shall soon have her again for my very own.

FATHER: Wait—I'll call her now. She's just down by the brook with the children. (*He walks upstage*) I can see them from here.

OLD WOMAN: How I have longed for this moment! And now that it's here I am ashamed, for I have nothing to offer her, none of the things that are her right . . . nothing but my love!

MOTHER: But there's no richer gift than a mother's love.

FATHER (*who has moved up and is looking off right*): Stella . . . Stella, my child, come here a moment, please. I have a surprise for you.

STELLA (*off*): After while, Papa Carl. We haven't finished our game yet.

OLD WOMAN (*restlessly*): I'm almost afraid to tell her who I am.

MOTHER: There now! Don't be so upset. (*She assists her to rise and walks her toward down left*) You stay here and let Carl break the news to her. (*She sits on bench beside door, as* STELLA *comes in.*)

STELLA (*entering up right*): Yes, Papa Carl, what is it? Where is this big surprise?

FATHER (*taking her hand*): My child, this may be a shock to you. I want to break the news to you myself. I . . .

STELLA: Oh, do stop stammering and chattering, Papa Carl. I'm in a hurry. What is it you're trying to say.

FATHER: Here, Stella, here at our own cottage door, your mother is waiting. She has come for you at last.

STELLA (*startled*): My mother? Where? Where is she? What are you talking about?

OLD WOMAN (*rising slowly*): She is here, Stella. I am your mother.

STELLA (*drawing back*): You! That ugly beggar woman my mother?

MOTHER: Yes, child, and she's been looking for you all these years.

STELLA: You're mad! I tell you you've lost your wits. I'm no child of yours! You're a beggar, and ugly, and in rags. Go away! I never want to see your face again!

OLD WOMAN: But Stella, listen to me! Long years ago I carried you in my arms as I fled from my enemies. Robbers held me prisoner, child . . . snatched you from me and left you to die. By some miracle this good man came upon you and saved your life. Look, my dear, here is the star cloak that I wrapped you in, and the amber chain that I put around your tiny white throat. Please come with me now . . . you are all I have left in the world. I need you, Stella.

STELLA (*bitterly*): If you *are* my mother, it would have been better if you'd never come here to shame me. (*To Father*) And I hate you . . . you and Mother Olga both, for letting me believe I was a mystic child of the sky!

FATHER: But Stella, I swear to you, we thought . . .

STELLA: You thought! Oooooooh! Well, you see what a mess you've made of everything.

MOTHER: But child—think! Think! You must understand that . . .

STELLA: Go away, all of you! Can't you see how miserable I am? Why do you stand there staring at me? Go away! (OLGA *and* CARL *go sadly into the house.*)

OLD WOMAN (*after a moment*): If you want it that way, I shall go too,

APPENDIX D: THE LONG PLAY

Stella . . . and I'll never trouble you again. But won't you kiss me good-bye?

STELLA: Kiss you? Never! I'd rather kiss a toad! Ooooooh! Go away! (*The* OLD WOMAN *rises slowly, weeping, disappears in the shadows upstage left. It is growing darker now, perceptibly so. At first* STELLA *follows the* OLD WOMAN *a few steps and then she comes down, falls on the doorstep and bursts into tears of disappointment. Her back is to the audience and it is at this moment, that she blocks out her features, lips, rouge, eyebrows with some pale flesh base which the stage manager has carefully concealed above the doorstep.*)

CHILDREN (*offstage*): Stella, aren't you coming back to finish the game? Hurry, Stella . . . it's getting late.

(ANYA *and* JAN *enter.*)

ANYA: There she is, Jan! Stella, what's wrong?

CHRISTINE: Didn't you hear us calling you?

ELENA: You promised to run a race with us. (*Children have all gathered around* STELLA, *whose face is buried in her lap. She lifts her head, an ugly child, and the children drop back in horror.*)

PETER: Oh, look! Look at her face!

ANYA: She's ugly!

CHRISTINE: She's ugly as a toad!

ELENA: Stella, what's happened to you?

JAN (*sadly*): You're not beautiful any more.

PETER: And we called her a queen, a princess!

ELENA: She looks like a clown! (*She starts to laugh, and the others join in, except for* JAN.)

CHRISTINE: She's been wearing a mask just to fool us.

ELENA: I'll never call you sister again . . . and you'll never share my room again, either! (*She goes into the house.*)

PETER: Come on, we don't want to waste our time with that ugly creature.

ANYA: Let's go find another playmate.

CHRISTINE: You go play with the snakes and the bullfrogs . . . that's where you belong! (*Jeering and laughing, they run off right.*)

JAN (*sadly*): Stella, I'm sorry I said what I did!

STELLA: Don't, Jan. Go away, please. I want to be by myself. (JAN *goes inside. It has grown almost dark now. There is a little light near the well. Slowly* STELLA *rises, feels her face, and goes to the well, almost afraid. She looks down into the water and draws back, startled. A green spot inside the well makes her appear more homely.*)

STELLA: It's true! It's true! I am ugly—ugly as a toad! (*She drops in center convulsed in sobs. Slowly and silently, the Spirit of the Well rises from the water and seats herself on the edge of the pool.*)

SPIRIT: Stella, Stella, my child . . . dry your tears. I have come to talk to you.

STELLA (*lifting her eyes slowly*): Who are you? Where did you come from?

SPIRIT: I am the Spirit of the Well, Stella. I live in the depths of the green water—so you see, I am an old friend of yours.

STELLA: But I never saw you before, never in all my life.

SPIRIT: Because you've only had eyes for yourself, Stella—but I've seen you every day, smiling at your beautiful reflection in the water.

STELLA: Was I really beautiful once, Spirit?

SPIRIT: Yes, very beautiful.

STELLA: Then why—why have I suddenly grown so ugly?

SPIRIT: It's been happening for a long time, Stella. You've been growing ugly in your heart . . . proud and vain and selfish, and cruel. Only when the heart is good and pure can the face be beautiful. You may not have known it, but little by little, you have been losing all the beauty God gave to you.

STELLA (*thinking*): I remember now. I laughed at the crippled boy, and . . . I smothered the neighbor's cat . . . I made Mother Olga cry last week . . . and I beat Christine's dog. That was cruel and ugly. Is that what you mean, Spirit?

SPIRIT: That's just what I mean. And today, this very evening—what did you do today?

STELLA (*looking toward up left where her mother disappeared*): My mother! I drove her away—my own mother! I was proud and cruel. Oh dear, I wish . . . I . . . How could I have said such things? And now it's too late.

SPIRIT: No, Stella, it's never too late. If you will search for your poor mother and ask her forgiveness . . . return the love she has for you, and try to be charitable and kind to all you meet, your heart will be soft again, and good. Beauty and happiness will come back—you'll see.

STELLA (*almost cheerfully*): Oh thank you, good Spirit. I'll start now, right away, and I won't give up until I've found Mother again. Thank you for helping me.

SPIRIT: My good wishes go with you, Stella. Somehow I think you have learned your lesson. Now I must go, for my children are waiting for me. Farewell. (*She disappears, and* STELLA *looks after her. She is just about ready to go off to look for her mother, when* JAN *sneaks quietly out of the house, and goes to her.*)

JAN: Stella . . . Stella . . . don't go away.

STELLA: I must go, Jan. I know now how cruel and proud I've been, and I've grown ugly because my heart is ugly.

JAN: It doesn't matter to me that you're not beautiful any more, Stella. I want you to stay. I'll miss you if you go away.

STELLA: That's kind of you, Jan. I'll miss you too—but I must go. I want to find my poor mother, and ask her forgiveness. When I've made things right again, I'll come back—I promise.

APPENDIX D: THE LONG PLAY

JAN: I'll be waiting, Stella. (*He watches her as she disappears in the shadows, up left, and the curtains fall.*)

ACT II

The action takes place in the forest near the royal walled city. It is early morning. Cutouts of trees or stumps suggest atmosphere. Bench sits down left. Several of the animals are just waking up. (*See Act 2 plans, page 193.*)

RABBIT (*peering out from behind tree, sees squirrel asleep, enters and runs over to him*): Hey there, Squirrel—wake up! It's a beautiful day. We promised Redbird and Bluebird that we'd all meet here.
SQUIRREL: Oh dear! Is it time to get up already? I was having a wonderful dream. You know, I dreamed that I had a whole pile of acorns all to myself. Yum, yum! Why did you have to wake me up?
REDBIRD (*entering upstage left with* BLUEBIRD): Good morning, everybody. (*Looking toward* SQUIRREL) Come on there, you lazy-bones! Are you just getting up?
BLUEBIRD: Don't you know the early bird always gets the worm? Why we've been up for hours.
SQUIRREL: Well, I'm getting up, so stop scolding. (*Stretches*) There, you see—I'm wide awake. But I'm still mad that I couldn't eat all those acorns that I had in my dream. (BOLOKOFF, *the magician's voice, is heard offstage right.*)
BOLO (*offstage*): Hurry, Poko, we haven't much time.
RABBIT: There's that wicked magician again. You can bet he's up to some mischief. We'd better hide.
BLUEBIRD: Yes—do you remember how he set those dreadful traps in the forest?
RABBIT: Indeed I do—got caught in one of them!
REDBIRD: Yes. And he was shooting those magic darts of his at all the birds, too.
BLUEBIRD: Look out, here he comes! And he's got that silly little dwarf with him.
SQUIRREL: Run, hide, quickly.
REDBIRD: We'll meet here later. (*The animals hide again as the magician enters upstage right, followed at a distance by* POKO.)
BOLO: Hurry up, fool! Why must I tolerate your laziness? Don't you know we must hurry? We've only a fortnight left.
POKO: Yes, Master, I know, Master, but what can I do?
BOLO: What can you do? Well, you haven't found the child we need. I sent you out to find a little girl with blonde hair and blue eyes. I told you to capture her and bring her back to me. Well, where is she?
POKO: I tried to find her, truly I did, Master. I tried to persuade little Katrinka, the soldier's daughter, to follow me. I even tempted her with magic candy—but the minute she looked at it, she began to scream. Then

her mother ran out and hit me with a rolling pin. And the dog chased me up a tree. So you see, I have tried. Little girls just don't like me, I guess. And I can't say I blame 'em very much. (*He sits down disconsolately down right.*)

BOLO (*pacing back and forth*): I tell you, you've got to find that child. We have to get those gold pieces. And a little girl is the only one who can find them. Those gold pieces will give me all the power I need. If I find them we can keep the royal family under the enchantment.

POKO: But what if we don't find them in time.

BOLO: Then, my dear Poko, we're lost—both of us. I lose all my power. The royal family will return in a fortnight, and I shall lose control of the kingdom. So you see, it's the end of both of us if you don't find that child.

POKO: But how, sir—how can I?

BOLO: I said find her, and I don't know how! You find her, or I shall throw you into my deepest dungeon. (*He exits upstage right in rage.*)

POKO (*following*): Wait for me, Master, wait for me. (*Exit.*)

(*The* SQUIRREL *enters and calls to the other animals, who are offstage.*)

SQUIRREL: Come on, gang, they've left. It's all right to come out now.

REDBIRD: Oh, goodie! Now we can have our game of ball.

RABBIT: You stand over there, Bluebird. No, no, no, farther away. That's right.

BLUEBIRD (*throwing a large plastic ball*): Here—catch. (*Improvisation during the game of ball. After a few moments,* BABY REDBIRD *enters from stage right.*)

BABY REDBIRD: Mama, I tried to fly, I really did—truly I did! Except I fell—but I almost flew!

REDBIRD (*angrily*): How many times have I told you not to try to fly when I'm not in the nest? You're much too little to do it by yourself.

BABY REDBIRD: But it was such a beautiful day. And I used a big leaf for a parachute!

RABBIT: Tch, tch, tch. You're a bad boy, Reddie. Do you want to be eaten by the cat?

BABY REDBIRD: Oh no, of course I don't. But I didn't see the cat anywhere—and I did see such a nice juicy worm crawling on the ground, right underneath our nest.

REDBIRD: Nonsense! It couldn't have been a worm at this time of the day. It's only the early bird that catches the worm.

BABY REDBIRD: But, mama, it isn't so very late. I know it was a worm, and it looked so yummy, and I was so hungry! Don't spank me, please. (*During this speech* REDBIRD *pushes him offstage right, and the other animals continue their game.* STELLA *enters up left, stands watching.* RABBIT *misses the ball, and it rolls toward* STELLA.)

SQUIRREL: Oops! You missed it, butterfingers!

BLUEBIRD: Get it, Rabbit.

RABBIT (*running for ball*): Well, I almost caught it. (*He is about to*

APPENDIX D: THE LONG PLAY

pick it up when STELLA *hands it to him*) Well, hello, little girl. Who are you?

STELLA: I am Stella.

RABBIT: Umm, that's a pretty name. Sounds like a star.

STELLA: That's what it means—star.

RABBIT: You look worried about something, Stella. What's the matter?

STELLA: Oh I am, I'm in dreadful trouble. Could you help me?

SQUIRREL: That depends on what you want.

STELLA: I want to find my mother.

BLUEBIRD: What makes you think she's here?

STELLA: When I chased her away, I thought she came in the direction of the forest. I want to find her so badly.

RABBIT: You chased your mother away? That wasn't a very nice thing to do. You must be just like that little girl who came to the forest last year.

SQUIRREL: I hope not—because she was very cruel, and selfish too.

BLUEBIRD: As a matter of fact, you look sort of like her—only she was beautiful. And yet . . . yet . . .

RABBIT: You know—I think you are that little girl!

SQUIRREL: Yes, come to think of it, her name was Stella, too.

BLUEBIRD: She used to throw stones at all the woodfolk. She was cruel, and very proud.

STELLA (*ashamed*): Yes, I know. I was that little girl, and I did do all that. I was hateful and mean, but I've changed now—truly I have. Can't you help me?

RABBIT: Help you? Stella, do you remember that once I had a long and beautiful tail? Then you came along and stepped on it. Now there's nothing left but a little piece of fluff. And after you stepped on it, you had nerve enough to laugh when I hopped away. You certainly can't expect me to help you, Stella.

BLUEBIRD: You hit me with a stone while I was trying to get a worm for my breakfast. And then when you found I couldn't fly, you clipped my nice, long, beautiful wings. Before that, I could go high above the trees, where I could see the whole countryside. But not any more! You see, if you hadn't hurt me, I could have helped you.

STELLA: I'm sorry—I'm so sorry for what I did.

SQUIRREL: My mother had a fine store of nuts saved for the winter, and you came along with your friends and hid them where she couldn't find them. She died last winter because there wasn't enough to eat.

STELLA: Oh, how dreadful! Honestly, I didn't really mean to hurt any of you. Won't you please forgive me?

RABBIT: I'll forgive you, but that won't bring my tail back. You should think before you act. (*Exit.*)

BLUEBIRD: Being sorry won't give me new wings.

SQUIRREL: Or bring my mother back. Next time you'd better be more careful, Stella. (*Exit with* BLUEBIRD.)

(STELLA *crosses the stage and sits down left, head in hands, unnoticed by the four children who enter up right. She is soon asleep from exhaustion.*)

1st CHILD: Here we are—this is the place I told you about.
2nd CHILD: Oh, it's nice!
3rd CHILD: Here's a stone I can use in my collection.
4th CHILD: Look, isn't that a bird's nest?
1st CHILD: Oh, I think I just saw a rabbit.
2nd CHILD: Where did he go?
1st CHILD: Over there—you can't see him now.
3rd CHILD: Look, isn't it a beautiful stone? (*The others stand around and admire it.*)
4th CHILD: It's a shame we don't have a basket. We could go over there and get some of those flowers to take home to Mother.
1st CHILD: Maybe we could weave a basket out of the tall grass.
2nd CHILD: Let's look for some! (*As they look around stage, the* 3rd CHILD *stumbles over* STELLA, *who is asleep.*)
3rd CHILD (*calling to others*): Look, look what I found!
4th CHILD: What is it, an evil spirit?
1st CHILD: She's certainly ugly enough to be one.
2nd CHILD: Is she asleep?
3rd CHILD: Maybe she's enchanted.
4th CHILD: I'm afraid of her—let's go home.
1st CHILD: You're a crybaby.
2nd CHILD: I'm going to wake her up.
3rd CHILD: Oh don't! Don't!
4th CHILD: She might cast an evil spell on us. (STELLA *is wakened by the sound of the voices, and sits up.*)
1st CHILD: Look, she's awake!
2nd CHILD: Who are you?
3rd CHILD: Are you an evil spirit?
4th CHILD: Please don't cast a spell on us.
1st CHILD: Why don't you answer us, you ugly thing?
STELLA: My name's Stella. I know I'm ugly, but I'm not an evil spirit.
2nd CHILD: Well, what are you doing here? Beggars aren't allowed in this forest.
STELLA: I'm not a beggar—I'm just looking for my mother.
3rd CHILD: Your mother?
STELLA: Yes—you see, I sent her away, and I thought she came toward the forest, but now I can't find her any place. I'm just so tired, I guess I fell asleep.
4th CHILD: Well, you can't sleep here.
1st CHILD: You're so ugly, you must be an evil spirit.
2nd CHILD: You could sleep in our barn, but I'm afraid you'd scare the cows.
STELLA: Oh, please, won't you just tell me whether you've seen an old beggar woman pass this way?

3RD CHILD: Goodness, no! We haven't seen a beggar in months.

4TH CHILD (*looking at the sky*): Oh look, the sun's nearly set—it's almost dinnertime. I'm hungry too—let's go home!

1ST CHILD: Yes, let's.

2ND CHILD: Look, here come two of the palace guards. (*To* STELLA) Maybe they can help you. (*The children exit up left as the two guards enter up right.*)

STELLA (*running to the guards*): Kind sirs, the children said that you might be able to help me. I'm looking for my mother.

1ST GUARD: So you've lost your mother, eh, poor little beggar.

2ND GUARD: That's too bad, but if you take my advice you'd leave these parts as quickly as you came, child. The real king of our country disappeared ten years ago, and there's a wicked tyrant ruling in his place.

1ST GUARD: And he has no love for people like you. He has decreed that any beggar found near the palace grounds will be shot. And the gate is just a stone's throw from here, you know.

STELLA (*troubled*): Then if my mother went inside the gates of the royal city, she . . . she was shot? (*She begins to weep.*)

2ND GUARD: I'm afraid so, little one. But there's no need to give up hope.

STELLA: Oh won't you please let me go inside the city to look for her?

1ST GUARD: But a poor, ugly child like you would be killed once you stepped inside those gates.

2ND GUARD: If only our beloved king would return, he would help you find your mother.

STELLA: When will he come back?

1ST GUARD: There are rumors about that the whole royal family will return sometime in the near future. We are living on that hope.

2ND GUARD: The wise ones say that the return is to be heralded by a blast of trumpets from the sky.

1ST GUARD: And a clap of thunder, and darkness at noonday.

2ND GUARD: And when it comes, it'll be the most joyful day in the history of Karakov.

1ST GUARD: But till that time comes, we wouldn't dare to help you, child.

2ND GUARD: The best thing for you to do is to leave here while you still can.

1ST GUARD: Well, we must be on our way now, Boris. (*The magician and* POKO *have entered up right and are listening to the conversation.*)

2ND GUARD: Yes, His Majesty will storm again if we don't get back soon. (*Exit.*)

1ST GUARD: Goodbye, child. You better heed our warning. (*Exit.*)

STELLA: Oh dear, I don't know where to go now. Please, God, won't you help me to find my mother? I'm sorry for the way I've behaved. (*She sinks to her knees in tears down center.*)

BOLO (*to* POKO): There, Poko, you stupid fool, there's the child that will answer the qualifications. A lost child with no place to go—we can use her.

Poko: Maybe we can capture her.

Bolo: No maybe's about it. She's got blue eyes and blonde hair—just the one who can discover the coins. I'll make her my slave, then I can force her to do my bidding.

Poko: But how will you do that, Master?

Bolo: Go, fool, speak to her! Hold her attention. While I creep up behind her and throw the magic shawl over her shoulders. That will make her powerless. Hurry, fool! (Poko *creeps around in front of* Stella, *and in the following conversation imitates her every word*.)

Poko: Hello, little girl.

Stella: Who are you?

Poko: Who are you?

Stella: I asked you first.

Poko: I asked you first.

Stella: But you didn't.

Poko: But you didn't. (*Magician throws shawl over* Stella's *shoulders*.)

Bolo: There, Poko, I told you we could do it.

Stella (*frightened*): What have you done to me? I . . . I can't move.

Poko (*still imitating*): I can't move! Ha, ha. Ha, ha!

Bolo: What's your name?

Stella: My name is Stella. But who are you?

Poko (*bowing low*): He is my master.

Bolo: Silence, fool! I am Bolokoff, the Royal High Exalted Magician.

Poko: Exalted magician! Exalted magician!

Bolo: Poko, will you keep still! Stella! (*Makes mysterious gestures*) You are now under my power. And you will consent to be my slave.

Stella: Will you take me inside the city gates?

Bolo: If you do what I ask.

Stella: Well, what do you want of me?

Bobo: I need three magic gold pieces at once. They're hidden somewhere near the royal city walls. My book of magic states that a girl with blonde hair and blue eyes will find them for me. You are that girl, and you must find the gold in a fortnight, or all is lost.

Stella: But suppose I can't find the gold—what will happen then?

Bolo: I will beat you with a hundred stripes, and cast you into my deepest dungeon for the rest of your life.

Poko: For the rest of your life, ha, ha! Ha, ha!

Stella: I will try to find them, sir—I'll do my best.

Bolo (*starting off*): Come then, follow me. (Stella *and* Bolokoff *exit up right*.)

Poko (*imitating* Bolokoff): Follow me—Follow me! (*Exit*.)

Curtain

ACT III

It is afternoon in the garden just before the King's palace gate. There are bright colored flowerbeds (cut-outs) below the two high stone walls that stretch the full width of the stage, well up, about 5 feet in front of the sky drop. The great oaken gate of the Palace stands in the center section of the wall. A small tree stump is downstage, left, and bench, down right. (See Act 3 plans, page 193.) Other wood wings or foliage borders may be used if desired. As the curtain rises, STELLA *is hunting frantically for the golden coins.*

STELLA (*sitting right, on bench*): Oh dear, what'll I do? What'll I ever do? (*She starts to cry.*)
    (NINA, *the gardener's daughter, and* STEFAN, *his son, come through the gates carrying watering pot and trowel. They do not notice* STELLA.)
NINA: Hurry, Stefan, Father will be angry if he comes home and finds we haven't done the flowers yet.
STEFAN: Oh dear, I wish Father were a groom instead of a gardener. Horses are much more fun than flowers.
NINA: But flowers are so much sweeter, Stefan, and much more beautiful.
STEFAN: Have you ever seen Boris's black pony?
NINA: You know I have, silly. I rode to the fair on it.
STEFAN: Then all I can say is, you must have kept your eyes shut. It's just like a girl to . . .
NINA (*noticing* STELLA *for the first time*): Shh! Stefan, look! who's that?
STEFAN: I don't know. She doesn't belong here—I never saw her before.
NINA: She's crying! Let's ask her what's the matter.
STEFAN (*disgusted*): All right, go ahead if you want to, but I don't like this meddling in other people's business.
NINA: Well, I do. When people are in trouble, somebody's got to help them out. (*Crosses to* STELLA) Good afternoon.
STELLA (*tearfully*): Hello.
NINA: Are you a stranger here? I don't think I've ever seen you before.
STELLA: Yes, I am. My name's Stella—what's yours?
NINA: I'm Nina, and this is my brother, Stefan.
STELLA: Hello, Stefan.
STEFAN (*stiffly*): How do you do?
NINA: Our father is the royal gardener, and we live here, right inside the palace gates. I thought maybe we could help you, if you're in trouble.
STELLA: I wish you could, but I'm afraid nobody can help me. I've asked everybody I've met on the roads for two whole weeks now, but nobody seems to be able to tell me anything.

STEFAN (*boasting*): Well, maybe you asked just ordinary people. Now, you see, we live in the royal city, and we . . .

NINA: Oh Stefan, don't boast so. (*To* STELLA) Honestly, aren't boys terrible? So proud and conceited. (*To* STEFAN) I'm glad I'm a girl.

STELLA: It isn't only boys that are proud and conceited, Nina. I used to be like that too, once.

NINA: Oh, you couldn't have been—at least not like Stefan. But do please tell us what's troubling you. We'll try our best to help.

STELLA: Well, you see, in the first place, I have a very hard master. He's given me a terrible job to do, and only a fortnight to do it in. My time's up tonight, and if I don't succeed, I'll be thrown into a deep black dungeon and left there to die.

STEFAN: Hmm! You really are in trouble.

NINA: Goodness! It's dreadful and wicked for anyone to treat a little girl like that! What is this job you have to do for him?

STELLA: I have to find three gold coins—one white, one yellow, and one red. They have been hidden for centuries, somewhere outside the palace walls, and they're supposed to possess some great magic power.

NINA: I never heard about them before—did you, Stefan?

STEFAN: No—and what's more, if I had, they'd have been in my pocket by this time. I think your master's just given you an impossible task, so he can have an excuse to get rid of you.

NINA: Oh no, Stefan! No one could be as cruel as that.

STEFAN: You just haven't read much, Nina. History's full of cruel masters.

NINA: Dear me, how dreadful! I do wish there were some way we could help. Maybe you could just give up, Stella, and come home with us. We could hide you from your master, and then you could escape the punishment.

STELLA: That would never do. He has strange powers over me. I think he must be a sort of magician. I've tried to run away before, but something always stops me—as though he had cast invisible chains around my feet. And then before I know it, I'm drawn back to his horrible cave in the hills.

STEFAN: Well, it looks like there's no help for it—and I must say, it's too bad.

NINA (*brightly*): Wait! I know! I'll go in and ask Aunt Kretaka. She's the oldest servant in the place, and the wisest, too. She just might know something about the coins. Go home, Stefan, and tell Mother what's happened—and tell her we'll do the flowers later. (*To* STELLA) I'll be back soon, Stella—and don't give up.

STELLA: Thank you, Nina.

STEFAN: I'm certainly sorry for you, Stella. (*Boastfully*) Just call on me if you need any more help. (*Exit.*)

STELLA: Thank you, Stefan—thank you very much. (*She wanders about frantically. There is a strange whimpering sound from upstage right.*

APPENDIX D: THE LONG PLAY

Stella *turns and runs over to a large bush. She stops, startled by what she sees.*) Oh dear, you poor little mole! What's happened to you?

Mole (*off*): I'm caught, little girl—caught in one of the gardener's traps, and I can't move my hind foot at all. If I do, it'll come right off, and I'll have to walk three-legged for the rest of my life. Oooooh!

Stella: That wouldn't be very comfortable, Mr. Mole—you mustn't do that. Perhaps I can find a way to unlock the trap. I know how it feels to be caught, because I'm in the same fix. I can't bear to think of anyone else having to suffer as I am. Here now, move forward just a bit. Now lie quiet. There! It's coming! It's coming, I think! Now pull while I hold it apart.

Mole (*freeing himself and appearing*): Hooray! You did it! I'm free again! You've saved my life, little girl, that's what you've done.

Stella: Oh, I'm so glad I could help you.

Mole: So am I. It was a narrow escape, I'll tell you that. Please, tell me your name.

Stella: It's just—Stella.

Mole: That's a pretty name. I like it! I wish I could do something to help you now, Stella.

Stella: I wish you could too, but . . . I'm in such dreadful trouble, I'm afraid nobody can help me out.

Mole: Well, I'm not very bright, because I spend most of my time under the ground, you know—but I sure would be glad to try. Tell me about it.

Stella: Well, my master has set a very difficult task for me to do, and only given me two weeks to do it in. My time is up at sundown today. I have to find three golden coins for him. His magic book says they've been buried somewhere near the palace walls, but nobody has ever found them.

Mole: Wait, Stella—wait a minute! I'm trying to remember something. (*The* Mole *makes strange circles about the ground before the gate.*) Let's see, I went under here, and around here, and. . . .

Stella: What in the world are you doing?

Mole: Trying to remember what path I took last night, when I came out of the royal city under the palace gates.

Stella: Under the gates—you mean through the gates, don't you?

Mole: No, no, Stella. I told you before, I spend most of my time under ground. That's the way moles travel—it's faster, and much more private that way. And at times like this, it's very useful.

Stella: You mean . . . you can help me. . . .

Mole: There! (*He points to a place behind the tree stump*) It was there I saw it, just behind the base of that tree—about a foot under.

Stella: What? What did you see? I don't understand.

Mole: An old metal box. I bumped my head on it, in fact. Right here . . . feel the lump? (Stella *feels his head.*)

Stella: Goodness, it's a big one.

Mole: I'll tell you, Stella, I'll bet that box holds the gold coins you're looking for. It was covered with mold and rust—must have been there for hundreds of years.

Stella: Oh let's dig, then, let's dig quickly. (*She stops suddenly*) But what'll we dig with? I haven't anything, and there isn't time for me to run to the village for a spade.

Mole: There's no need to! You forget—digging's a mole's job.

Stella: Of course—I did forget! How lucky I am to have found you, Mr. Mole. (Mole *starts to dig as* Stella *watches. A tired, sick beggar comes in up right, and looks with interest as he rests beside the gate.*)

Mole: Must be six inches now—must be getting pretty close.

Stella: Oh dear, I do hope you've got the right place.

Mole: Stella, wait! I've got it! It's hard and it's square! Yep, here it is! (*He pulls out the box and hands it to her. It has been placed on floor back of stump.*)

Stella: I'm almost afraid to open it.

Mole: You might as well.

Stella (*lifting the lid*): Look, little mole, look! it is—it's the coins I've been hunting for! Three gold coins—one white, one yellow, one red! How can I ever thank you? You've paid me back a hundred times now for getting you out of the trap.

Mole: Nonsense, Stella! I haven't done anything. You see I just live by that old saying, "One good turn deserves another"—that's all. Well, I must be getting back to my little family now. Goodbye, and good luck! You'd better take those gold pieces to your master!

Stella: Oh yes, I will—I'll run all the way. (*As she looks at the coins, she whispers, "Thank you, God, thank you." As she is about to run off, up right, past the beggar, he calls to her.*)

Beggar: Little girl.

Stella (*looking back*): Did you speak to me, sir?

Beggar: Yes, I did. Won't you have mercy upon a tired, sick man? I'm dying of hunger. Can't you give me a few coins, please? Please have pity!

Stella: I'm so sorry for you, sir. I wish I could help you. But I only have these three gold pieces, and if I don't take them to my master before sundown, I will be beaten to death.

Beggar: Just one, then! Couldn't you spare just one of your coins? I've had neither food nor drink for three days, and I am ill—very ill, indeed.

Stella (*after a moment's pause, realizing that she must help the poor man, opens the box and hands him the coins*): Here, sir, take them all. Your need is greater than mine. (*As she hands him the coins, there is a great crash of thunder, and the stage is in complete darkness. Strange crashing music blends into music that is regal and peaceful. There is the sound of a trumpet—first far off, and then closer. The lights dim on again, and the stage is empty except for the beggar, who is now standing tall and*

APPENDIX D: THE LONG PLAY

straight, as though great strength had come back to him. The gates swing open, and the two soldiers, accompanied by a lady-in-waiting come through, talking excitedly.)

1st Soldier: It's the prophecy come true.

2nd Soldier: The crash of thunder! Darkness at noon!

Lady: And the heavenly sound of a trumpet, just as the story said. (*Six villagers enter, three from each side of stage, they gather about the gate.*)

1st Villager: It was as black as if it were night.

2nd Villager: And thunder, like a summer storm.

3rd Villager: That was to be the sign, remember—the sign of their return.

4th Villager: Rumor has it that at the sound of the trumpet, our own King and Queen and Princess will return to us.

5th Villager: Do you suppose they're somewhere nearby in hiding?

6th Villager: Do you think they will come at once? (*As the villagers have gathered, the* Old Woman *too has slipped in from stage right, to stand beside the beggar, who now reaches for her hand.*)

Page (*running through the gate*): News from the Royal Bedchamber, friends. The tyrant Olensky has been stricken. It is said that he lies dying. (*He goes through crowd and off stage, shouting*) "Olensky is dying! The tyrant's rule is over!"

1st Soldier: There, there! What did I tell you? It's the prophecy.

2nd Soldier: It's all coming true! Our own royal family must be near at hand.

Lady: I would give my life to see our dear Queen, and that precious little Princess again.

1st Soldier: Are you sure you would recognize the little Princess, Sonia?

2nd Soldier: She was nothing but a wee babe when our dear Queen was driven out of the palace by Bolokoff.

Lady: I tell you, I'd know that beautiful little face anywhere. (Stella *has entered right, frightened, trying to discover the cause of the excitement. She is now more beautiful than ever.*)

1st Soldier: Look—look at that child!

2nd Soldier: Could it be . . . ?

Lady: It is! It's the little Princess herself. (*She kneels at* Stella's *feet*) Dear Princess, thank God you have come back to us.

1st Soldier (*kneeling*): Your Royal Highness.

2nd Soldier (*also kneeling*): Welcome to Karakov, Your Highness.

Stella (*drawing back pathetically*): Oh please, please don't make fun of me. I'm no princess—I am the child of a poor beggar woman. I just came into the crowd to look for my mother.

2nd Soldier: Indeed, we too are looking for your holy mother, our good Queen.

1st Soldier: And your father, our rightful King. They should return at any moment now, Your Highness.

LADY: You are still so beautiful, my child—as lovely as on that day ten years ago, when I sat beside your cradle for the last time. I can scarcely believe my eyes.

STELLA (*hiding her face*): You're mocking me, all of you. I know I'm ugly. It was my own punishment, because—oh dear!

1ST SOLDIER: Nay, little Princess, Sonia is right. You are more beautiful than on that day ten years ago, when we brought our gifts to your cradle.

2ND SOLDIER: Come, Your Highness, see for yourself. (*He holds up his shield and as* STELLA *looks she is astonished at her beauty, which has returned. There is a strange sound of the music of the Spirit of the Well, and she hears the voice of the Spirit as if from a great distance.*)

SPIRIT (*offstage*): Only when the heart is good and pure and kindly can the face be beautiful. It's never too late. Beauty and happiness will come back to you, Stella.

STELLA: I can't believe it. I simply can't believe it! Something very strange has happened to me.

2ND SOLDIER: And to us, Your Highness. For the prophecy which we hardly dared believe till now, has been fulfilled.

STELLA: But my mother . . . ? I don't understand? My mother was a beggar, and poor!

1ST SOLDIER: Because she was under the spell of Bolokoff, the evil magician who drove her forth.

STELLA (*to herself*): Bolokoff! My master! The very same! (*To others*) Oh if I could only find her! I so want to ask her forgiveness. I . . . (*She suddenly sees the* OLD WOMAN *in crowd and rushes to her*) There . . . there she is now. Oh dearest Mother, can you ever forgive me? I was proud and cruel, but I have learned my lesson. (STELLA *kneels at Mother's feet*) Please, please forgive me. (THE OLD WOMAN *is silent and* STELLA *lifts her head to the beggar to whom she gave the gold*) Please, sir, beg my mother to speak to me. I tried to help you, sir. Please tell her that my heart is kind! (*She bows her head again in a flood of tears.*)

OLD WOMAN (*dropping her cloak, displays a queen's robes*): Rise, my child, with my forgiveness. You have indeed done well. Rise, and take your father's hand.

STELLA (*looking up breathlessly*): My father?

OLD WOMAN: It was he to whom you gave the magic coins.

BEGGAR: And it is your mother's royal feet that you have washed with your tears. (*There are murmurs of pleasure from all the crowd. Some kneel, some cannot refrain from shouting, "The King and Queen!" . . . "Your Majesty!" . . . "They have come back" . . . "Long live our good rulers!"*)

STELLA: It's like a dream—or like the perfect ending of a fairy story, Mother. At least, it would be perfect, if only . . .

BEGGAR: If only what, my child?

STELLA: Well, you see, for many years Mother Olga and Papa Carl and Elena have been so good to me—and Jan . . . I promised Jan that one day I'd come back to him. And now . . .

JAN (*stealing out from the crowd, which has been watching, kneels*): Jan is here, Your Highness.

STELLA: Oh, Jan, I'm so glad and so happy! (*To the Queen*) Please, Mother, may I have one wish granted now—just one?

OLD WOMAN (*smiling*): I think the Princess of Karakov might be permitted a single wish, don't you, my dear? (*She turns to the* KING.) What is it, Stella?

STELLA: May I please have Jan and Elena and Mother Olga and Papa Carl come live here in the royal city with us?

OLD WOMAN: Indeed you may. No one in the whole kingdom has a better right to a place in our palace than they.

PAGE (*running through*): More news, friends! The tyrant is dead! Long live the King and Queen!

ALL: The King and Queen!

POKO (*running in, wild with joy*): I'm free too! Old Bolokoff has gone up in the smoke of his own fire. Long live the royal family of Karakov!

(*Others take up cries again as the curtain falls.*)

Production Notes

Since no definite time or locale is indicated in the original story, the choice rests with the group producing the play. Some of the names of characters suggest a Slavic background, and the plot itself seems to concern a mythical, medieval kingdom in Central to Eastern Europe. These ideas form the basis of the present design plan.

Setting. The description of the setting at the beginning of each act assumes the use of cyclorama, or draped, stage, with a permanent blue sky drop against the upstage wall. Since all scenes take place out of doors, the upstage section of the "cyc" will always be drawn to reveal the sky drop. "Legs" or screen-type wood wing pieces, may be used with foliage teasers, to further suggest an outdoor set. The necessary units to be constructed are:

Act I

1. A corner of the woodcutter's cottage, which includes the doorway.
2. The wall of the well, circular or hexagonal in shape, about 28 inches high and 4 feet in diameter. (The well area should not be completely enclosed; the upstage portion must be left open to facilitate the business of the Spirit.)
3. Two or three low bush or rock cutouts, to serve as upstage ground rows.

ACT II

1. One or two tree cutouts, which can be suspended from the teaser battens, to give the impression of a forest.
2. Several tree stump or single rock silhouettes. (The ground rows used upstage in Act I can be employed in a different combination.)

ACT III
1. A six-foot wall, stretching across the full width of the stage well up, the center of which contains a double gate about five feet wide.
2. Two flower bed cutouts, which stand before the two portions of the wall to the right and left of the gate.
3. A two-step platform, which is placed center, directly below the gate.
4. A tree stump to conceal the box of coins, in the downstage left area. (The cutout from Act II can be used.)

Costumes. The medieval peasant style provides the basic pattern for the costumes of Stella, Papa Carl and his family, the children, and the other peasants in Act III. The dress of the men and women of high estate might follow the designs for the nobility, suggested in Chapter 11. The animal costumes, and those of the magician and his servant, give free rein to the creative imagination; no limitations are set by the style of the period. The child's sleeping suit, dyed, provides an excellent base for the costume of the mole, rabbit, or squirrel. An appropriate and interesting headdress and tail will define the character. The most significant features of the birds' costumes are the headdresses and the wings. There should be unity of color and pattern in the costumes of Bolokoff and Poko, who often appear together. The design for Poko should stress the comedy aspect of the character.

Lighting. Three important acting areas should be accented:
1. Down right—incident: the action around the well in Act I.
2. Down left—incidents: business at doorway in Act I, Stella's scene with children and animals in Act II, business of finding the coins in Act III.
3. Up center—incidents: Jan's goodbye to Stella in Act I, climactic scene at gateway in Act III.

These areas should all be covered by special spotlights controlled on separate circuits. The dimming of the rest of the stage at important moments will intensify the interest in a particular spotlighted area.

The general illumination, which can be provided by strips or additional spots, should include two sets of light: (1) the daylight color, for certain parts of all scenes; (2) the blue color, to suggest the coming of evening in the latter part of Act I, and the early morning in the first part of Act II.

The play requires two special effects: (1) the green light (flood or spot), placed in the well to stress the entrance of the Spirit: (2) sudden flashes of lightning in Act III. (This effect can be achieved by pulling the main switch on the board at irregular intervals.

Sound. Child of the Sky offers an excellent opportunity for the use of creative background music.[2] An original motif that represents Stella, the

[2] For information regarding an original background musical score for *Child of the Sky* (in manuscript), apply to Director, Children's Theatre Association, Baltimore, Maryland 21212.

lost princess, can be used effectively at many moments throughout the play; its development toward the climax will stress the exultation of the final curtain and add unity to the whole production. The entrance of the Spirit of the Well is far more effective if covered by her own musical theme. Repetition of this musical theme in Act III, when Stella hears the Spirit's words again, will create the illusion of her presence. Several long pantomime sequences will be more compelling when the action is backed by appropriate mood music (i.e., the waking of the animals in the early morning, at the opening of Act II). A metal sheet, placed offstage, can be used to produce the effect of thunder. Two strips of wood should be nailed to the top and bottom edges of a piece of galvanized steel, measuring about 2' x 4'. A screw eye placed in the top of wood will serve to support the sheet backstage. The operator can use the bottom wooden strip as a handle. If the metal is shaken in irregular rhythms, it will make a sound resembling thunder in the distance.

Appendix E:
YOUTH SPEAKS FOR ITSELF

Prepared by alumni of the Children's Theatre Association, Baltimore; Editorial Committee: Christopher Parsons, Joseph Patterson, and Elissa Kaplan.

We're growing up now! We've made it to college! The business of starting on one's life work seems only minutes away! All that we have gathered in thoughts, feelings, and changing philosophies must soon be blended and shaped into a reliable rudder to steer a straight and, we hope, a safe and profitable course! Strangely enough, agreement exists among members of this Editorial Committee, which individually is temperamentally far apart, that it has shared the effects of certain profoundly driving development forces that do, and shall, both point the way and motivate the human reactions of every one of us. These forces sprang from the stimulating, exciting, often exhausting and disturbing years we have spent in creative dramatics workshops at the Children's Theatre Association in Baltimore. For some of us the years are nine or ten, for some, as few as five or six; for all they were important growing-up years. As one of our colleagues has so aptly described them, "years when ideas and ideals are being shaped and when we're all inclined to be more than a little selfish."

Some of us have had a desperate urge, for a long time, to climb on the proverbial soapbox and shout a special message to the blasé or incredulous audience of peers with which we are surrounded most of the time! We have wanted a chance to tell other teenagers, and the people who teach them, the exciting story of thousands of us, and what we feel the influence of the creative dramatics experience has been in our lives.

We asked for a chance to speak in the Second Edition of Isabel Burger's book (we who know and love her call her "Dearie"). It was granted and we are grateful. We wanted to be heard NOW, because we believe that now, more than ever before, young people and teachers need to know about the benefits we've found in creative drama. There are teachers who think that this kind of experience is only for the elementary school. Well, we disagree! And we hope that by putting down some of the dramatic situations that we have found exciting and challenging, we may be able to change their minds. We're not great writers; we don't pretend to be! But we are enthusiastic believers; and we want to help other young people like us! That's the only justification we can claim for asking for a few pages in this book, which we realize is largely meant for teachers. Just to prove that there was another generation of young people, who were part of CTA in 1941, who share our opinions whole-heartedly, we have asked permission to quote from several alumni letters that were received during CTA's twentieth anniversary celebration in 1963. They all focus on four or five basic philosophies and needs that we also believe: 1) human understanding and compassion; 2) acceptance of one's self; 3) the building of security and self-confidence through a sense of satisfaction in accomplishment; 4) the joy of service and sharing in a worthwhile task.

CHARTER MEMBERS SPEAK

The following quotations are from letters from charter members of CTA (membership 1941–43). They are now men and women twenty-eight to thirty-five years of age.

"CTA has been a cornerstone in the growing and learning process—of my life and work. Knowing and understanding people vicariously through the many dramatic play exercises was both an educational and a pleasant experience."

"It created a desire in me to value people for their achievement through contribution to society and not their 'social status.'"

"For ten years the hours . . . were the most rewarding ones I have ever spent . . . (when) I went away to college . . . I realized the deep values that had been implanted from those simple situations which we acted out . . . all these instilled in us a compassion for our fellow human beings, a confidence in ourselves, and the ability to make a decision. With each new role that I have assumed as an adult, from camp director, to my present one of wife and mother, these values have repeatedly presented themselves."

"The lessons we learned in our weekly classes were truly a 'child's rehearsal for his role as a grown-up.' Here we learned to both give vent to and control our emotion. I believe that CTA experiences, second only to my faith in God, were a tremendous help to me when I was suddenly left to be father as well as mother to two wee children."

"As a shy, withdrawn child, I found a place where I could express my emotions, where I could be myself. My experience helped me to communicate with others. . . . I am grateful for the feeling of gladness one senses in contributing one's time and energy to a 'cause' one loves."

"I gained at CTA classes a self assurance that has helped me to overcome many difficulties, and to appreciate myself and others and acquire a deeper understanding of people."

"CTA has meant . . . understanding myself and others, the ability to communicate with all kinds of people on many levels, self-confidence, and self-respect."

"More than aiding in expressing my own ideas and emotions, more than a deepening of my own imagination, CTA classes gave me an awareness that other people had thoughts and feelings, and their own private world of hopes and dreams. Perhaps the word is tolerance, a tolerance of what others were and wanted to be."

"In CTA I have come to know the great personal satisfaction that can be found in accomplishment. I have discovered what it means to be a part of something that is of real importance. CTA helps one understand and appreciate life and our fellow-man. To understand others, even in part, is to have compassion. . . . I can never again find what I have found in CTA but I will never lose it."

"Being a charter member of CTA was the most important possession of my youth. Whatever sense of beauty and of sympathy for others I may have developed over the years I discovered first with the help of Isabel Burger and the extraordinary students she attracted to her classes. . . . most important, the predominantly emotional climate in class and on stage probably offered us the best chance, at the most formative time of our lives, to help each other learn and grow. . . . It often took time to find out what we had acquired. The realization may only have come to some of us when we walked in the midst of hopelessly enslaved peoples in East Berlin, or as we took time out to cheer up a hospitalized friend at Christmastide, or, for all of us, as we read *Peter Pan* to a little child for the first time."

VALUES OF CREATIVE DRAMATICS

Several of us have tried to analyze our own reasons for believing in the values of creative dramatics. May they be sufficiently convincing to persuade teachers and administrators to include this kind of course as "required" rather than "elective."

"Creative dramatics has helped to shape my entire life. Perhaps it can best be summed up in four words:

1. AWARENESS —The experience has made me aware, not only of myself but also of others—of those I know well—of those I see on the street. I am now aware that my way of acting and reacting is not the only way; that the ways of others are as justified, meaningful and important as mine.

APPENDIX E: YOUTH SPEAKS FOR ITSELF

2. INTEREST —I am not only *aware* of my fellow man—I am *interested* in him. I am interested not only in how and why he is what he is, but interested in discovering how I can help him realize his full potential and the full meaning of life.
3. PERCEPTION—This quality helps deepen my interest in men—the ability to sense what is right or wrong without being told—to know when a friend or stranger needs help or a comforting word —to look inside and see what and why a person IS.
4. CARING —I have learned to be truly concerned with what happens, to me—to my friends, to the world. I care that I have been taught awareness, interest, perception and I am thankful that others may also have this chance."

"By experiencing, in CTA workshop, many dramatic situations with which I may be faced in later life, I have acquired many qualities which are necessary to a successful adult life. Perhaps the most important of these is a highly developed awareness. Success in life surely depends upon the degree to which one can communicate with others in a myriad of real-life circumstances. Awareness is essential to sensitivity; it helps one recognize other people's needs and also excuse their individual eccentricities. I have also, through my CTA experiences, developed a striving for perfection. Nothing is worth doing unless it is done as perfectly as we can do it! The ability to concentrate and express emotion freely but with control and direction has greatly increased for me. I attribute this entirely to the opportunities to shut out present environment, and extraneous thoughts and feelings, in order to become another person in a different environment. Because all of these attributes are so essential to a happy, contributive adulthood, I feel that creative play acting, according to our CTA methods, is an important supplement to the developmental forces of home and school."

"When one attempts to analyze and evaluate the CTA experience, it is difficult to put into words. My four years have been filled with enjoyment, excitement and above all a sense of belonging. From the very first time when I walked into the Carriage House, for my first rehearsal of *Tom Sawyer* in which I played Joe Harper, I felt that I was needed and wanted. I could also sense a remarkable enthusiasm; everyone connected with the play wanted to do a 'perfect' job. They wanted to do their best and they expected me to do mine. I was swept along with this inspirational, workmanlike attitude which is the spirit of CTA. I think it can be stated simply that *everyone tries*, and *everyone cares*. Even the very youngest members seem to concentrate and give their best efforts. Although everyone in the program is relaxed, happy in his job, and has a variety of interests, the CTA project makes an important contribution to his life, because it represents a worthwhile endeavor to which he can contribute. The knowledge that one has helped create a successful artistic program of high quality brings real joy and satisfaction."

"When I first entered CTA, I was, to my knowledge, a typical teen-ager; in reality, completely centered in myself. Immediately I was thrown into a situation which I could neither comprehend nor modify: that situation in which one is unafraid to care. From a mentor who cared so much, I slowly forgot my self-limiting fears and learned to accept, relate to and even appreciate others.

"In reflecting, I realize that this feat was accomplished subtly through classes where Isabel Burger nurtured us with the importance of being, and then communicating, whatever character we assumed—whether it was groping for a way to apologize to a dying friend for a lifetime of negligence or bubbling with excitement over a surprise party.

"From this knowledge comes a freedom and a discipline which have allowed me to become sensitive to, and understanding of, people, their thoughts, feelings and innermost desires. In learning to give of myself, I have learned to receive from others—and thus, to love. As I leave CTA, secure in my new found faith, I can face an insecure world with courage and confidence in the strength of CTA, a binding force which molds, changes and influences one to accept responsibility to self and others."

"One finds it extremely difficult to analyze, evaluate and put into words the benefits derived from CTA's Teen-age Workshop; because each class or work session represents a new flowering and unfolding of one's way of life, it seems impossible to make a check-list of values in chronological order.

"Specifically, the creative drama experience, the chance to put one's self in another's place, to react as he would to a given situation, provides many welcome opportunities to grow in understanding of one's self and one's friends and neighbors. As we gain insight, through developing sensitivity and awareness, we make new and important discoveries about people and the world about us which help to make our life relationships much more significant and meaningful. This sensitivity in response to others is perhaps the greatest attribute one can possess.

"Generally speaking, a creative drama program like CTA, with its varied group activities, offers a special chance, so lacking in many of our experiences today. We, the teen-agers, become involved deeply in all facets of the project. We know that we are directly responsible for 'both sides of the footlights' at production time—for helping with publicity, or the 'house' or putting costumes away if there is work to be done in these areas. Our reward is that soul-satisfying sensation of being a necesary part of a worthwhile goal; one experiences no better feeling than that which comes from doing something important, and seeing the efforts take shape in tangible form. Young people today desperately need to feel that they can contribute something real to the world—that they are considered responsible individuals. In a skillfully handled creative drama project, these longed-for satisfactions can be realized; one can feel, at last, that

APPENDIX E: YOUTH SPEAKS FOR ITSELF   221

one's opinions and abilities are accepted for what they are, and not qualified or discounted because of age."

"The most profound influence which can emanate from such a teen-age creative drama project comes from the personal strength of the leadership. In 'Dearie' at CTA, many of us have found a religious leader, a teacher, a mother, and above all, an understanding friend. This kind of friendship is inspiring, demanding, and challenging! Only the best one has to give is acceptable; and this kind of attitude is splendidly contagious. The receiver of such friendships goes out into the world expecting to give his best and is only satisfied to receive the best. How great is the need for this philosophy in today's world where the casual, blasé, indifferent if not indolent attitude is so prevalent.

CTA or any similar project for teen-agers can be a source of inspiration, support, understanding, and warm friendship; it can be a school where one's courses all lead to the same diploma—in the joy of full self-realization through selfless giving and creative interaction."

"One who has participated for a dozen years in such a creative drama project as CTA in Baltimore, honestly feels, as he looks back from his 'college outpost' that whatever he is can be largely attributed to this creative group experience. Such a project is so much more than just a succession of classes. It represents a place where one can be himself without fear or pretense—a place where everyone is nourished by a warm sense of belonging, sharing, believing.

"The two words that seem to state the core of the 'creative drama' experience are AWARENESS and COMMITMENT. One first becomes aware of one's self, and then in quick succession, gains a deeper awareness of others. To be aware is to understand, to experience, to feel, to live. The process of understanding one's self is sometimes a frightening experience, sometimes embarrassing, but always it is revealing. Commitment means the total giving of one's self, the dedication of all one has, to a worthy humanitarian cause. This lesson, once learned, carries over into all aspects of one's daily life and, when practiced, returns the greatest benefits and rewards. To be committed is to care—and caring is what makes life worthwhile."

EXERCISE MATERIAL

The following exercises represent only a few of those experiences that the members of the editorial committee feel have contributed so much to our "growing-up" years. From the materials submitted, we have selected those that we believe will be most stimulating and challenging for use with groups of young people between the ages of fourteen and twenty. It seemed more practical not to give credit to a particular individual for any of the following contributions; we agreed that we would all want it that way!

1. The following scene can be played in pantomime or in dialogue. If it is done in pantomime several people could try it at the same time. Each would be assigned a certain part of the room and imagine the presence of the invalid in the hospital. If dialogue is used, it should be done with two people, the visitor and the invalid.

Situation: You are a young person who has been reared in an orphanage, knowing almost nothing of your background. Life has been hard; people have been *taking*, not *giving*. One day a lawyer sends a request to you to visit someone who is dying in a nearby hospital. He says that this individual is your sister (or brother) to whom life has been kinder than it has to you. Now, at the end, she wants to find you and ask your forgiveness for deserting you during your childhood. As you enter the hospital room you are filled with bitterness and hate, which is increased by the vision of flowers and luxurious gifts with which the room overflows. Then . . . suddenly your eye is caught and held by a picture of this sister's husband, on the table. He is aristocratic, but hard, unfeeling, authoritarian even in the set of his shoulders. He is the reason for her silence; he has stood between you; she was helplessly caught in his wealth and his social obligations. Poor thing! Your sister is sleeping, restlessly, in pain. Scribble a note . . . telling her that you understand, you forgive, you will return, and leave it standing before the picture . . . Quietly exit. (If played in dialogue, the sister awakens, calls you weakly, a short dialogue follows . . .)

2. To discover, in a single line, how differently three people can feel about life, is interesting. The line is this: "What a wonderful world this is." It is spoken as one stands out of doors, observing a magnificent sunset. The three individuals are:

1. A bitter, disillusioned pessimist, middle-aged.
2. A young person, who has recently become engaged to be married.
3. A middle-aged person, who has led a happy, full life, and has deep faith, who has just been told that he has only four more weeks to live.

3. The following exercise appealed, perhaps, because it helps one understand human relationships through positions and movement in space. Six of us were asked, one at a time, to move into a designated space that was a room, any room, anywhere. There was no motivation for the position we took, or the character's movement. We must simply be aware of the space and position ourselves to make a pleasing and balanced picture.

This was then repeated; but we must justify our own positions, and also relate in some way to the others. Positions remained static as one after another entered the scene; there could be a little shifting if an imbalance seemed to occur and by small movement this could be remedied.

The third time, the same thing was repeated, but one was asked to be-

APPENDIX E: YOUTH SPEAKS FOR ITSELF   223

gin dialogue, and gradually we made an effort to weave a story, still maintaining the characters we had assumed, motivating honestly any crosses or stage business, and attempting to keep the stage picture balanced and pleasing at all times.

4. This rhythm exercise in 4/4 time has always seemed very real and impressive. You are watching a boat pull away from the dock. On its deck stands a loved one from whom you must be separated for a long, long time.

```
11111111  (run to the edge of the dock)
1111      (move to look at the far end of the deck)
1111      (come back to look at the other end)
1---      (stop, as you discover her there waving)
1111      (wave, in return)
11--      (wave and then stop suddenly as you realize the ship is pulling out)
1---      (drop hand to side . . . as ship moves farther away)
1-1-      (turn away and drop head in sorrow, as full meaning of separation
           comes over you)
```

5. *Individual Pantomime, Motivated by Music.* Music, with a wide range of moods, is played; something unfamiliar and, if possible, spontaneously created is desirable. You are asked to listen, and to let the music suggest an object, or a place, or a dramatic situation in which you find yourself. When you are ready, you build in pantomime your own scene, with the music as background, heightening your action and mood changes.

6. *Group Dialogue.* A group of people are waiting for a bus; they may be sitting, standing, pacing. Each has his own individual reason for catching this special bus. Someone rushes into the scene to say that someone has been hurt. He asks for help in getting this person to safety. Do you offer help? Do you give an excuse? Do you pretend indifference?

7. Imagine yourself walking down the street in an unfamiliar town. Suddenly, seeing a crowd looking up, you do the same. There is a man walking along the window ledge of a high building about to jump. Three endings are possible from which you are to choose one:

   a. He will jump off and be killed.
   b. He will be persuaded to come in by a friend, and will not jump.
   c. He will jump off and into a trampoline, which is hidden by the crowd, and come bouncing up again, waving.

In the last case he is a part of an advertising stunt. Although this may seem simple, it is rather demanding because there are so many different reactions possible, depending upon your own characteristics and your potential relationships with the man, the town, your job, etc.

8. Take the single word: THERE! Think about it until you have developed a little scene that could be played in pantomime beginning with or leading up to the use of this one word.

9. Come into a half-dark room in your own house. Go to the light

switch and turn on the light. See one of the following individuals and react as you would to his presence:

  a. A member of your family with whom you've had a serious quarrel
  b. A business associate whom you have been trying to avoid
  c. A friend whom you love, but from whom you have purposely separated yourself for the past six months
  d. A stranger who has no right to be here; he is obviously in hiding and looks dangerous.

10. This exercise is a study of growing anger. You come home from a trip a day early; your younger sister, who lives with you and whom you have brought up, does not expect you until tomorrow. As you enter the house, you see lying on the couch a familiar cigarette case. It belongs to a worthless friend of your sister's whom she has promised you she will never see again. She has broken the promise and thinks that she will never be found out. When you realize the full impact, you are disillusioned and disappointed but basically angry. Then, as you hear the two voices, laughing over some foolish remark, your anger reaches its peak. Rush through the door, to order him out!

11. You live in a small cabin in an area subject to flash floods. You have always feared that tragic moment when all will be destroyed but so far it has never come. It has now been raining for six days and nights; the river has risen alarmingly. Your young husband has insisted upon staying with the gang that is trying to save the bridge and the dam. He has promised that he will come home when his shift is over. He is now two hours late and you are pacing up and down, anxiously. From time to time go to the window and look out into the storm-torn night. Suddenly, you hear the sound of steps . . . then a door opens . . . and above the wind, your name is called. "Thank goodness! He is home and safe!" Rush off to meet him.

12. You are standing or pacing restlessly outside your father's study. You have had trouble with the car which you borrowed last night when you shouldn't have. You had to have it towed to a garage . . . The time has come when you must make a clean breast of the affair. But how can you face him? What will you say? Finally get up the courage to go in—or give up and go running off because you can't face the ordeal.

13. Try to relate yourself to a single article—a ring. Decide that you must get rid of it. Walk along an old dock at night and carefully drop the ring into the water. It is important to know who you are, why you want to get rid of the ring, and how you feel afterward. The thought patterns should come through clearly and tell this story.

Editorial Committee, YOUTH SPEAKS FOR ITSELF
Christopher Parsons, University of Carolina
Joseph Patterson, American University
Elissa Kaplan, George Washington University

AUTHOR'S POSTSCRIPT

The author has been granted permission to add a postscript to what, in her opinion, is one of the most significant and revealing parts of this text. To read on the printed page what young people themselves feel about experiences in creative drama, to know what a deep and lasting influence for good it has exerted in their lives, is to suddenly be assured that one's whole life objective has not been in vain and that the labors of thirty-odd years have reaped rich rewards. This is a rare experience granted to few. To our CTA young people I am deeply grateful!

But these pages carry a message far more significant than mere personal gratification. This is a poignant message to educators the world over. These young people are indirectly condemning us who teach, and guiding us with good advice at the same time. They are reminding us of a sin of omission of which most of us are really aware, but about which we have done little. They are saying, frankly, that their potential for self-understanding is usually neglected and underestimated. While we busy ourselves pushing them to learn about the Gold Rush, the Dark Ages, or the dates of bygone wars, we casually ignore a study of human motives and the inner life of man. We seem afraid of encouraging children to face and analyze their own personal concerns, as though this had nothing to do with the subject of education. . . . And yet, if we really made the effort to question some of our younger people, we would find most of them troubled by one fear or another, one doubt or another! Most of them harbor some grievances and attitudes of insecurity or hostility. Surely it is our responsibility, as teachers, to provide them with the kind of experiences that help them to understand and accept themselves. Until a child can regard himself as someone who is worthy even if he is not perfect, and accept the limitations that are his lot without blaming himself or others about him, he cannot use his own capacities to think or feel, nor can he enter into friendly and rewarding relationships with others. Many of the statements in this chapter that our young people have written, and the dramatic situations that they have suggested for use with teen-age creative drama groups, point to their obvious need for, and joy in, self-realization and self-acceptance, which will lead them to loving acceptance and concern for their fellowmen. Let us heed their wise words and not forget, in our hurried curriculum planning, that "the proper study of mankind is man."[1]

[1] Alexander Pope, *An Essay on Man,* Ep. 11, *The Best of Pope,* ed. George Sherburn (rev. ed., New York: The Ronald Press Co., 1940).

Bibliography

Adix, La Vern. *Theatre Scenecraft—For the Backstage Technician and Artist.* Anchorage, Ky.: Children's Theatre Press, 1956.
Allstrom, Elizabeth. *Let's Play a Story.* New York: Friendship Press, 1957.
Anderson, Virgil A. *Training the Speaking Voice.* 2d ed. New York: Oxford University Press, 1961.
Andrews, Gladys. *Creative Rhythmic Movement for Children.* Englewood Cliffs, N.J.: Prentice-Hall, Inc., 1954.
Bridge, William H. *Actor in the Making—A Handbook on Improvisation and Other Techniques of Development.* Magnolia, Mass.: Expression Co., 1936.
Brown, Corinne. *Creative Drama in the Lower School.* New York: Appleton-Century-Crofts, Inc., 1929.
Chaplin, Dora P. *Children and Religion.* Rev. ed. New York: Charles Scribner's Sons, 1961.
Chorpenning, Charlotte. *Twenty-One Years with Children's Theatre.* Anchorage, Ky.: Children's Theatre Press, 1962.
Cornberg, Sol, and Gebauer, Emanuel L. *A Stage Crew Handbook.* Rev. ed. New York: Harper & Row, Inc., Publishers, 1957.
Corson, Richard. *Stage Makeup.* 3d ed. New York: Appleton-Century-Crofts, Inc., 1960.
Davis, Jed H., and Watkins, Mary Jane Larson. *Children's Theatre—Play Production for the Child Audience.* New York: Harper & Row, 1960.
Davis, John E. *Play and Mental Health—Principles and Practices for Teachers.* New York: A. S. Barnes & Co., Inc., 1938.
Dean, Alexander, and Carra, L. *Fundamentals of Play Directing.* Rev. ed. New York: Holt, Rinehart & Winston, Inc., 1965.
Dolman, John, Jr. *The Art of Play Production.* Rev. ed. New York: Harper & Row, Inc., 1946.
Durland, Frances. *Creative Dramatics for Children—A Practical Manual for Teachers and Leaders.* Yellow Springs, Ohio: Antioch Press, 1952.
Fisher, C. E., and Robertson, H. G. *Children and the Theatre.* Rev. ed. Stanford, Calif.: Stanford University Press, 1950.
Fitzgerald, Burdette S. *Let's Act the Story.* San Francisco: Fearon Publishers, Inc., 1957.
Gassner, John. *Producing the Play.* Rev. ed. New York: Dryden Press, Inc., 1953.
Jersild, Arthur. *Child Psychology.* 5th ed. Englewood Cliffs, N.J.: Prentice-Hall, Inc., 1960.

LEASE, RUTH, and SIKS, GERALDINE B. *Creative Dramatics in Home, School and Community.* New York: Harper & Row, Inc., 1952.
LEES, CHARLES LOWELL. *A Primer of Acting.* Englewood Cliffs, N.J.: Prentice-Hall, Inc., 1940.
LOWENFELD, VIKTOR, and BRITTAIN, W. L. *Creative and Mental Growth.* 4th ed. New York: The Macmillan Co., 1964.
MCGAW, CHARLES J. *Acting Is Believing—A Basic Method for Beginners.* New York: Holt, Rinehart & Winston, Inc., 1955.
MEARNS, HUGHES. *Creative Power—The Education of Youth in Creative Arts.* 2d rev. ed. New York: Dover Publications, Inc., 1958.
NATIONAL ASSOCIATION OF TEACHERS OF SPEECH. *Guides to Speech Training in the Elementary School.* Magnolia, Mass.: Expression Co., 1943.
OMMANNEY, KATHERINE A., and OMMANNEY, PIERCE C. *The Stage and the School.* 2d ed. New York: Harper & Row, Inc., 1950.
ROSENSTEIN, SOPHIE, HAYDON, LARRAE, and SPARROW, WILBUR. *Modern Acting.* New York: Samuel French, Inc., 1947.
SAWYER, RUTH. *The Way of the Storyteller.* Rev. ed. New York: The Viking Press, Inc., 1962.
SELDEN, SAMUEL. *The Stage in Action.* New York: Appleton-Century-Crofts, Inc., 1941.
SELDEN, SAMUEL, and SELLMAN, HUNTON D. *Stage Scenery and Lighting.* 3d ed. New York: Appleton-Century-Crofts, Inc., 1958.
SIKS, GERALDINE B. *Creative Dramatics: An Art for Children.* New York: Harper & Row, Inc., 1958.
SIKS, GERALDINE B., and DUNNINGTON, H. B. (eds.). *Children's Theatre and Creative Dramatics.* Seattle: University of Washington Press, 1961.
SIMOS, JACK. *Social Growth Through Play Production.* New York: Association Press, 1957.
SLADE, PETER. *Child Drama.* New York: Philosophical Library, Inc., 1955.
SMITH, MILTON. *Play Production.* New York: Appleton-Century-Crofts, Inc., 1948.
TUTTLE, HAROLD SAXE. *Drama as a Device for Cultivating Basic Social and Civic Attitudes.* Washington, D.C.: American Educational Theatre Association, 1945.
WARD, WINIFRED. *Drama with and for Children.* Washington, D.C.: U.S. Government Printing Office, 1960.
WARD, WINIFRED. *Playmaking with Children—From Kindergarten Through Junior High School.* 2d ed. New York: Appleton-Century-Crofts, Inc., 1957.
WARD, WINIFRED. *Theatre for Children.* 3d ed. Anchorage, Ky.: Children's Theatre Press, 1958.
WASHBURNE, CARLETON W. *A Living Philosophy of Education.* New York: The John Day Co., 1940.
WHITING, FRANK M. *An Introduction to the Theatre.* Rev. ed. New York: Harper & Row, Inc., 1961.
WITTENBERG, RUDOLPH M. *So You Want To Help People.* New York: Association Press, 1947.

INDEX

Acting unit, 74, 77–78
Activity pantomime, 25–32
   creating an appropriate climate for, 21–24, 26
   definition of, 25
   difficulties with beginners, 29–30
   as dramatic play, 25
   exercises in, 31–32, 150–52
   first classes in, 26–28
   follow-up classes in, 28–30
   objectives of, 25
Alice in Wonderland, 135

Balance
   in creating the stage picture, 106, 114–16
   psychological, 106
Blocking
   the long play, 89
   pin-and-blotter method, 106
Border lights, 130, 131 (fig.)
Box set, 117, 118 (fig.)
Bridge, William H., 61
Budget
   for long play, 84, 88
   for trailer theatre, 140

Casting, 84–85
   double cast, 76, 85, 92–93
   longer short play, 78
   outdoor production, 138
   short play, 76
Change-of-mood pantomime, 12, 43–54
   as a bridge from dramatic play to drama, 43
   discussion before, 45–46
   exercises in, 48–54, 155–59
   in a group working as a group, 48
   in a group working as individuals, 48
   selection of material for, 46–48
   several changes of mood, 47
   single change of mood, 44–47
   sources for, 47

Chaplin, Dora, 34
Characterization
   assuming the role offstage, 107
   through imitation, 110
   motivation, 105, 106
   use of oral and written biographies, 110
Child of the Sky, 191–215
   set plans for, 193 (fig.)
Children's stories, as source for pantomimes, 47
Children's theatre
   growth of, 103
   research and development in, 103
Christmas Carol, A, crowd scenes in, 86–88
Church school, as setting for creative dramatics, 13, 14–15, 16
   disadvantages of, 15
Cinderella, 135
Classroom, as setting for creative dramatics, 13–14, 16, 77
Color
   common emotional associations of, 120
   in highlighting an important character or object, 109–10, 116
   as integrating medium in costumes and settings, 100, 118–20, 124
   psychological effect of, 119–20, 132
Concentration, 25
Contrast, in creating the stage picture, 108–9
Costumes, 120–24
   and the actor, 121
   and the budget, 121
   in episodic play, 98
   in fantasy, 122–23
   in historical setting, 121–22
   importance of color, 100, 120
   in long play, 83, 89, 93
   materials for, 122, 124
   medieval, 122, 123 (fig.)
   and outdoor production, 134

Creating an appropriate climate, for creative dramatics, 21–24, 26
Creative dramatics, 3–11
　definition of, 5–6
　and human development, 4–9
　objectives of, 3–11
　subdivisions of, 6
　and total growth, 10–11
　transition from, to formal drama, 81
Critique period
　after each acting unit of short play, 77
　after mood pantomime, 37
Crowd scenes, 85–88
　disadvantages of, 88
　as improvisation, 86
Cyclorama, 107, 117

Dancing, in pageants, 101
Davis, Jed, 84, 106, 148
Dialogue, 55–69, 111–13
　elementary practice scenes for, 57–60
　exercises in, 66–69, 159–67, 222
　group, 60–62
　　exercise in, 223
　　improvisation, 61
　improvisation, 55, 61–62, 111
　introductory approach to, 55–57
　silent, 112
　single-word, 56–57
　in different settings, 56
Dickens, Charles, 86–87
Dienesch, Marie, 81
Dimmers (rheostats), 100, 130, 132
Directing
　the episodic play, 98–101
　formal, 88
　the long play, 88
　outdoors productions, 134–35
　suggestive, 104–5
Director of creative dramatics project
　personal qualifications, 21–22, 71, 88, 103–4, 148
　responsibility of, 104
　　for creating an appropriate climate, 21–24
Double cast
　in long play, 85, 92–93
　in short play, 76
Draped stage, 117–18
Dress rehearsals, 93
Dunnington, H. B., 82, 84, 88, 103, 106

Emphasis
　in creating the stage picture, 109–10
　methods of highlighting an important character, 109–10
　through use of color, 109–10, 116, 119–20
　through use of lighting, 109–10, 116
　word, 111–12
Entrances, 107
Episodic play
　costumes in, 100
　definition of, 95
　direction of, 98
　essentials of, 97–98
　importance of lighting, 100
　integration of, 99–101
　intermission during, 101
　vs. pageant, 101–2
　rehearsals, 98
　setting in, 100
　uses of, 95–96
Exits, 107–8

Fantasy
　costumes in, 122
　lighting of, 129
　makeup in, 126
Floodlights, 129–30, 131 (fig.)
Footlights, 130, 131 (fig.)
Formal dramatics, 6, 13
　definition of, 6
　transition to, from creative dramatics, 81
Formal settings, 116

Gelatins, 132
Graham, Kenneth, 82
Group dialogue, 60–62
　exercise in, 223

Hansel and Gretel, 135, 139 (fig.)
Heidi, 135

Improvisation, 57, 61–62, 75–76, 111
　crowd scenes as, 86
　in long play, 80
　musical, 17, 18
　in short play, 75–76
Interest levels of children, 71–73
Intermission, disadvantages of, 101

Jersild, Arthur, 4, 11, 60, 146

Kierkegaard, Sören, 146
King Arthur's Knights, 84
King of the Golden River, 84
The King's Birthday, 182–90
Knights of the Silver Shield, 84

Leader; *see* Director of Creative Dramatics Project
Lighting, 93, 127–32, 133
　border lights, 130, 131 (fig.)

INDEX

dimmers, 100, 130, 132
effect of, upon colored materials, 132, 133 (fig.)
emotional impact of, 127, 128 (fig.)
in the episodic play, 98, 100–101
for the fantasy, 129
floodlights, 129–30, 131 (fig.)
footlights, 130, 131 (fig.)
gelatins, 132
in highlighting an important character or object, 109, 116
hints for amateur directors, 132
in long play, 82, 93
major functions of, 128
and makeup, 125
and outdoor staging, 134
for the realistic play, 128
spotlights, 129, 131 (fig.)
switchboard, 130
use of color in, 120
   effect of colored light upon colored materials, 133 (fig.)
Little Women, 111
Long play, 80–94, 191–215
   application of creative technique, 91–92
   blocking, 89
   crowd scenes in, 85–88
   double cast for, 85
   formal directing of, 88
   improvisational vs. formal approach, 80–82
   objectives of, 82–83
   organization and planning of, 88–89
   rehearsals, 90–91
      final, 93–94
   selection of material for, 83–84
   touring, 84
Longer short play, 76–77, 182–90

Magazines, as source for pantomimes, 47
Makeup, 124–27
   character, 126
   fantastic, 126
   influence of lighting on, 124–25
   mustaches, wigs, and beards, 127
   purpose of, 124–25
   removal of, 127
   straight, 126
Mearns, Hughes, 5
Mind-pictures, 25, 33, 37
Mood pantomime, 12, 33–42
   as a completely different person, 37
   critique after, 37
   divisions of, 37
   exercises in, 38, 40–42, 153–55
   growth of sensitivity through, 34–38

music used with, 38–40
   as one's self, 37
   thought patterns, 34, 36
   transition from activity pantomime to, 33
Motivation, 105–7
   character, 106
   invented, 106
   story, 106
Music, use of, 16–21, 38–40, 45
   as background for the creative play, 21, 38–40
   in episodic play, 98, 99–100
   in individual pantomime exercise, 223
   in long play, 83, 84

Newspapers, as source for pantomimes, 47

Outdoor staging, 134–143
   costuming for, 134
   direction of stage business for, 134–35
   lighting for, 134
   sound effects, 134
   special problems in, 134–35
   trailer theatre, 135–40; *see also* Showmobile, Trailer Theatre

Pageant
   definition of, 95, 101
   vs. episodic play, 101–2
   favorite subjects of, 102
   importance of settings in, 101
   pantomime in, 101
   singing and dancing in, 101
   uses of, 95
Pantomime, 12; *see also* Mood Pantomime, Change-of-Mood Pantomime
   exercises in, 222, 223
   in pageants, 101
Personality development, through creative play acting, 12, 148
Pin-and-blotter method, of staging the play, 104
Pinocchio, 135
Play acting and living, 5, 144–49
   helping the problem child, 61–62, 145, 146–48
   self-realization through play acting, 145–46
Poems, as source for pantomimes, 47
Properties, 93, 107
   for short play, 76
Puss in Boots, 135

The Queen of Hearts, 177–82

Realistic settings, 116
   lighting of, 128–29

Recreation center, as setting for creative dramatics, 13, 15–16
   disadvantages of, 15–16
Rehearsal unit, 90
Rehearsals
   dress, 134
   for the episodic play, 98
   final, 93–94
      characterization improvement during, 93
   for long play, 84, 90–91
   for longer short play, 78
   method of conducting first, 91–92
   music, 132, 134
   sample rehearsal schedule, 90–91
   for short play, 76
   technical, 93, 134
Rhythm, 16, 19–20, 168–71
   exercises in, 19–20, 168–71, 223
      rhythm patterns that tell a story, 168–70
      simple activities played rhythmically, 170–71
      as an expression of a life situation, 19–20

Scale models, of setting, 89
Selection of material, 8
   for long play, 83–84
   for short play, 71
Self-realization, through play acting, 145–46
Sensitivity, growth of
   through creative dramatics, 4, 34–37
   in long play, 82
Settings
   box set, 117, 118 (fig.)
   color as an integrating medium in, 100
   draped stage, 117
   in the episodic play, 98, 100
   formal, 116
   in long play, 83, 89
   in the pageant, 100, 101
   qualifications of, 115–116
   realistic, 116
   in short play, 76
   suggestive, 116
   underwater, 117
   use of scale models, 89
Short play, 70–79, 177–90
   casting, 76, 78
   characteristics of good, 70–71
   developing the play, 78
   improvising the, 75–76
   introduction of the story, 73
   longer short play, 76–77, 182–90

   for the "older teen," 72–73
   outlining, 77
   properties in, 76
   preparation for, 74–75
      character analysis, 74
      discussion of the story, 73
   rehearsals, 76, 78
   scenery in, 76
   selection of material for, 71
   treatment of material for, 77–78
Showmobile, 135–40; *see also* Trailer Theatre
   drawing plans, 136 (fig.), 137 (fig.)
   repertoire of, 135
Siks, Geraldine, 5, 16, 22, 73, 81, 82, 84, 88, 103, 106
Silent dialogue, 112
Songs
   dramatization of, 14
   in pageants, 101
   as source for pantomime, 47
Sound, 93
   in the outdoor production, 134
Speech drills, 62, 64–65
   disadvantages of, 62
Speech improvement, 55, 62–65
   of grammar, 59–60
   use of verses for drill, 64–65
   in voice production, 55, 62–65
Spotlights, 129, 131 (fig.)
Stage business, 105–7
   in outdoor productions, 133–34
Stage terminology, use of by the director, 106–7
Staging the play, 108–110, 114–143
   balance, 108, 114–16
   contrast, 108
   emphasis, 109–10
   entrances, 107
   exits, 107–8
   outdoor staging, 134–35; *see also* Outdoor Staging
   pin-and-blotter method, 106
   student participation in, 85, 140–43
Stellar roles, disadvantage of, 85
Student participation, in staging the play, 85, 140–43
Suggestive settings, 116
Summer camp, as setting for creative dramatics, 13, 15, 16, 76, 77
   advantages of, 15
   disadvantages of, 15
Switchboard, 130

Tales of Robin Hood, 84
Technical rehearsals, 93, 134

INDEX

Tillich, Paul, 146
Touring, 84; *see also* Showmobile; Trailer Theatre
Trailer theatre, 135–40
   assembly of Showmobile for production, 138–40
   cost of, 140
   equipment for, 139–40
   essential attributes of cast, 135
   learning experiences, 138

Tuttle, Harold Saxe, 8
Twain, Mark, 82

Verse, as a speech drill, 64–65

Ward, Winifred, 81, 85
Whiting, Frank, 88, 103–4
Wittenberg, Rudolph M., 148

York, Eleanor Chase, 5